Weatl
Permitting

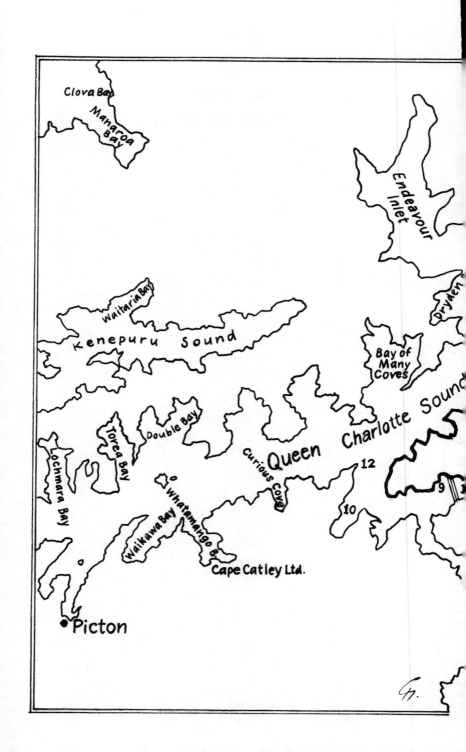

Ship Cove

Long Island

solution

Blumine Island

East Bay

Arapawa Island

24 25

23

18

COOK STRAIT

2 1

4

3

13

14

TO WELLINGTON

Channel

Tory 8

7

15

16

17

26

21

22

19 20

13. EAST HEAD
14. WEST HEAD
15. JORDY ROCKS
16. LUCKY BAY
17. RUNUNDER POINT
18. WELLINGTON BAY
19. MARCH ROCK
20. PERANO HEAD
(PREVIOUSLY WELLINGTON HEAD)
21. CAPE KOAMARU
22. THE BROTHERS
23. WHAREHUNGA BAY
24. PURIRI BAY
25. AOTEA
26. ONAUKU

1. OKUKARI BAY
2. WHEKENUI BAY
3. FISHING BAY
4. TE AWAITI
5. DEEP BAY
6. NGARURU
7. TE PANGU
8. WIRIKARAPA
9. TE IRO
10. MARAETAI BAY
11. POWER CROSSING
12. DIEFFENBACH POINT

WEATHER PERMITTING

by
Heather Heberley

CAPE CATLEY LTD

First published April 1996

Second edition May 1996

Third edition August 1996

CAPE CATLEY LTD

Whatamango Bay, Queen Charlotte Sound
New Zealand

Design by Bill Wieben
Cover photograph by Ian Garrod
Typeset by Central Typesetting & Imaging, Wellington
Printed in Hong Kong

ISBN 0-908561-49-0

Contents

In memory of Tom and Rene Macauley

Acknowledgements

A NUMBER of people have helped me with this book.

Gary Hebley is a direct descendant of Frederick Heberley, Worser Heberley's brother. Over the years the name lost one syllable. Gary designed the decorative heading for the recipe section, and did the map.

I'd like to thank Paul Palmer for many of the photos that he took while spending time with us, and Ian Garrod for the cover photo and the experience of my one and only 'photo shoot'.

Many people helped me with technical information.

In 1994 I enrolled in a writers' workshop run by Chris Cole Catley for the first Picton Sounds Spring School. Then in the next January I attended another of Chris's workshops at the Marlborough Summer School of the Arts, in Blenheim. The Picton workshop gave me the courage to start my book and the Blenheim one the courage to keep on. Since then we have worked together, often by fax from our two remote Sounds homes.

But most especially I'd like to thank Chris for the time and effort she has put in. She believed in me.

In this book I haven't written about the many times in my thirties when I went to hospital for surgery. Some of these hospital stays were accident-related, others were to deal with threatening lumps in my breast. Perhaps one of the surgeons planted a seed in my mind when he said, after my protests at having to be incapacitated during a long convalescence, that I should go home and write a book.

Without my family I couldn't have begun to write. They are the book. And as for my dear Joe - I must congratulate myself for having the foresight to marry him. Without him there would certainly have been no book.

Heather Heberley

My Life In The Sounds

Correspondence School essay by Rachael Heberley, 1995

HELLO, my name is Rachael. I live on Arapawa Island, in the Marlborough Sounds, on my grandparents' farm. I am 11 years old and I'm the oldest daughter of Joe and Joy Heberley. I have a nine-year-old sister called Angela. Dad is a fisherman who fishes in Cook Strait which is very close to our place because we live right at the entrance to the strait.

Dad runs the *Fugitive*, which is a 40-foot wooden fishing boat. He catches crayfish in the winter and sharks and groper the rest of the year.

Sometimes when Dad's crew has a weekend off we all go out fishing with him. Mum takes the crew's place. Angela and I fill up the bait bags with fish called rats and gurnard frames for the crayfish to eat. It is fun looking for the brightly coloured floats bobbing up and down on the sea.

Mum gaffs them and helps Dad put the rope on the winch to pull the pot aboard. Dad takes the crayfish out, measures them and throws the undersize ones back. He puts the crayfish we're allowed to keep in a tank full of salt water on the deck. We hook the bait bags in the pot and Dad sets the pot again. We do this for about 120 pots each day. If it's rough weather, Angela and I sometimes have to stay in the cabin because it can be very dangerous on deck with ropes, floats and pots everywhere.

When we get home we put all the crayfish into a crate in the sea, in our bay. When it is full we take the crayfish to town and they go live to Japan after being sent to Oamaru.

When Dad puts the boat on the moorings for the night, Angela and I usually row the dinghy out to get him and bring him ashore. I like rowing the dinghy around the wharf if it's not blowing too hard.

When it's low tide, we get paua off the rocks. We always get very wet up to the waist. If Dad is home he comes pauaing too, but he is clever, he doesn't seem to get so wet.

We get mussels too. We can find big ones in our bay, but they are always quite sandy.

I like swimming in the sea, but it is very cold here, so I usually just splash and play around in it.

Mum teaches us school. As there is no road access to town, we can't go to a local school, so Mum has to teach us correspondence lessons. We have school days quite often, where lots of families meet and have lots of games and activities together. It is fun because we get to see our teachers and friends.

In my spare time I like riding my bike, sewing on my little sewing machine, reading books and doing Lone Guides. Angela and I build huts in the pine trees by our house. You can make them out of big branches and pine needles. We have made one hut and it's got two rooms. One is the kitchen and the other one is a bedroom.

Angela and I like listening to music and jumping on our trampoline at night after tea. I can do high flips and somersaults. If it's a calm night we play badminton or tennis on our front lawn. I enjoy painting pictures for Mum to hang on the fridge door.

When it comes to doing anything around the farm, I will ask Mum or Dad if I can go and help. I always enjoy going mustering. We always take the motorbikes and I ride with Uncle James or Grumps on the four-wheelers. I sometimes have to bring one of the bikes home. I have to put it in low gear because the road is very windy. When I get back to the flat paddocks, I put it back in high gear, so I can go faster.

When we tail the lambs, I get to hold some of the small ones while they have their tails cut off, ears marked and injections. I don't like listening to them crying out to their mothers.

I like shearing time too. My jobs are to either sweep the board, fill up the catching pens, jump down the wool in the wool-press or skirt the wool to make it tidy and clean.

We will always hire a couple of shearers because we need the people who live here to work on the board and at the wool table.

The thing I like most about living down here is you can enjoy the advantages of living on a farm or near a beach because you can go fishing and swimming, as well as all the things that are right outside your back door step waiting for you.

CHAPTER ONE

To The Island

FOUR grey and red vinyl chairs. One grey Formica table with shiny chrome legs. These were the only objects in this huge room, a room which probably seemed even bigger to me, fresh from my Auckland suburban street. They gave me my first impression of the house on Arapawa Island where, in 1963, I would make my home.

This furniture of ours – and how grand the word furniture sounds – was sitting in front of a wonderful painting. As long as I lived here it would be mine. Not the usual painting one sees in art galleries, or on an artist's easel, waiting to spring to life. This was a living painting. The sea. My companion in the years ahead.

From my picture window I gazed at Tory Channel stretched out until it disappeared around Wirikarapa light on the 18-mile journey into Picton. The water was a dark blue. Green hills reached into the sea on the western side. Why ever did fashion pundits say that "blue and green should not be seen"? I could smell the freshness.

Two whale chasers cruised slowly across the water from Peranos' whaling station to West Head at the entrance of Tory Channel. They were the only moving things in view. Their ripples ran on to the beach and slapped against the white sand which was the foreground of my painting. The silence was deafening.

No canvas would have been big enough to take in what I had left behind in my earlier life in Auckland. In all my 20 years, material things had never played an important part. These were easy to leave behind. But Mum, Dad, Betty – my only sibling and six years my senior – two nieces and a nephew along with 20 years of friendships; they were hard to say goodbye to. Paradise would have been if my new home, Arapawa Island, could have been placed in the Hauraki Gulf close to Auckland. The Gulf had been the scene of some of my very happiest days.

It was here on New Year's Day, 1961, on Great Barrier Island where my family sailed each year for Christmas, that I met Joe Heberley.

I went again to the Barrier for Queen's Birthday weekend in 1962, a 30-minute flight with Freddy Ladd. The words he was famous for – "A shower of spray and we're away" – and the ducking and diving over isolated farm houses to drop off the *New Zealand Herald*, made a fairytale flight. He drove the plane up on the beach alongside the whaling station, and I jumped out.

Joe's father Charles, called Charlie, had managed the whaling station in

1

Whangaparapara Harbour since 1959. Whaling is well and truly in Joe's blood. His father is descended from James (Worser) Heberley. Worser began whaling in New Zealand in 1830 for the whalebone which was sold for 80-100 pounds a ton, and the black oil which was worth 30-35 pounds per ton. He whaled round the Marlborough area until 1842 when he became Wellington's first pilot. Joe's mother, Ruby Heberley, was a Guard, a direct descendant of Captain 'Jacky' Guard, father of John Guard, the first white child born in the South Island.

Charles Heberley continued his forbear's whaling tradition. Before going to the Barrier, he had worked for 15 years as a whaling gunner for the whaling family, the Peranos, at their whaling station which had been established in 1923 at Fishing Bay. He fished out of boats with 36-foot planing hulls, some equipped with aircraft engines and capable of speeds up to 45 knots.

Later, Charlie had combined fishing and farming, buying a farm in the Marlborough Sounds in 1945. Then, in 1959, Charlie had gone to the Barrier to manage the whaling station in Whangaparapara, but he kept returning to check on his land in the Sounds.

Joe, too, seemed to be following the family tradition. At 17, and already the youngest gunner in the Southern Hemisphere, he shot whale after whale.

On the beach where Freddy landed were sheets of baleen. I gazed at them. In those few countries which still go whaling, it's the only part of the whale not used today. In earlier days it was used for the boning in ladies' corsets. The humpback whale had hundreds of these baleen sheets, tapered towards the tip and fringed on the inner side. Although it is called whalebone, it is actually a horny, flexible material. Pressed together like the leaves from a book, the baleen forms an effective sieve to trap krill, the small creatures from the sea that the whale lives on.

Ruby, Joe's mother, waited for me at the top of the beach. Neat and ladylike, she wore pearls and pearl earrings and a twinset, but if I hadn't been coming I knew she would have been on the chaser with Charlie and Joe. Only wet windy days kept her at home. Recently I'd read in the paper how she'd taken the helm of the chaser while Joe's father, in charge of the gun, had harpooned a 50-foot whale. The paper said the usual gunner could not go because of illness. But when I rang to see if this "usual" gunner – Joe – was seriously ill, I found that, for once the press was being kind, while being wrong. Joe had been in the lookout hut when the whale was spotted. His parents had remained on the chaser. As all the crews raced down the hill to be the first, Charlie couldn't resist the temptation to start up the chaser and leave everyone in his wake.

I followed Ruby up the track to the house built for them by the whaling company 300 feet above the station. Ruby and Charlie had selected the site for the view – close to the station, but far enough away from the noise and the smell. The track wound up through gnarled pohutukawa trunks to where the

2

house nestled among native trees and ferns. The whaling station was left behind, and at the house I stepped into another world. Visible from miles out to sea, the house was surrounded by kowhai, puriri and tree ferns, perfect housing for the kaka, whose shrieks were nature's alarm clock. Windows from floor to ceiling scanned the Whangaparapara Harbour.

I heard the loud humming of the three chasers' engines long before I saw their navigation lights when they swung round the point into the harbour. When the chasers were moored the men rowed ashore to their accommodation. Joe slept in one of the huts within the camp, but drew the line at eating in the cookhouse. His mother's cooking brought him home for meals.

Early next morning, well before sunrise, I was aboard the chaser with Joe, and with Charlie at the helm we headed for Cape Barrier, the southernmost tip on Great Barrier. The cabin space was filled with the engine, and no conversation was possible in the noise. I later asked Joe how skipper and gunner related to each other, and he told me it was all by hand signals. Ashore, we climbed a steep muddy track to the tiny lookout hut overlooking the sea to the south and east. Our cold hands warmed quickly, wrapped round thick mugs. As the sun rose over the edge of the ocean, eight keen eyes behind binoculars scanned the empty sea for the betraying "spout" of the humpback. I waited in vain to hear, "Thar she blows." The first year of whaling at the Barrier had seen 106 whales caught. Over the last two years whaling catches had decreased. There was no doubt that stocks of whales were being wiped out in the Antarctic where the main whaling countries of the world were operating with fleets of chasers and factory ships.

The very next month, on 7 July 1962, whaling at Great Barrier ceased. Only eight whales had been caught that entire season. Whaling in that part of the world had ended for ever. Joe's parents returned to their Marlborough farm. Joe and I became engaged that July and our love for each other became part of the love that had wrapped round me all my life.

My mother had always been there, all five foot one of her, and her love was her greatest strength. My father was a big man with a heart to match, and plenty of good advice. On our wedding day he had told Joe and me, "Never let the sun go down on your anger." I was often pulled up with, "If you can't say anything nice about someone, don't say anything at all." A wise man, he lived up to the standards he expected of me and my sister. It was after we were married that Joe told me he was never jealous of my other boyfriends. He knew Dad was his biggest rival.

After his parents' return to their Marlborough Sounds farm, Joe stayed in Auckland, working for a panel beater. We had planned an 18-month engagement, but the city didn't agree with Joe. He needed space, so in January he flew home to work on the farm. That meant Joe was in the South Island while I was in the North. We wanted to be together, so we halved our engagement period. Joe returned to Auckland one week before our wedding on 27 April, 1963.

I was a bride with a dowry. I couldn't imagine life without a piano. I had used my savings to buy myself one, to be delivered to Picton and then to my new home in Tory Channel after we were married. Wedding presents and all my belongings including my sewing machine were packed and then shipped to Picton. Our car would have to be left in Picton but it was loaded with cartons of items we'd need when we first arrived at our new home, before our furniture could be sent up by barge.

As our ferry came into Tory Channel from Cook Strait, the first bay to greet us on the right was Okukari. The white sand glistened on our curving beach as it swept around a rocky point and on into Whekenui Bay. The old woolshed painted by years of rust sat in the middle of the bay above high water mark, on the edge of a six-foot bank. My eyes followed the green valley until it disappeared from sight behind a stand of pine trees at the head of the flat. I saw Joe's parents' house among tall pine trees, and ours 100 yards to the left. The steep hills framing the bay, their tops wreathed in thick mist, were home to 1500 romney sheep.

The ferry skipper's voice came over the intercom. "You have now entered Tory Channel. We will be arriving in Picton in one hour." What a long way to go if I ran out of anything, I thought. And how strange to sail past our home then have to turn round and come back by small boat.

As the *Aramoana* cruised slowly into Picton harbour I viewed my new home town through new eyes. I had visited Okukari for a fortnight 15 months earlier while Joe and his parents were at the farm for dipping and the culling of the old or rejected ewes that were to go to the sheep sales in Blenheim. That time I had flown into Blenheim, and my first view of Picton had been from the road as we'd driven over the Elevation, when I'd looked straight down between golden-clad hills to the small township built closely to the dark blue water's edge. Going back to Auckland, I'd left Picton behind on the *Rangatira* not long before the ship's retirement. There'll be no traffic lights here, I thought now as I studied the picturesque scene. Driving will be a piece of cake and I certainly won't get lost.

"What's that big brick building on the edge of the scrub, Joe?"

"Picton hospital. The left wing is maternity and the opposite side is for general."

"It's close to the bush, isn't it. I wouldn't like to be there if a fire got away."

"A fire sweeps over the hills every few years and it's still standing, so it must be okay."

To the left of the hospital there was a small cleared area where three or four new houses had been built. Three hotels – Oxley's, Federal and Terminus – dominated the waterfront. A smoothly mown grass strip sloped to the beach.

"It's crowded on New Year's Day for the rowing regatta. Next year, weather permitting, I'll bring you in for it."

Joe's parents had come to meet us in the *Wheke*, their farm boat. I began to feel concern. The prospect of a boat trip itself didn't worry me. I'd grown up on boats. I was three when my parents had bought the *Awahou*, their first family yacht. A 26-foot mullet boat, with her low flat cabin and most of the interior taken over by the centreboard, she wasn't designed for families. With the centreboard raised, the yacht would become a flat-bottomed punt, ideal in shallow waters. The boom hung well out over the stern, making a massive sail area. Exciting boats to sail, mulleties, but definitely not boats for a young family. It was said you didn't need to go away on a mullet boat. Instead, all you had to do was take a box of food, a dozen beer and a roll of bedding and sit under the kitchen table with a grey blanket draped over it. With such limited space aboard, this wasn't far wrong.

Then, when the house desperately needed painting and the *Awahou* was becoming too small, the boat was sold. We became landlubbers. A year later, when the house looked as if someone loved it again, Dad developed salt water withdrawal symptoms so we bought another yacht.

The *Mangawai* was a 28-foot yawl. A 12-foot beam gave plenty of cabin space with a well-equipped galley, five bunks and a toilet. After the *Awahou*, the *Mangawai* was the *Queen Mary*, and every fine weekend we'd swap the city for the Hauraki Gulf.

The *Mangawai* was a living history book. The tiller came from one of the *Elingamite's* lifeboats, sunk off Three Kings in 1902. Shelves built under the deck beams in the cabin were edged with intricately turned mahogany washed ashore from HMS *Orpheus* when she was wrecked on the Manukau Bar. It was on the *Mangawai* we began our regular sailing to the Barrier.

Although she never learnt to swim, my mother had sailed with Dad, but was terrified when it was rough. It wasn't until I became a mother myself that I realised her cries of anguish – cries that still echo in my mind – were not for herself. They were for her children, and what could happen to them.

But, as a new wife standing on the wharf at Picton, I didn't realise that then. At that point I was realising that all of the *Wheke's* 26 feet was piled up with our gear from the car, and the things I'd bought in Picton. Carrying everything from the car to the wharf and on to the boat was difficult, but at Okukari there wasn't even a wharf, so it would all have to be rowed ashore in the dinghy, put on the tractor-trailer, and driven to the front gate. From there the last 100 yards would be by wheelbarrow or shanks's pony. I'd had to try to think of all the groceries I'd need until the next trip to town. I knew my mother-in-law wouldn't let us go without, but, in my newly-married independence, I wanted to have remembered to put everything on my list.

Once our stuff was unloaded, our car was garaged in Picton and we were on the last leg of our journey. I was longing to see the inside of our new home. When I'd been down from Auckland the previous year the farm manager still lived in it and I hadn't been able to see the interior.

As Picton became smaller behind us, a cold void in my chest grew bigger and squeezed out the warmth. I hungered for my parents' loving arms, and quickly brushed tears away with the back of my hand. My wedding ring felt cold against my face. Joe gently took my hand in his.

Arapawa Island is 18,500 acres, or 7487 hectares. When I first came to Queen Charlotte Sound there were nine farms on the island. Now, more than 30 years on, only three farms remain – ours, Whekenui and Onauku in the head of East Bay. Land that hasn't been swallowed up by pine plantations has reverted to native bush. The eastern side of Arapawa's rugged coastline guards the entrance to Tory channel, while, on the other side, the grassy hills join the waters of Queen Charlotte Sound. Boats cruising out through the northern entrance of the Sound leave Arapawa behind on their right.

One mile south of Okukari in Tory Channel is Te Awaiti, scene of the Guard family's historic whaling station. Worser Heberley made his new home here when he arrived from England and began whaling.

On my journey to my own new home the strong flood tide was against us so Joe's father kept close to the shore to stay out of it. Punching the tide can add extra 20 minutes to our two-hour trip, I was told. We were so close to the beach I saw a gravesite and whaling pots – relics of the longboat whaling days.

We smelt Fishing Bay before we saw it. Peranos' whaling station was being run by Joe and Gilbert Perano.

"The little huts up the gully are for the workers to live in during the season," Joe told me. "The long one in the front is the cookhouse."

Smoke poured from all the chimneys, rising and mixing with the steam from the whaling station. A whale lay against the breastworks, waiting its turn to begin its last journey up the steep ramp to the top deck for processing. It was the blubber that smelt so foul as it cooked.

Turning into our bay my father-in-law pointed out the whaling lookout opposite us, on the other side of the channel. "They must be chasing a whale. The boats aren't there," he said.

Gilbert's wife, Nan, waved to us from her front verandah as we passed Whekenui before dropping anchor a short distance off our beach. Three farm dogs stood waiting at the water's edge, and I was welcomed with sandy feet jumping up on my shoulders, frantically wagging tails and lots of rough licks.

Everything from the dinghy was loaded on to the tractor, and while my father-in-law took the boat out and put it on the mooring, Joe drove the tractor to the front gate.

During the three months Joe had spent at home before our wedding he had painted our house. It looked very smart. The gaily painted red door opened into the back of the house. Two concrete tubs, my agitator washing machine alongside, sat beneath windows overlooking my in-laws' vegetable garden. A dark narrow passage lined with cupboards led into the kitchen. Space greeted me. The sink with its long Formica bench top and cupboards underneath ran the length of the room. The coal range was opposite but at that moment my eyes feasted on the view from the front window.

Just now there wasn't time to stop and stare. Everything had to be carried from the gate. When it was all inside, my arms felt at least one foot longer and I was hot, hungry and exhausted. Real married life had begun.

The sound of the lighting plant starting up invaded the silence. Only five kilowatts, it generated enough electricity for my in-laws to have lights and use most electrical appliances, but not a stove. When it was on we had lights too, and with care and choosing my time I could use my washing machine, jug, toaster and iron. Too big a load on the power caused the lights to dim and black smoke to belch from the exhaust of the poor overloaded engine. I rapidly learnt that the electric jug used 1500 watts and my toaster and iron both used 1200.

Ruby and Charlie had had the thermostat removed from their deep freeze, and with no temperature control it kept on freezing down whenever the power was on. Frozen foods held down well but the fluctuating temperature caused food to deteriorate within two or three months. All the same it was a wonderful appliance to have, and made food storage much easier. From 6-9am, then again in the evening for about three hours, the engine ran. During summer the freezer needed a cold boost in the middle of the day so we'd have power for an extra two hours. Ruby had invited us for dinner that first night so we took our perishables with us to store in her kerosene fridge and the deep freeze. Our fridge, a wedding present from Joe's parents, was coming on the barge. Decent kerosene fridges were hard to come by so we hoped our electric one, with its thermostat removed, would be as successful as the deep freeze.

"Don't buy a deep freeze," Ruby had said. "I'd rather you helped fill ours up. Things stay frozen better if it's full and I don't like filling it up for myself. If the generator breaks down we'd lose the lot unless it's fixed quickly."

A major breakdown meant two hours to Picton to pick up the auto electrician and two hours to return before any work could even be started. Joe or his father usually fixed any breakdowns. Over the years I became adept at running repairs myself, rather than sitting in darkness waiting for a man to get home. As we left their house this first night, Joe's father flicked a switch on his switchboard and we opened our door into electric light.

We left unpacking until the next morning. Tired bodies sleep anywhere, even on a mattress on the bedroom floor. Our bed was among the things still to arrive in Picton.

It seemed everything was waiting for something. The barge waited for our belongings to arrive. We waited for the barge to bring them to Okukari but the weather was in charge. Nothing would arrive until the weather permitted. The dull thump of the generator merged into the still sound of the night and lulled me to sleep.

About 6am the sound that sent me to sleep woke me with a start. It also disturbed the farm dogs. They yodelled their "Good mornings" above the noise of the engine. Joe was already up and rummaging through boxes to find our electric jug and toaster.

"Give Mum and Dad time to have their breakfast, then we can use the power for ours. Later I'll light the coal range for you." From our bedroom window I saw my in-laws' chimney already smoking. "It's a Wellstead, a heat storage. Burns all the time," Joe explained. "If it's banked up at night it only needs the dampers opened in the morning. A quick rake and it's away."

That morning the pile of possessions inside our door seemed much smaller. By the end of the day our house was looking lived in and I'd had my first lesson on the coal range. Joe made it look easy. My trials began once I was on my own.

With the party line intended for five or six telephones and already overloaded with 13 households, we'd had no joy when we approached Post and Telegraph and asked if we could have a telephone. Any calls for us meant we had to tear across the lawn to my in-laws.

At last came the call we'd been longing for. Everything from Auckland had arrived in Picton. Our fridge from Blenheim was there, too. In no time our house would be completely furnished. Best of all, my piano would be there.

Joe was whaling now. I needed my piano for company. I longed to run my fingers over the keys and let the music take over. Now I knew it had arrived in Picton my need was even greater. The man whose help I needed was Charlie Tarrant, an old Picton identity who ran the barge, that essential Sounds transport.

Charlie lived a hermit's life on the boat he used to tow the barge. He was a scruffy individual. I never did see him in clothes other than those he worked in. He'd stay on his boat enjoying a yarn whenever he came into our bay. Hoping to get him ashore and have morning or afternoon tea, I always got the same answer. "Thanks, missus, all the same, but I dinna want to wet me good shoes." One day my father-in-law decided to get him ashore anyway. When he picked him up we nearly died. Charlie's shoes had no soles.

The night before he hoped to leave Picton, Charlie phoned us. "Tomorrow, weather permitting, I'll be arriving with your furniture."

I was so excited. Sleep didn't even shorten the night. I lay in the darkness, my fingers running through the Rustle of Spring.

There was no spring next morning. A gale and rain battered the windows.

"No barge today, love," Joe said, studying the weather.

"Tomorrow then?"

"Not a chance. After this the wind will swing straight round to the south. Always does." He left for work, and I spent my day hating the weather.

Sure enough, three days of strong southerly followed. Even my "painting" lost its power to cheer me up. Salt spray whipped off the tops of waves crashing on the beach and covered the windows with a thick film of salt, making it hard to see out. Until the weather improved, our things would stay in Picton.

At last the weather came round in our favour. No wind or rain, and the swell had gone down.

"You'll get your piano tomorrow, love, weather permitting."

'Weather permitting' indeed! I shrugged away those last two words, with no sense that they were to shape the remainder of my life.

The next morning I stayed by my window. From the whalers' lookout high on the hill Joe watched the progress of the barge up the channel. Charlie Tarrant slowly steamed his boat into the shallow water and nudged the bow of the boat on to the beach. Two planks quickly made a ramp from the barge's flat deck to the sand.

Whales were scarce. There had been no sightings all day, so, leaving one man to keep watch, five men came over in the whale chaser with Joe to give a hand. Tea chests heavy with our wedding presents came down the bending planks. Then our fridge and bedroom suite. Finally – my piano's turn.

Six men struggled down the makeshift ramp. It moved in the gentle swell lifting on the beach. I waited for the straining planks to crack and tumble my piano into the sea. Miraculously nothing happened and my piano with 12 black legs clad in thigh gumboots slowly made its way on to the beach. These days, of course, the sight would have reminded everyone of Jane Campion's epic film, The Piano. But my drama was to come.

Rather than bumping the piano around on the tractor, the men carried it all the way up the hill. Amid laughter and jokes about what a great sing-song they were going to enjoy, it reached the house.

Our door was quite narrow. The men struggled. They heaved and they pushed but it simply would not go through that door. Then it jammed. My piano wasn't going anywhere.

"Don't worry," one of the men laughed. "If we can catch whales we can fit a piano through a door." I was still trying to see the joke when someone yelled "The flag's up!" No goodbyes. I didn't even have time to thank them. Everyone was gone.

The lone whaler on the lookout had seen a whale. In the early days of whaling, before radio communications, the Union Jack was flown high above the hut to alert the whaling station and mother ship, the *Tuatea*, that a whale could be coming in shortly. Tradition was still maintained. When a whale was sighted, up went the flag.

But now the piano was stuck in the doorway, and I had another problem. There was only one door into our house. All our things except the piano were inside. I was outside.

I ran my fingers over those of the keys I could reach. At least the piano still played. I went round the house, heaved myself up, and used our bedroom window as a door. That meant I could bring in the wood to light my stove, but I wasn't happy. If anything else had stuck in the door I might have seen the funny side. But not when it was my piano.

The pieces of our bed were inside, and after assembling them I felt we were becoming civilised. The hours ticked by. Always I'd envisaged myself at the piano when Joe was away. Now I felt very much alone.

Two whales later, six tired but jubilant men arrived to finish what they'd started five hours earlier. More heaves and pushes, more trying the piano from other angles, lots of swearing, and finally the piano slid through the door. I played in triumph.

Nothing was broken in transit and with all our possessions around us the house became our home.

Trying to compile a grocery list from scratch, and one which would last a month, was a mammoth task. Cut lunches for Joe, breakfasts, large meals at night, ingredients for baking – taking my list with me I went through Joe's mother's cupboards for ideas with her. If I ran out there was no corner shop here.

Joe was whaling so I was going to Picton with my in-laws.

"We'll see you on the beach at 7am. Better to get an early start, then we can be home early," I was told.

Next morning it was freezing, but I was looking forward to time in Picton. My enthusiasm kept me warm. Stumbling down to the beach in the dark, I made a mental note to add a torch to my list. With a skirt and stockings in place of slacks, and make up on, I felt feminine again. As Charlie rowed us out to the *Wheke* I couldn't help giggling. Here I was dressed for town but my skirt was hitched up to keep it out of the water sloshing around in the bottom of the dinghy, and black gumboots were on my stockinged feet.

The tide was flowing in and as we swung out of the bay I felt the boat surge ahead a little faster. Looking back through the channel entrance I saw the early morning sky transform Cook Strait into molten lead. Nothing broke its surface. A light wind brushed over the water and soft ripples ran before it. The horizon was empty. A lone seagull followed us, screeching and diving into our wake in its endless search for food.

Dieffenbach Point, named after Ernst Dieffenbach, was our halfway mark. This German botanist came to New Zealand in 1838 on the Tory, the ship which gave Tory Channel its name. He and Worser Heberley lay claim to being the first European men to climb Mount Egmont. The year was 1839.

Coming home our boat was once again loaded up, mostly with my stores. The trip took an age. My mother-in-law sat busily knitting, wriggling around to get comfortable on the hard seat. The chugging of the engine made me drowsy; I was in Auckland, the car pulled up next to the back door. Fancy having to lift all those boxes of groceries from the car, I dreamt. My father-in-law's voice woke me. "Home, love. Into the dinghy with your things. I'll help you up to the house with them. Joe's not home yet."

All those trips up the hill from the beach. This was different from my dream. With four hours' travelling behind me, I decided a day in Picton was definitely not my favourite thing.

Homesickness. This was the sickness I had to beat. I had come from such a close family circle and I was desperately lonely at times. I had Joe, and his parents were caring, but many times I only wanted my mother and my father and my sister.

Today we use the telephone without a thought of toll calls, and I can phone friends in Picton and Blenheim without cost. In the first few years I lived in Okukari it was a toll call to phone anyone unless it was a person on our own party line on the island. I didn't know anyone to ring on the party line except my in-laws, and the only brief calls I made were to order stores. I restricted myself to one call a month to talk to Mum and Dad. I had to do that or I would have spent more than our budget allowed. My father was a wonderful letter writer and our twice-weekly mail bag always brought me a letter from Auckland. I lived from mail day to mail day.

The first four months I was at Okukari were the worst. Joe was away from daylight till dark, whaling. Two people in a house make little mess and muddle. It didn't take long to make one bed and dust one bedroom suite and one piano. My days stretched endlessly out in front of me. Quiet. I longed to hear a busy noise. But the only sounds were the wind in the tall pine trees that grew around the houses, and the cries of the birds. Then I would turn to my piano, making it speak to me. I played the haunting music of Schumann and as I played his Traumerei, or Longing for Home, I'd let the tears run down my face and I'd feel Schumann's sadness as I played his beautiful chords. Dvorak's Largo from the New World Symphony was another one of my 'sad day' pieces. After the tears had flowed I'd feel much better and out would come the old favourites. Chopin's wonderful waltzes would sound around the bay and I'd feel ready to face the world again.

When I cleared the long grass up one side of the house and across the front I discovered two low flower boxes. I tidied them up and suggested to Joe that I put some flower plants in them. "Waste of time until after the winter. The first southerly will burn them off." So gardening was out.

11

The sea became my best friend. I loved its strange beauty and constantly changing moods. I came to know them all. I'd leave the loneliness of my house behind and walk down and along the beach to the rocks that lay between Okukari and Whekenui. From there I could see Cook Strait through the entrance of Tory Channel. Our bay, and as far as I could see, would be deep blue, calm and sparkly. Sometimes I'd see graceful yachts with their full white sails sailing off to somewhere else. A fishing boat would pass by, on its way out or coming back loaded down with fish. At 12.10pm and 3.20pm the new Cook Strait ferry *Aramoana* passed our place on her daily trip into Picton and on her return to Wellington.

The cold clean water looked crisp as it lay against the white sand. My favourite sea mood is still when the sea is dressed in aquamarine, especially where it swirls around the rocks and catches the air on their jagged edges. Fingers of bubbles pull back through the water, leaving streaks a lighter shade of this delicious colour. In those early times, days like that sent me home happy, my homesickness forgotten.

But sometimes the sea is full of sorrow. Its heavy heart has often matched my own as I've stood by it in a thick fog. I've smelt it as I've licked the salt taste off my cold lips. I've heard the waves lifting before they dump themselves on the shore with a relentless insistence. You cannot see them. You know only that they are there, bearing down.

The days I'd walk along the beach in a howling southerly made me feel great. I'd shout and sing out loud. I could yell and scream and no one could hear me above the gale-force winds and crashing seas. I'd stand at the top of the beach and feel the hurt of the sand as the wind drove it against my bare skin. Patches of foam blew up the beach. The constant heaving of the water against the land changed its colour to a dull green. I still loved it, and the flotsam it gave up. I'd come back to the house with glass floats washed off Japanese fishing boats within our waters, and sometimes the 5000 watt light bulbs the squid boats use for their fishing at night. In the house it was hard to imagine that these delicate glass treasures could arrive on our beach unbroken.

All sorts of fish washed up – casualties of the southerly weather. Leatherjackets, porcupines, mackerel, frostfish and the John Dory with the distinctive black spot on each side of its body were frequent casualties of southerly weather. Tradition has it that St Peter obtained his tribute money from the John Dory. The spots are said to be the imprints of the apostle's finger and thumb. Sadly for tradition, St Peter's fish were the inhabitants of a lake.

After one southerly storm I was out exploring. In the middle of our beach is a pile of flat rocks. I had been told they were the Canterbury Rocks but I hadn't given the name any thought. At the high tide mark, above the rocks, the stem of a ship was poking up. I excitedly scraped away the sand. I could see the copper fastenings. The lust of a treasure hunter surged through me. I might find all sorts of treasure. I dug carefully. It was buried deep in the sand. It got too hard to dig by hand and I gave up and ran to my in-laws to tell them about my find.

It had all been found before. Hundreds of times. Whenever there was a southerly the stem became visible. It was the remains of the *Canterbury*, a 59-foot schooner. She was anchored in Okukari Bay, sheltering from a southerly gale, when her anchors dragged and she was blown ashore on to the rocks on 4 March 1878. Hence their name. I was pleased to hear no one had drowned on my beautiful beach. The sea has since claimed the wreckage back and we haven't seen any sign of it in the last 20 years.

Some days I wanted to run as far as I could, just to go somewhere. Anywhere. The sharp craggy skyline drew my eyes and I'd walk to the top of the hills.

The highest hill on the farm is 1200 feet and I'd feel immense satisfaction on reaching the top and flopping down into the grass. I'd lie on my back staring into the sky and try to shake myself out of my homesickness. Sometimes I'd just sob. I often asked myself if I should have married Joe and come to live in this place, so far from home. If only I could've visited my parents without a boat trip to Picton, then a ferry trip to Wellington and that train trip to Auckland. It's all too far away, I'd decide. I can't stand it.

Hours later I'd look at my watch to see what the time was. I'd been there only half an hour.

Looking down into the valley that made up the flat land of the farm I saw three similar-sized paddocks with two larger ones taking up each side of the foothills. A fast-flowing stream ran down the side of the flats and, where it broke out to the sea, a lagoon had been formed. Some geese had found their way to Okukari and nested in the rushes. Above the lagoon under an old macrocarpa tree was a fenced-off grave site.

Buried here are Daniel Godfrey, who died in 1885, his wife Emma, who died in 1889, and their son Charles, who died in 1907. On the gravestone I read that Charles was the appointed keeper of the Tory Channel leading lights, which were first shown on 1 January 1882. He lived in Okukari and kept the lights at Whekenui until he died. The same lights still guide ships into Tory Channel entrance today but of course do not have to rely on a keeper to light them. I thought the words inscribed on the stone suited the man he must have been.

Light in the Darkness Sailor
Brightly Gleams Our Father's Mercy
To Send A Gleam Across The Wave.

There is one other grave on the farm. On a knob in the bottom paddock overlooking the sea there is a small sandstone headstone. Four words are written on it. Baby Hood. Aged 2. Over the years the constant sandblasting of southerly-driven sand whipped up from the beach has smoothed the headstone, her name and age now only a memory. I found out that Baby Hood lived in Okukari Bay with her parents, Caroline and Captain Augustus Hood. He was a trader and sailed between Wellington, Nelson and the Marlborough Sounds in his ketch, the *Augusta*. I'd look at her headstone and I'd wonder if her mother had had to bury this child on her own if her husband was away – he must have been away quite often. My heartache seemed small in comparison.

Joe finished whaling for good, it was spring, I could start to grow a garden, the farm got busy and Joe and his father diversified into fishing. Now I had lots to do and was over the worst of my homesickness. I had Joe at home and could spend my time with him out on the farm or on the boat. Homesickness had gone. By then this was my home.

CHAPTER TWO

Dictator in the Kitchen

MY PIANO became one of my best friends. My moods never bothered it. I would come away in a better frame of mind after playing some of my favourite Chopin and Mozart and Beethoven. The piano's traumatic entry into our house made it seem even more special.

I needed a friend. The wood-burning stove was a malevolent presence and I felt threatened. But sometimes it behaved well and then I'd rush to the piano and play in triumph. A sultana cake slowly baking in a moderate oven became a perfect accompaniment to any of Chopin's brilliant waltzes. I would be in control of my stove, not have it in control of me.

Poor Chopin suffered. His haunting Nocturne No 2 and some of his preludes matched the many days I couldn't get the fire going. Wet wood, no wind and a dirty chimney all conspired to give poor combustion. The thing would be constantly smoking and I'd be groping around for something to wipe my eyes with. If smoke alarms had been in use then, as they are today, I'd have been unable to keep up with the batteries.

In what should have been the hottest part of the oven, the cold black enamel meat dish with a shoulder of mutton still sitting in its juices would wait patiently to begin cooking. More than once Joe arrived home to meat still struggling to be cooked, vegetables waiting their turn to go in the oven, and me in tears. I dreamt electric stoves. Any type, any age. Anything in place of the monster green and cream Shacklock 501 that squatted in the corner of my kitchen.

I had married a very patient man. Without a word Joe would rake the embers round, select the 'right' wood and in no time the top would be red hot with the oven thermometer creeping up. But the relief of having the fire going never made me feel better. Why couldn't it do this for me? The round dial of the thermometer on the oven door became a face, and as the red gauge slowly moved up I'd see red lips stretching into a mean grin at me.

The whaling season had begun and was in full swing when I first came to Okukari. Each day Gilbert Perano steamed his whale chaser across the bay and put the bow on to the beach to pick up Joe at 6.30am. Across the channel the boats were moored beneath the lookout perched on West Head at the entrance of Tory Channel. The whalers clambered up to their lookout hut and waited for first light to begin their vigil for the humpback whale as it swam through Cook Strait.

One extremely cold morning I was delighted to be told to stay in bed. "I'll get my breakfast and light the coal range. The house'll be warm when you get up." Not needing to be told twice, I quickly snuggled into the warm bed.

Auckland never had frosts like this. The two hours before first light would push the temperature down two or three degrees. The stillness outside would wake me before the cold did. I would see a new picture out my window.

This particular morning the moon still hung in the sky just above the black waters of Tory Channel. Black hills, their crinkled skyline standing out in sharp relief against the sky, merged into the sea. Trees burnt black by the moon's light stood still. I gazed from my bed and felt as primitive people must have felt at the beginning of time. Nothing moved. Everything waited for the frost to settle gently.

I heard the door slam, Joe's gumboots crackle across the frosty lawn and the protesting creak of old age as the gate swung on its hinges. The chaser's engine slowed down as it came in to the beach to pick Joe up. I slept.

Something woke me. The fire was roaring. I could smell the heat. The thick taste of diesel was in my mouth. I leaped out of bed and into the kitchen. Joe had used diesel from a plastic container to coax the wet wood to burn. It had certainly worked. Now there was this odd shape slowly melting on to the red-hot stove top. Diesel oozed out to feed the fire.

I tried to lift the thing off. It had stuck to the stove top and all I did was make a bigger space for the hot diesel to pour out. Black acrid smoke filled the kitchen. I knew about petrol, but until I'd come to the farm I'd never met diesel. Would it explode? How hot could it get before it did? My mind raced.

I didn't even notice the ice crunching under my bare feet as I raced over to my in-laws' house and shouted for help. In later years my mother-in-law told me she always knew when something was wrong and how serious it was by the sound of my pounding feet. Now she quickly came over. We poured water on the fire and shovelled out the firebox. Then it was easy to scrape the lump of plastic from the stove top. Among all the wet greasy mess I noticed that my oven thermometer had gone around the dial out of sight. It would have been a wonderful scone oven.

I learnt that diesel has a low flashpoint. I could relax. But it might just have been coincidence that when Joe arrived home that night he heard me struggling to play the Warsaw Concerto, the theme from the old film Dangerous Moonlight. He wondered if his hat should be thrown in the door first.

The oven door made a very efficient clothes dryer. Joe always arrived home damp when he came back from the sea. Thick shirts, cord trousers and woollen jerseys were a struggle to air. I draped a piece of newspaper over the door, hung the clothes over and soon they were dry and back into drawers. That was until I scorched his new cords. I didn't think it was very noticeable. They were brown, anyway. Perhaps he wouldn't notice the burn when he dressed. Why don't my scones brown like that?

Next morning we slept in. The chaser's engine coming across the bay woke us up. Clothes were hastily dragged on. When Joe turned to leave the room I couldn't believe what I was seeing. The trousers must have been folded evenly across the door. A symmetrical burn spread across his bottom. No ordinary burn, this. A screen printer couldn't have come up with a better butterfly than I had managed. With every step the butterfly's wings fluttered tentatively, waiting for flight.

Its life was shortlived. The trousers became an angry discarded heap. The butterfly lay still, wings still outstretched.

Joe was five minutes late for work and I acquired a floorcloth.

In all the years when the coal range was my cooking, water heating and warmth source, we learnt to tolerate each other. I could never bake what I wanted to. Always my oven did the dictating. It organised me. A windy day, dry wood and clean chimney put pastry, biscuits and scones in my store cupboard. If it just didn't want to burn well, something cooked slowly would have to suffice. Sultana cakes were my standby then, and I became great at cooking them as I had so much practice. Fortunately Joe loved them and I always used my mother's recipe.

One particular cooking disaster stands out in 33 years of marriage. I'd decided a steamed pudding would be just right this particularly cold night. It hadn't been cooking long when the stove went out. By the time I had cranked it up and had the water boiling in the pot again, an hour had gone by. "I've plenty of time anyway," I thought, so the stove never even got a kick.

After the main meal I proudly turned out my superb pudding from its bowl. Perfect, I thought. It seemed a bit small and heavy, though. It was the first thing I'd made since we'd been married that Joe couldn't eat. "Sorry, love, it's just too rubbery." He had struggled through heaps of flops very bravely up until now.

We had a pet pig, Isabelle. Joe had brought her home as a piglet when he'd been hunting. She was a Captain Cooker, a descendant of the few pigs Captain Cook had left on Arapawa Island in 1774. All the scraps went up to her sty in the morning and she had fared particularly well in the first months of my cooking. On this occasion, a couple of days later Joe's mother asked me if I knew where the pig had got the ball from. Apparently she was rolling it around her pen and having a great time with it. I had no idea. Perhaps it was a stone, I said. But as soon as I could I went up to check it out. Yes. I'd been right. It was my pudding. Not even the pig could eat it. Lesson learnt – keep a steam pudding on the boil – don't let the heat die out.

My stove couldn't always be blamed for my flops. A perfect oven persuaded me to cook a sponge. The generator was going so I could use my cake mixer.

My mother-in-law's recipe guaranteed me a sponge at least four inches high. I visualised Joe coming in and seeing it on the kitchen table, dredged with icing sugar and cream oozing from the middle. I'd sit it on our Country Rose cake plate.

The cooking time completed, I opened the oven door carefully. My sponge sat in the bottom of the tin. It hadn't risen at all. Was it possible I'd left out a vital ingredient? Biscuits for afternoon tea again.

I still smarted from Isabelle's refusing the steamed pudding.

"I'd rather give it to the dogs than offer it to the pig," I told Joe.

"I've a better idea," he said. "Post it up to your Dad. Put a note on the outside saying 'If it won't fit in the letterbox, slip it under the door.'"

Time found me getting as smart as my stove. Kindling put in the oven overnight meant a quick crackling fire in the morning. Keeping the chimney and around the oven free from soot helped too, and I discovered a bushy branch of manuka tied to a long stick made an excellent chimney brush.

My stove taught me well. My piano sweetened the lessons.

Keeping up the wood supply for the fire was almost a full-time job. Occasionally a gale blew down a pine or a macrocarpa tree. I felt sad for the fallen tree, one day so proud and tall, another day the chainsaw's blade cuts cleanly through the green wood, slicing up rings as if they are cheese. Cream slabs framed in callused bark lean drunkenly against each other. The trunk lies, a broken line over the grass. The fragrance of fresh pine sap oozing out of cut wood intoxicates the senses. The pure notes from cheeky birds sound louder. Drunken bumble bees slam into anything in their path and insects whose homes have been destroyed seem quite content to laze in the sun on the big log.

A month out in the weather would leave the wood dry enough for Joe to split up into bite-sized pieces for the stove. Stacking it in the woodshed was my job. I made sure I had those 'right' pieces handy for the days when my stove and I were at loggerheads. Bark and pine cones were carefully stored. These were gold on cold wet days. They started the fire well and a firebox filled with cones or bark soon had the oven red hot and the water boiling in its tank. Even the small branches were tied in bundles and stacked in a corner of the woodshed and used as kindling.

Homesickness still hit me at times and left me feeling miserable. One such evening in an attempt to cheer me up Joe said, "Tomorrow, weather permitting, I'll take you down to Lucky Bay. With all the southerly weather we've had there'll be a lot of driftwood washed ashore there."

Lucky Bay lies three miles south of the channel entrance out in Cook Strait. The vagaries of the tides push driftwood into the bay and the ocean swells dump it high up on the stony beach. When the swell is low a dinghy can be rowed ashore and the wood gathered. The mere thought of the boat trip brightened me up.

18

Next afternoon we steamed through the narrow mouth of Tory Channel. The ebb tide pushed us along an extra five knots. Whaling was finished for the season, and high on the lookout only the closed shutters kept watch from the whalers' hut. The strong current pushing hard against the rudder made Joe grip the wheel tightly to stop the boat yawing in the tide.

The seals are the only inhabitants of this barren coast. Stretched out on the warm rocks they keep watch on the water below where thick bull kelp surges in the ocean swell. I saw one spot a fish. It splashed into the sea, no longer a lumbering creature of the land but a deadly streamlined fisher. Teeth clenched on the flapping fish, it hauled itself back on the rocks. A quick shake of the head flicked the fish around, head first, and with one gulp it disappeared. The meal completed, the proud fisher, its fur glistening and whiskers spiked with water, rejoined its friends, flopped on to the warm rocks and lazily rolled over to begin its patient vigil once more.

Steaming past Jordy Rocks I spared a thought for Jordy, a whaler from the longboat days. My father-in-law had told me how Jordy often needed to have a 'nervous one' during a whale hunt and insisted that he be put ashore. The longboat would put in close to the tiny island of bare rocks, Jordy would leap off, go to the 'toilet' and then rejoin his boat. Legend has it that one day a whale was spotted and before Jordy could clamber back into the boat it took off, leaving him behind. One whale later the crew returned to pick him up.

Today the swell broke gently around his namesake, making a frill of white lace lying on a dark blue velvet background.

Off Lucky Bay we dropped anchor, made sure it held on the rocky bottom, and rowed ashore. Logs stripped bare of bark from their constant tumbling in the sea covered the beach. Above the mean high water mark a wall more than five feet high of smooth white logs had been left by the crashing seas. Hundreds of roast dinners with crisply baked vegetables lay here. It didn't take long to fill the dinghy up with wood and, perched on the top, Joe paddled out to the *Wheke* to unload. From the shore I saw our woodstack mounting high above the bulwarks of the waiting boat.

"My woodshed will love this," I told myself. After Joe had done a few trips in and out I noticed the swell was slowly rising. Out from the shore the sea looked flat calm but close inshore the waves lifted roundly and swelled over the smooth rocks.

"We'll have to get out of here soon. The tide's changed. This will be our last load," Joe decided.

This time we were greedy. It was the biggest load of the day. The swell had grown bigger in the last half hour. The waves crashed into hollow corners of the beach, then dragged the gravel back to the sea. As we pushed the heavy dinghy out, a wave, bigger than any others, broke over us.

"Hold the bow into the sea. Don't let her get broadside or we'll lose her!"

Joe yelled. The wave left the sea calm. "Quickly, hop in now before the next one breaks," he ordered.

Both of us leaped into the dinghy, grabbed an oar and paddled frantically to clear the shore.

"Look out, here's the big one!" Joe shouted. Above us a towering green wall of water blocked the sun. It crashed down, swamping the dinghy before overturning it, leaving Joe, me, and the wood all struggling to reach the surface first. Both of us swim well in open water but we were surrounded by heaving logs that slammed into our bodies. We clawed frantically at the upturned dinghy as it surfaced, found the painter, and pulled it ashore. We got through the breakers on our second attempt but we left that wood for another day.

Constant stoking, especially on cold days, boiled the water in the old cylinder. The ancient plumbing rattled and thumped in the walls. When the tap was turned on the water rumbled along the rusty pipes to escape. Depending on how long it had boiled, varying shades of brown water spewed out. It stained the bath, and the rust flakes that settled on the bottom weren't the most comfortable things to sit on.

Visitors running a bath received a shock when they were greeted by the steaming brown water. Arriving in from fishing wet and cold, my cousin, John, turned on the taps. A short time later one disgusted 'townie' boldly stated, "I can't have a bath in that. It's dirtier than I am now."

We finally persuaded him not to be stupid. "It's only rust. The boiling water kills the bugs anyway," Joe told him.

Not completely convinced he shut the door. We heard the cold water running, then came a loud shriek. Out shot John.

"That's it! I'll have a rusty bath but I'm not sharing it with an eel!"

When we went in to investigate, the hapless eel was completing its final dance of death. Its swim down the pipes from the dam in the creek was its last. It was only a small eel.

Washing became discoloured by the rust, its crisp new look gone. I kept the doors of my linen cupboard firmly shut on its dull contents. My over-enthusiasm with bleach soon found me selecting new linen with an eye to bold bright colours.

Over the winter months the coal range was the central point of the kitchen. A cup of tea tasted much better when we were sitting around with the oven door open, thick-socked feet curled over the bottom oven slide and toasted nice and warm. The top of the stove kept the huge pot of soup simmering all day and the stove's radiating warmth spread through the house. After the trouser mishap Joe rigged up two lines in the kitchen. I didn't like seeing my washing strung up inside but it was great getting it all dry. I baked more when it was cold. With the stove gobbling wood to heat the house my hot oven had to be utilised. My Scottish ancestry made me feel guilty if I didn't.

Our kitchen trapped all the afternoon sun. In summer the coal range was unbearable. Butter melted in its dish and if I cooked a hot meal at night we enjoyed it only if we ate very late or outside. I lit the fire in the early mornings, heated the water, cooked what I needed for the day, and we lived on salads with cold meat rather than having to bear that heat inside.

With summer came the blowflies. As soon as the stove was lit and I started cooking, my windows became the landing zone for the big black blowies from the bush. Someone suggested sprinkling pepper on the hot stove top to make the blowflies disappear. With the next invasion out came the pepper and I covered the top of the stove. It got rid of the blowflies. It also got rid of me. Burning pepper made tears roll down my face and had me gulping for fresh air outside.

As I sat on the doorstep waiting for the air to clear enough for me to go back inside I realised that blowflies and I were going to have to learn to live with one another. I couldn't live in my pepper-created environment so I'd either have to keep all the windows and the door shut and swelter, or have everything open and let the blowflies in and the hot air out. This was before the days of fly screens.

Not long after the pepper incident my coal range and I created another problem. The top of the range was dirty and dull from years of neglect. I thought how lovely to have a sparkling, white-topped electric stove. After each use I could wipe it clean. Not like my coal range. Any spills danced up and down on the hot top and stuck hard before the top cooled enough to be able to clean it.

"I used to buy Zebo when I had the old coal range," Ruby told me. "It was cast iron, and I used to blacken the whole thing." When I was told how shiny it used to look, I decided I'd try it.

But I wanted to do it now, and our next mail day was three days away, so I used black shoe Nugget instead. My stove top glistened. I was so thrilled with it that I put on a second coat. I had plenty of elbow grease, and ended up with a stove top that looked every bit as shiny as a new pair of shoes.

I lit the fire and went outside to fill up the coal bucket. When I came back inside a blue haze pouring off my beautiful shiny range met me at the kitchen door. As it became hotter, thicker smoke billowed up. Once again I was driven outside to wait until the air cleared. Once again my coal range was the victor. I decided once and for all that the only thing I'd put on the top of my stove ever again would be pots and pans.

CHAPTER THREE

If You're a Heberley

HEBERLEY means boats, sea, fish. Six generations of Heberleys have been involved with the sea as harbour pilot, whaler or fisherman.

My Joe lived for whaling. His work was his sport. He loved the excitement of the hunt and the satisfaction of the kill. Whaling was something he'd grown up with. It was part of the country's economy. He was lucky to be in a job he loved.

Today he is loud in his protests about continuing whaling, and wholeheartedly supports the conservation of the whale.

Back when we were first married, the whaling at Peranos' was a winter job. Joe's father, Charlie, was a true Heberley and he had to get back on the sea. Since he had left the Barrier a year ago, the farm had taken up all his time, but salt water ran in his veins and it was getting thin. He decided he needed a boat to go fishing, and the *Wheke*, the boat they owned, was too small.

Ruby's father, Maurice Ivanhoe Guard (better known as Ivan), had been a commercial fisherman. About this time he died, and his boat, the *Midlothian* (now named *Mariner*), a 36-foot double ender, came up for sale. Before Port Underwood was opened up by road he had delivered the weekly mail into the Port, using the *Midlothian*. Charlie bought this boat, steamed it down the Opawa River from Blenheim, over the bar and up the coast to Okukari. The *Wheke* was sold. A new era had begun.

Joe finished whaling in September 1964, and both he and his father got to work making crayfish pots. They designed their own style and built the pots three-foot square with a wooden-framed base. They drilled holes in the base and hooped supple-jack frames over from each side. The pot was then covered with wire netting. Bricks wired in the corners were used as weights and when these began to get low I noticed them eyeing my chimney. Ruby had a retaining wall of bricks on the outside of her garden. They even started prising them out of the bank until she realised where the muddy-looking bricks were coming from. Then flat stones off the beach had to suffice.

The boat was changed from a trawler into a cray-boat. Coils of rope and boxes of buoys, which all had to have some distinguishing mark, arrived at Okukari. At last the pots went out and as the *Midlothian* steamed out, laden down with pots, we could hear the laughter in Joe's and Charlie's voices carrying over the bay. The Heberleys were fishermen once more.

Local fishermen laughed too. "Only thing you'll catch in those will be chickens." But they fished well and before the end of the first cray season, using the new pots, we noticed the loudest scoffers had lots of similar-looking newly-built pots in their boats.

Joe and Charlie fished the coast north of the channel entrance as far up as Cape Koamaru. Crayfish were plentiful and our bank balance grew, but it was hard work and often dangerous.

One episode I'll never forget. It was our second wedding anniversary. Joe and Charlie were setting nets for butterfish up the outside coast north of the channel. The day was eerie, with the leaden sky making the water in the bay black. Not a breath of wind ruffled the water. Down south a southerly bank had been bulging over the hills all day although sou'westerlies were predicted. Just on dark the wind swung to the south, and gale-force winds hit with a vengeance. Ruby and I heard Gil Perano's boat coming into Whekenui Bay and knew our men would also be in at any minute, as they had been fishing nearby. We went out to the bank to see if there was any sign of them. The wind was so strong it pushed us to our knees and we both crawled to the edge of the bank that overlooked the bay. Salt blown off the top of the waves stung our faces. We couldn't look into the wind. But the boat we wanted to see was nowhere there.

"I'll ring Gilly. He might see their lights coming from his place," Ruby said when we got in out of the wind and could hear ourselves speak.

Gil's words made us feel sick. "They were only a mile behind us but we lost sight of them when we turned to come in the channel. I would've thought they'd be in by now. They've probably turned and are running with it, Ruby. I'm sure they'll be okay."

The storm lashed the windows amid the noise of the rain, and the sea crashed on the beach. The *Midlothian* had a radio telephone but we didn't have a receiver. Why didn't they send a message through Wellington Radio to us? The terrible hours dragged past. At last, at 11pm the call we'd been praying for came through. They'd called Wellington Radio as soon as they were around Cape Koamaru. They had done as Gilly thought. They were all right and would be home in about four hours, steaming through the northern entrance of Queen Charlotte Sound and back up Tory Channel.

I was up and had the stove burning well when Joe walked in the door. He broke down. "I never thought I'd see you again," was all he said as he wrapped his arms around me.

The day had been perfect to begin with. The little wind they'd had all day had drawn in from the sou'west. Their nets had been full all day and the boat was loaded with butterfish. They were pulling in their last net when without warning the wind switched to the south-east. By the time they got the last net aboard and rowed to the boat it was over 60 knots. They didn't even clear the net as they pulled it up, and they left all the nets in the dinghy to get underway more quickly. They fastened the dinghy and hauled the anchor up. They followed Peranos' lights and saw them turn into the channel but by the time they reached Wellington Head they knew it was too risky and rough for them to try to get through the rip.

"Dad said we'd have to run with it and try for the northern entrance. After we turned the seas were so big the boat kept trying to broach on the huge seas that tucked themselves under the stern. Dad yelled at me to make a sea anchor. 'Use those two car tyres,' he said. 'Don't need them as fenders now, and that school shark we caught should do the work of another sea anchor once they're tied together. If she broaches we're goners.' They sure helped," Joe said.

Behind them the dinghy was struggling to survive the seas. She'd sit up on the top of a wave as it crested behind, then rush down and race past the stern of the boat until the rope jerked it to a standstill. As the boat kept on steaming ahead, the dinghy painter would tighten with a loud crack, then begin its ride down the seas once more. When it became dark it was worse. They heard a bang and knew their dinghy was gone. With it she tore the railings off the top of the bulwarks. "That's when I was really scared. Specially when Dad told me to go and put on a life jacket and bring one up for him."

They wanted to call Wellington Radio but it was too rough to get anywhere near the radio. Going up the coast they couldn't see a thing through the wind and hail. It was pitch black. Every now and then the skyline was lit up in a sheet of lightning. Joe told me how glad he was to be with his father who knew that coast like the back of his hand. All they could hear were the seas crashing against sheer cliffs. If the boat had gone down they wouldn't have stood a chance of getting ashore. Then as they steered into the shelter behind Koamaru the seas flattened, the wind stopped whipping the air away from their mouths, and they could relax. They'd made it, they'd be all right. They called Wellington Radio. "I'll tell you one thing the sea has taught me tonight," Joe said. "Respect."

As so often happens after a southerly buster, the next morning was fine with a clear blue sky and not a breath of wind. Joe and his father thought there might be a chance that the dinghy had got ashore. They were positive it would be smashed up but the possibility of salvaging some of their nets sent them out. We all went out. How could this glassy water have been so violent less than 12 hours ago? Nothing was found – no nets, not even any wreckage from the dinghy. The sea hugged their whereabouts to itself.

There was a farm still to be run, and trips to town, whether on business or otherwise, took the *Midlothian* away from fishing. One particular day Joe's parents had to go to town. The tides and the moon were at their best and catches had been excellent over the last few days. "Tow Heather and me out in the dinghy and we'll pull the pots around Wellington Head and in Wellington Bay as we work our way back."

"You mad bugger," was Charlie's answer.

All the same I found myself cast adrift in a 14-foot clinker dinghy, each of us with a pair of oars – and me four months pregnant. I watched the *Midlothian* disappear from sight and felt very insignificant in our small boat. Joe noticed my glum face. "C'mon, love. Imagine my grandfather. He caught whales in a boat like this." His words did nothing for me. I wasn't his grandfather, Arthur Heberley, and I had no wish to catch whales.

At least it was flat calm as we started pulling our pots around Wellington Head and working north. We had four cases of crays sitting in the bottom of the dinghy when we'd finished those pots but by then the tide had changed and the rip around Wellington Head was too rough to go through. We had a choice. Go outside the rip, which meant an extra hour's rowing, or through the gap between Wellington Head and Arapawa Island. This gap often went dry. Sand bars altered in it and the water was only about 20-30 feet wide. We opted for the gap.

When we got closer it didn't seem such a good idea. The swell had built. Waves were building on either side, then rushing in the gap from both sides to meet head on and rear up with a loud clap – like two dogs rearing up on their hind legs and fighting.

We stood off while Joe studied the pattern. "There's a lull between every fourth and fifth wave. You watch." It seemed all the same to me but I trusted his words. He knew the sea and I didn't.

As we made for the gap my heart pounded. Then Joe yelled, "Now!" We dug our oars in and rowed frantically into the narrow stretch of water. The rocky beach was only a few feet away. Out of the sea behind us a wave grew until it towered over us. I screamed as I turned around to Joe sitting in the bow of the dinghy, and saw one just as big in front of us. Just before the waves met, Joe ordered me to jump out and run up the beach out of it. The waves hit, the dinghy filled with water, and it was washed up on the sand. "Quickly, bale out the water before the next wave hits!" Our baler was still floating in the dinghy with our precious crayfish. Using it and our hands we managed to get rid of most of the water, push the dinghy through the gap and begin our long row home around Wellington Bay. Joe said he never forgave me for my words as I ran up the beach away from the towers of water. "Save our crays! Don't lose them!" I wasn't worried about him.

We still had more pots to pull around the bay and by the time we reached Tory Channel I was exhausted and had blisters hanging off my hands. Rivalry between boats was fierce and no one liked to let any other fisherman know what they were catching. Jim Fishburn Senior came around East Head into the channel in his boat, the *Northern Star*. My flagging spirits lifted. He'll offer us a tow, I thought. He came up close and shouted over the water. "Like a tow to your bay? I'll throw you a line." In absolute disbelief I heard Joe's reply. "She's right, Jim. We're nearly home. Thanks all the same." To me he said, "We don't want them seeing what fish we've caught." If the crew of the *Northern Star* had turned around as they steamed past they'd have seen one pair of oars being dumped in the dinghy and Joe rowing on his own.

Crayfish have to be unloaded live, and rather than our making daily trips to Picton to unload, a holding tank was built and moored in the bay. Once a week, unless it was full sooner, it was towed ashore by tractor and emptied out into boxes. Then these were rowed out to the *Midlothian*. To prevent all this double handling, a wharf was the answer.

In 1965 Dig Thacker from Te Iro Bay came with his pile-driving gear he had set up on the *Oria*. This was an old whaling chaser, built for Joe's Heberley grandfather, and because of her long narrow shape she was affectionately known as the Splinter. He began the job of driving railway irons for the piles. The stringers underneath were Australian hardwood and had come from the original railway viaduct, built in 1874, in Picton's Essons Valley.

Visitors arriving at Okukari for Christmas in 1965 were met on our new wharf. Meeting the mail boat was no longer by dinghy. When I arrived home from a day in town with a load of stores, and later with tired children, I'd feel like the Queen Mother as I stepped up on to our new wharf.

Only once did I wish that the wharf had never been built. It was summer and a lot of tourists were on the *Reo Moana* with Bill Kenny. I heard him giving his passengers the Heberley history as he came alongside the wharf, and the well-dressed tourists stared at me as I wandered along to meet him, followed by one of the farm dogs. Bill had a corgi, and he came on most mail runs. The corgi strutted up to the bow of the boat, past many of the passengers who were sitting on the outside seats, put his front legs on the capping rail of the *Reo Moana* and growled at our dog. That did it. Immediately our dog jumped across on to Bill's boat, landed among the passengers, then lifted his back leg and let out a stream of urine on a very new-looking white leather handbag. All I could do was swap mail bags, call the dog and get off the wharf as quickly as possible.

My first trip up the Sounds had made me think that for this place to have been created there must be a God. Such a beautiful place couldn't evolve without a gentle touch or a nod of the creator's head.

Maori mythology recognises the hand of the gods in the making of the Sounds. In a story handed down through generations, Maori gods came down from the heavens in a canoe. They'd travelled such a long distance from their source of power that they'd become weak. The canoe capsized. Its keel rose and formed the Southern Alps, and the intricately carved prow shattered and formed the Marlborough Sounds.

Western scientists have different, though strangely allied stories. They speak of immense tectonic forces that heave, twist, push up, lower and shatter the rock of the area. Land once raised from the sea was lowered, and what were river valleys have become the waterways of the Marlborough Sounds. It's a process that is still continuing – scientists estimate the area is still subsiding about one metre every 100 years.

In the 33 years I've lived in the Sounds I've experienced violence in storms, the hell of earthquakes and the worrying tedium of droughts. But once these natural forces pass over, the Sounds again become a place of haunting beauty where steep hillsides slide into deep water so clear that fish can be seen swimming among the forest of kelp below the surface. Mussels and paua grip the rocks, ignoring the swirling currents which try in vain to pluck the shellfish from their home and toss them into deeper water.

In many places the water laps against sheer rock faces, and boaties can tie up to a hanging bough which has reached out over the water and become the nesting place of cormorants, or shags as they are more commonly called. With glinting eyes the birds swoop down, their screeches silenced only when the waters close over the sleek black and white bodies. They dive deeply to snatch a blue cod, butterfish or a lowly sprat from the depths, then surface with the fish clasped tightly in their hooked bills before it is gulped down head first.

The thick sweet smell of the clematis hangs in the air, and the white flowers are easy to spot as the clematis twists through the regenerating bush. Ponga ferns grow thickly in steep gullies and on unfarmed land. On a fine day millions of cicadas sing their hearts out, or less romantically rub their legs together in a song of summer.

I envy those passengers arriving in Picton for the first time on the Cook Strait ferries, or aboard the cruise ships that now have Picton on their itineraries. I try to imagine their feelings as they travel in these waterways for the first time. Do they stand and drink in the beauty of the carpet of pongas laid to the water's edge on Picton Harbour's western shore, and smell the freshness and hear the silence above the cadences of the cicadas?

I thought my 20 years in Auckland had taught me about strong winds. I remembered how Auckland was frequently hit by gale-force easterlies in March and April, as depressions of tropical origin formed in the Pacific to bear down on New Zealand. They'd create a hell of horizontally-driven rain and spray as the wind roared up the Waitemata Harbour, turning it into a seething mass of foaming water. The port would be closed and not even the faithful 'Blueboats' were allowed to leave their berths.

I remembered these storms when as a child I stood with my back to the wind and leaned into it, lying so far back that the minute the gust died I'd collapse in a heap on the ground. During one such storm the *Mangawai*, our yacht, started dragging her moorings towards Northcote's Sulphur Beach. With estimated wind gusts of 90-100 mph, the port was closed and no assistance could be given from the harbour board. This was my father's boat, his pride and his joy, and he wasn't going to stand on the beach with the rest of us, watching helplessly as each sea lifted her bow high out of the water. Each lift dragged the mooring closer to the beach where the breaking waves foamed over the mud flats. There they formed pools of water in the hollows made from the feet of spectators who'd come to watch a crazy man and a youth probably drown themselves. These two men were my father and Bill Kells. They rowed through the seas that day, reached the *Mangawai*, freed her from her mooring, and steamed through the maddened sea to Western Viaduct on the southern side of the harbour, to tie up in the calm waters of the basin. This was to be the first but certainly not the last rescue of my life.

In the days before the Auckland harbour bridge was built, these winds occasionally prevented the ferries berthing at Northcote wharf, and buses transported commuters to Birkenhead wharf where the ferry boats could berth. If the harbour was closed it meant a long trip around the top of the harbour through Riverhead and Henderson.

Oh yes, I knew all about strong winds, I told myself when Joe regaled me with some dreadful stories of the gales they'd had at Okukari.

"I've seen chooks flattened against a fence," Ruby told me.

"And cows kneeling into the wind," added Joe.

I nodded. I understood.

But nothing, nothing on this earth had prepared me for the naked fury of the first storm I experienced at Okukari. I'd first felt the rage of the southerly and the northerly winds when I was waiting for my piano to arrive but when nature unleashes all her power on Okukari it sends grown men to their knees as they crawl through the winds.

My first such storm came at us from the north. During the night, winds tore macrocarpa trees out of the ground. Their roots, caked with dirt and more than 10 feet high, were drying out in the sun when I looked out the window after the worst night I'd ever spent in my life. Ninety years of growing time meant nothing to this wind, and the trees now lay in Ruby's and Charlie's back yard, their branches scratching against window panes along the back wall of their house which was amazingly still intact. Their garden was destroyed and it took weeks to clean up the mess and rebuild the garden.

But our woodsheds bulged.

Storms of this intensity are infrequent so they remain vivid in my memory. During one such storm I'd lain through the darkness, willing the night to end. Rain and wind thrashed our bedroom window all night. I could hear the pane of glass protesting with each onslaught. Joe sleeps on the window side of the bed and with each gust I'd tell him this was it. The window would blow in.

"Don't be so bloody stupid. Get to sleep," I was told, but sleep was not on my agenda that night. With each crack of the wind on the glass I buried my head under the pillow and made sure I was covered completely with the blankets. "We'll be cut to bits when it goes," I muttered from beneath the bed clothes.

Just as the first hint of light was peeping through the gap in the middle of the curtains, the forces of nature became too much for the glass. One loud crack and the bedroom was showered with glass, driven across the room on the wind and rain. In all the mess and confusion I still had great delight in telling Joe from beneath my pillow, "I told you so."

The curtains hung in shreds, and glass lay over the bed and the furniture. It drove us from our bed to find a sheet of plywood to place over the window frame. Carrying this up to the house from the woolshed was a fight all the way as the wind tried to wrestle it from our arms. The wind held the plywood in place while Joe hammered in the nails.

Next we heard loud crashes and bangs in the generator shed. When Joe went in to start the power he found the end blown out and a window gone as well. We still had a lighting plant which was just as well, as anyone who was brave enough to poke their noses outside needed a change of clothes. Wet clothes were peeled off and put straight into the clothes dryer and it ran non-stop until we turned the lighting plant off about 9am.

Nature was trying her hardest to rip us off the hillside and blow our house right out into the bay. We sat around the kitchen table, watching. The wind tore across the water, lifted the tops off the waves and blanketed the hills on the opposite side of the channel with salt spray. Around the wharf, woolshed and boatshed, anything not tied down was lifted by the wind and carried out into the bay.

"What's that?" yelled Joe as we watched something big bobbing off the end of the wharf.

"God knows. It's something white, I think." I peered through the gloom.

Something similar joined it. Wind-borne rain blotted out our vision. Through binoculars Joe tried to fathom out whatever was bobbing in the bay. He swung the binoculars to the woodshed.

"Jesus Christ! It's the roof."

Corrugated iron was peeling off the roof as if a giant hand was flicking over the leaves of a book.

"I'll get Dad!" Joe yelled as he tore out the door. "And don't anyone come outside. It's too bloody dangerous."

I watched Joe as he crawled towards the woolshed where he met up with his father. Each wind gust brought heavier sheets of rain and they disappeared from sight. Catching glimpses of their yellow smockies through the rain brought me some relief. Sheets of iron blew over them, some bouncing along the wharf as if they were no more than autumn leaves dancing in an April's breeze.

It was impossible to climb on to the roof in these conditions so they had to work from the inside. I'd seen them do it once before when the roof had lifted in places in gale-force winds and we'd lost some roofing iron. Joe climbed to the rafters and his father passed him some timber, a plank this time, but oars can be used if nothing else is to hand. They pushed the plank through the gap where the iron had blown away and placed it so it lay over the iron that was still fast to the shed on each side of the hole. Then it was wired down to stop more iron from peeling off. They worked without speaking as the noise of rattling iron and the straining building fighting for its life against the wind and rain made it impossible to hear. At last I could see that they had beaten the elements. No more iron was flying out into the bay. This storm had taken one-third of the woolshed roof, and the end truss from the front of the shed.

But now we had another worry. After a violent northerly gale we can expect the wind to switch straight around to the south and blow as hard from this opposite direction. The northerly wind died during the afternoon, and already strong to gale-force southerlies were being predicted for the following day. Our woolshed had to be repaired before the next blow or we might lose the whole roof.

Our local timber merchants were only too pleased to open up their yard on a Sunday afternoon and deliver the materials we needed to our boat in Picton. That same evening with the help of some neighbours and working with hastily erected lights we had a roof back on the woolshed. It still needed finishing off, but at least we could fall into bed that night knowing that if the southerly arrived before daylight our shed was secure.

Four days later, on our usual Thursday mail day, we received a large mail. It was the truss, or framing, from our roof. The mail boat driver had picked it up in Maraetai Bay, nine miles down Tory Channel.

A gale from the south is compounded. Not only do we have the wind to contend with but also the salt spray. The flats look almost as if an atomic bomb has been detonated and its blast has roared over the farm. Green grass is burnt black, trees lose their leaves and any plants with soft leaves curl up and die. The southerly is nature's lawn mower.

One morning we woke after a southerly to find the foreground of my picture strewn with pine logs. They'd broken loose from a raft of logs in a neighbouring bay. Nothing could be done till heavy equipment arrived, when the logs were laboriously collected and carefully counted before being loaded on to a barge. If even one log had escaped and floated off, partially submerged, small boats would have been endangered. Logs are still milled in the Sounds but they are no longer rafted.

One southerly storm no one who lived through it will ever forget was when the inter-island ferry *Wahine* sank at the entrance to Wellington Harbour, with the loss of 51 lives. The book, *New Zealand Shipwrecks*, says of it: 'On the day of the disaster, April 10, 1968, Wellington and the surrounding area was savaged by a storm, the force and violence of which had never before been recorded in New Zealand.'

In Okukari, tucked inside the entrance of Tory Channel, 25 miles away from the ongoing tragedy, we were in a different world. The day was calm and sunny. The only sign of a possible storm was the huge sea breaking on the beach and a black southerly cloud bank passing through the strait. Waves curled out of smooth sparkling waters to thump down with an angry roar before sucking hungrily back to race up the sand once more.

We couldn't believe what we heard on the radio – what was happening just over the water from us. The Kelburn weather office in Wellington was recording gusts of 100-123 mph. All we could do that day was listen to news broadcasts telling us of a ship losing its battle against the sea, and feel the pain of the survivors because they existed and their loved ones didn't.

Rain storms usually come with the wind. Slips leave the farm with yellow scars over the hillsides, unusable farm roads and broken fences. The flats become deserts of silt and stones. These have spewed from torrents which used to be meandering creeks, but now rage down the paddocks to burst into the sea.

One of the worst of these storms lost us more than 50 sheep. The pre-lamb shearing had been done three weeks earlier. We'd expected the heavy rain, but not the strong northerly winds as well. Cold sheep trying to escape the driving rain huddled in creekbeds that couldn't cope with the volume of water pouring off the hills. Some sheep died of the cold. Others drowned. Many were carried out to sea, and others were washed against fences and lay dead on the flats after the storm was spent. All were heavy in lamb, and we cleaned up in the aftermath of that storm with saddened hearts.

Hot summer days take away the pain of winter but bring a new crisis to Okukari. Three houses, as we have now, and a fish freezer that needs a garden hose of water running through it constantly for cooling, cause our water supply to become very low. Some years are worse than others. We have endured summers when the water has been so low we have had to cart all our drinking water from the head of the flats, and share showers every other day or go swimming instead of having a shower.

One summer, long after I'd had my family, the pushchair came out of retirement and down out of the rafters of the shed, and became our water tanker. I fitted six flagons into it and it became a daily pilgrimage to push the pram as close to the creek as possible, then carry each flagon to the water to be filled. People who live in towns don't realise there are times when water becomes liquid gold.

One Christmas we had 15 people in the house. Water in the dam was low, and then a stomach bug swept through the bay. The smell that emanated from the taps told us the water was to blame. "It's because the dam's so low," Joe said. "Don't drink water from the taps. We'll cart it from the head of the flats."

The pushchair came out again, and the flagons. I changed from being a Virgo to become an Aquarius. Our James with Greg, the son of Picton friends Maureen and Cedric Stewart, whom we had met because of one tragic search and rescue exercise, offered to help out. They loved an excuse to take the motorbike up the paddocks with my big stock pot tied on the back, and bring it home filled with water. They'd leave it sitting on my bench with the lid on until the water was needed.

We began to feel we were going to live again once the tummy bug had left the house. Long gins sipped on a hot evening tasted great. Then I lifted the lid off the pot to take out some clean water. There, swimming lazily around, was an eel.

Greg and James must have waited all day for my screams, and no doubt had been disappointed when I hadn't noticed it. I scooped the eel out – it was only about six inches long – and put it in the bottom of my uncle's glass. It curled around like a snake waiting for the charmer's music to entice it from its basket.

I added ice blocks, squash and water. I couldn't bear to waste the gin on an eel so I left that out.

"I love the sound of tinkling ice on a hot day," my uncle said in anticipation as I handed him the glass. He had the glass in his hand when the eel rebelled at its small swimming space. The head popped out, and a disgusted uncle let out a roar. Once he knew I'd left out the gin he enjoyed the joke and settled back to have his gin without eel.

Summers leave our bay dry, and as the hills become more yellow we wait for the time when we can burn off. It is one of the best methods of land clearing on the rugged terrain. Sheep are mustered off the blocks, and fires sweep over the land. Blackened hillsides soon have tender green shoots of grass growing where patches of gorse and manuka have stood. After the first rains it isn't long before the hills green up, and once again I feel that nature has triumphed and beauty has returned.

We expect dry summers, and storms are usually predicted so we can prepare ourselves for them. But earthquakes hit. The only warning is the rumble that precedes them. Dogs seem to sense an earthquake. I've noticed them whining, running around in circles with their tails between their legs and huddling close to people. And I've been on the beach and been surprised to see crabs scuttling out of the water and up the beach. Then in minutes I've felt the tremor and watched the sea rise and fall on the sand, and wondered how the crabs have sensed this force which had sent them scurrying from their homes.

Until I lived at Okukari I'd felt only an occasional earthquake in Wellington and those were when I was young. I'd forgotten my fear of them.

My first earthquake in Okukari happened one evening as I was cooking paua fritters. I'd collected the paua from the rocks that lay between our place and Whekenui, and minced them with an onion, and now they smelt delicious as they sizzled in the pan on top of my burning-well coal range.

Earlier in the day my mother-in-law had remarked that it was earthquake weather. The day was still. Noises seemed to be louder than usual and echoed round the bay in the airless atmosphere. "It's the eerie stillness. Even the birds are quiet," she said when I asked her what she meant.

I heard the rumble and remembered her words. Later everyone was to laugh at the memory of me running outside clutching the frying pan, my paua fritters still spattering. I could hear the swish of the tall pine trees around the house and loud crashes came from inside. I squatted on the path outside the door, arms wrapped around my head, waiting for the world to end or the quake to stop.

Later we heard it was 4.7 on the Richter Scale but its epicentre was only half a mile from Tory Channel entrance in Cook Strait. "You've got to expect the odd quake, love. We're on the fault line," did nothing to pacify me when Joe arrived and found me still outside, my cold paua patties soaking up all the oil in the pan.

Inside our house nothing appeared to be broken but my coal range had gone out. Joe lit it so I could start cooking our paua once again. Smoke poured out of every nook and cranny of the coal range. The earthquake had caused bricks to fall down inside the chimney. Joe took off the chimney damper, and with my smaller hands I groped around and pulled out the fallen bricks. "See," Joe said. "Let it be a lesson. Never run outside in an earthquake. They could've fallen on you if they hadn't gone down the chimney."

It was a lesson well learned. I've now lived through dozens of earthquakes but I'll never get used to them. We haven't had major damage from any but I've lost bottled fruit as it's tumbled from shelves, and some ornaments. We've had a cracked chimney and our house has one or two cracks in the bricks.

The most terrifying time was during the Inangahua quake in May 1968, even though we had no damage. Joe and his father had both left to go line fishing in the strait when the angry tremors woke me. I jumped out of bed and flung open the window at the same time as Ruby was doing this in her house. "Are you okay?" she yelled across the lawn. My answer was drowned by the clamour coming from behind our house. It sounded as if the whole hillside was crashing down. We heard a sound like boulders rolling down the hills but no boulders came. The noise stopped and the silence returned. Later we heard of the devastation and the loss of three lives on the West Coast.

Out fishing that day, the fishermen had no luck. They always know when there has been an earthquake as the fish simply don't bite. Jim Fishburn was fishing out at Cook's Rock on his *Northern Star*. He told us he felt the boat being thrown around and when they pulled up the lines they found sharks foul-hooked in their tails and stomachs as they'd been tossed around when the seabed heaved in the quake.

The roaring I heard during the Inangahua quake and the jolting as the land moved beneath me remains with me. Sometimes on still sunny days when the Sounds are their most beautiful, my mind hears that terrifying noise again and makes me think of the magnitude of these different natural forces that continue to shape this region.

CHAPTER FOUR

The Production Years

I CALLED the years between 1964 and 1968 my production years. They produced four children and our first fishing boat.

In December 1963 the doctor told me I was pregnant, and that our baby was due the next June. I was 21 and I hadn't imagined I would become a mother quite so soon.

Once the idea had sunk in it was exciting, but I also had many anxious hours wondering how I would cope. It was just as well I had no idea of all the things I could be anxious about. I was a long way from the hospital. In Auckland the doctors had always lived up the road from us. And there was no Plunket nurse to give that reassurance which town mothers receive. What if something goes wrong out here? What if the baby gets sick? Will I be able to breast-feed, and, if I do, how will I know if I'm doing it right?

Questions swirled constantly in my mind and I'd voice my thoughts to Joe the moment he walked through the door at nights. In exasperation one night he said, "Well, what the hell's wrong with me? Mum managed to bring me up, plus my two sisters. I don't think we turned out too bad." That's when I decided I'd been stupid. Joe was right. I thought of the pioneer women who'd had their babies out in the bush, and they certainly didn't have a hospital or a doctor two hours away.

I was so well throughout this pregnancy – in fact I was well for all my eventual four. I never suffered morning sickness, fainting or feeling ghastly, and I ate whatever I felt like. The months flew by and I hadn't been back to the doctor as I had been advised to. I certainly knew I was pregnant by my shape, but I was so fit and well that going to a doctor didn't seem necessary.

Ruby, my mother-in-law, kept telling me I should go and have a check, especially as this was my first baby. But that boat trip to Picton – the thought of it made it easy to find excuses not to go. Then Ruby found she unexpectedly had to go into hospital in Blenheim. I knew she was worried about me because I was going to be in the bay on my own a lot, so to keep her happy I made an appointment to see the doctor on the same day that she was going into hospital.

It was 11 May. In the early hours of the day that we were going to Picton to keep our appointments, I woke up in a pool of water. I had read about births and so I was aware that my waters must have broken. "Joe, Joe!" He always sleeps the sleep of the dead. "Wake up. My waters have broken."

"Yeah? That's good. I'll take you to town in the morning." I still swear to this day that he started to snore. Then my words must have seeped in. He leaped out of bed. It was 2am. This time it was his bare feet, not mine, that never felt the newly-settled frost as he tore across the lawn to wake up his parents. I was thankful that my mother-in-law had made me pack my suitcase for the hospital. "You never know what might happen out here," she'd said.

In the darkness we all piled into the dinghy. Charlie, Ruby with her hospital suitcase, Joe and I began to head out to the boat. "Hang on. Where's my bag?" I said.

"What do you need a bag for?"

"I'm probably going to have a baby some time today," I reminded the father-to-be. "And I left it for you by the door." Back at the beach he flew up to the house – I think he imagined I might have the baby in the dinghy.

Our individual thoughts kept us silent. The oars creaked in the rowlocks and that and the splash as they dipped in the black sea were the only things to break the stillness. I heard the curious sound the gentle wind made as it brushed over the surface of the sea. An ageless sound. The wake looked like white hot metal boiling up behind our stern, and the phosphorescence in the water lit up the oars with each stroke Joe made. Once we were aboard the boat and on our way down the channel, the noise of the engine should have made me sleepy but I was too excited to sleep and the thought of the unknown hours ahead were making me feel scared.

Joe's married sister, Jocelyn, lived in Picton and when we arrived in town we drove to her home for a 5am breakfast. Now I was near the hospital I felt better but I wasn't in labour so I decided hospital was not the place for me. Jocelyn, a mother of five children, reassured me. My fears disappeared and I felt only the natural anxiety of any first-time mother about to give birth. The morning was filled in quite leisurely. I didn't have to rush round to get things done, ready to go back home again. It was wonderful.

Picton is a very small place and shortly after lunch the hospital tracked me down.

"Why haven't you come up to the hospital?" an angry voice enquired. "Come up at once. We want to examine you."

I felt like a humble little schoolgirl who had done something wrong as Joe drove me to the hospital and I climbed out of the car. All this fluffing around – and I was fine. Perhaps I wasn't going to have a baby today after all. I was wrong. At 5.50pm Joseph Thomas, four weeks early and weighing 5 lbs 9 oz, roared out his arrival to the world.

How times have changed for young mothers today. They are in and out of hospital so quickly unless there are complications. I had to stay in Picton Hospital until Joe had regained his birth weight. At two weeks he finally reached the magic weight, and I was allowed home. My mother flew down from Auckland and came to Okukari for two weeks. By the time she left, my confidence was firmly in place, breast-feeding was going well and I had a contented baby.

He stayed content as long as I kept up the milk supply. Four-hourly feeds day and night. How I hated that night feed. The nights, sitting up in bed and feeding the baby by the light of a candle, were some of the loneliest I have spent. The loud silence outside was profound. It accentuated the greedy swallows as Young Joe gulped his milk. The flame of the candle spluttered when a moth, mesmerised by the glow, fluttered into the hot wax. Joe's steady breathing as he slept beside us kept forcing my heavy eyes shut. I dreaded going to sleep on top of our baby on those nights. I'm sure he was often put back to bed without his wind being brought up. Tiredness would get the better of me but he always went back to sleep, wind or no wind. I really looked after my milk supply, and sometimes imagined how it would be if I lost it. With no electricity, the coal range would have to be lit and the milk warmed before a crying baby could be satisfied. There was no doubt about it. Milk on tap was the best option for both the baby and me.

With no Plunket nurse I never knew Young Joe's weight, but by looking at his rapidly filling out body I knew he was doing fine. I was the one who wasn't doing so well. Weeks of nights being woken up at 1am and 5am were taking their toll. I was desperate for sleep.

"He's big enough now to sleep through the night," said my mother-in-law. "When he wakes just change him, put him on his other side and he'll soon learn it isn't feed time."

That first night was hell. He wasn't going to be tricked into thinking he had been fed, then changed and turned over. When he realised he wasn't getting his usual nightcap he let roar. Nothing appeased him, not even the rocking of his cot. He made me feel a dreadfully uncaring mother. I was determined not to give in. The roars at last woke Joe who wanted me to feed him so he could get back to sleep.

"Let him suffer, he's the father," I muttered to myself as I blocked my ears and buried my head under the pillow. Joe had never sat up night after night, feeding a baby, and now he was being kept awake just one night. But that one night continued for more than a week. The house was so small, and the furthest away place I could put the baby was in the bathroom. Then I found I couldn't shut the door, so he was dumped unceremoniously in his baby cot in the bath, and the door slammed on the noise. A mother's ears still listened to the screams, but at last I won. My nights became mine again.

I enjoyed our baby. When I was told I spoiled him my answer was that if I couldn't spoil our first child heaven help the others we might have. He'd lie in his pram beside the piano as I played it, making contented baby noises as long as I kept playing. I still had problems with my stove but it was no longer the central pivot in my life. Often I'd leave it, when it wasn't burning well, to attend to the baby and when I came back later I'd find it smouldering in the grate. I was learning to cope with it better.

I still needed the occasional burst of salt injected into my veins, and after Young Joe was born I couldn't go out in the boat as I used to do. He was three months old and my mother-in-law must have recognised my symptoms. "Go out with Joe. I'll mind the baby." I needed to be told only once.

"You'll need plenty of warm clothes. It'll be cold out there," Joe told me as I dragged an extra jersey on.

I felt good as we left Okukari behind and headed out to the pots. With gumboots, waterproof leggings and a coat over all my clothes I certainly didn't feel the cold. I had to find my sea legs and I was having a lot of trouble with the gaff when hooking the ropes of the floats and passing them to Joe so he could put them on the winch to haul the pot up to the surface. It finally got too much for Joe and in exasperation he told me I'd have been better off at home, and at the rate we were going we'd miss the tide. I was so angry with him I swung round, slammed the end of the gaff on the deck and in very unladylike language told him what I thought of him.

The devil struck. The boat lurched and I went over the side, still abusing Joe. When I opened my eyes under the water everything was very green. I'd gone down very deep. I surfaced at last at the same time as the offending pot broke the water. All I could see were red flapping things alongside me. I stretched out my hand to Joe. "Give me a hand."

"Cool off. I have to get this pot aboard first. The crays'll swim out if I leave it on the surface."

That fishing trip was short-lived and I was taken home in disgust as there were no dry clothes on the boat. It was quite some time before I was asked out fishing again, time to have another baby, in fact.

When Young Joe outgrew his baby bed and needed to move into a big cot we built on another room so we became a two-bedroomed house. He seemed so grown up when he moved to his own room, and I loved having our room to ourselves once more. This bliss lasted only a year as number two was on the way, and the baby's cot was back in our room waiting for the new addition.

On 27 October 1965, when Joe was 17 months, Helen Patricia was born. Helen was my only full-term baby, born one day before her due date. Strangely she is the smallest in our family today but her birth weight of 6 lbs 12 oz was the heaviest of our four children. The morning of her birth I'd woken up feeling my usual self. I'd cooked Joe's breakfast and listened to his complaints about a sore back. "It's killing me, right in the small of my back."

"Perhaps you're having a baby," I laughed as he left the house. Two hours later I was the one who was having a baby. There was no way I could get hold of Joe on the marine radio. He was fishing now on the *Midlothian* with his father. They were crayfishing and usually came in the bay during the morning to put their crays in the holding tank before steaming up the coast to pull the rest of the craypots. My mother-in-law shared my anxiety and came up with a good idea.

"I'll light a fire on the bank. Surely then when they come into the bay they'll realise something's wrong."

"I hope so! But when Joe left I was fine." I admit I had the breeze up, but was trying hard not to show it. My contractions had rapidly gone from 20 to 15 minutes apart. We heard the boat and Ruby ran out to light the fire and attract their attention. The engine of the boat stopped and I breathed a sigh of relief. Joe would soon be with me.

Joe had bought a 16-foot plywood hull, built a cabin on it, and installed an engine so now we had a fine-weather runabout that would get us to Picton in an hour. Just now we were having problems with it. The gearbox was overheating and it was running like a hairy goat. "I think we'd better go in the faster boat and hope it gets us to town," Joe decided.

Young Joe was left with his grandparents and we took off. Ruby rang folk down the channel to ask if they could watch out for us, and told them what time we should pass. She followed our progress by the phone calls. On the boat Joe kept feeling the gearbox and seemed to take great delight in telling me how hot it was getting. Then he spat on it and little balls of spit danced up and down. I sat on the seat, concentrating, and willing the contractions to go away for a while.

We reached Picton without a breakdown and I had three whole hours to spare before Helen was born. This time I stayed in hospital 10 days. Helen's discharge weight was 7 lbs. Once again my mother came down from Auckland to stay and give me a hand.

Joe came in to Picton to pick us up in our small boat. As so often happens in the Sounds, the nor'westerley wind had increased and by the afternoon when we were about to leave it was a gale at home and pouring rain. Certainly it wasn't small boat weather, especially with a new baby on board. Joe organised a ride home for Mum, the baby and me in the *Friendship*, the flag-ship of the Kenny fleet of charter boats, while he brought our little boat home. When we turned into Okukari Bay the wind hit us. From the northerly direction it funnels down the gully and screams out the bay. White water torn off the tops of waves hit against the boat's windows, making it hard to see.

Our wharf was in the process of being built, and six piles had been driven in. If only we had a finished wharf to tie up to, I thought. Mr Kenny brought the boat as close in to the beach as he could and Joe, already home, came out in the dinghy to collect us. He didn't have time to put the oars in the dinghy because once free of the beach the dinghy simply blew out to the boat. Joe grabbed the side of the *Friendship* with both hands to prevent himself being blown out the bay. "I'll take one of you at a time. Your mum first." As we helped Mum into the dinghy the force of the wind and rain made it impossible to look up. It stung bare skin. Helen was certainly going to have a rough welcome to Okukari.

Soon it was my turn to scramble into the dinghy after I'd passed down the bags and a few stores I'd hurriedly bought before I left Picton. Mum and I watched as Joe made his last trip for Helen. He hung on to the boat as Helen was handed down, her carrycot swaying in the wind, and placed in the bottom of the dinghy. When Joe arrived ashore I ran to check the baby. She hadn't stirred and lay snuggled up in her blankets, completely indifferent to the weather.

I was never organised with Helen. Her longest sleeping time was 20 minutes during the day. I'd feed her, put her down, she'd sleep for a short time and then she'd be awake until I fed her next. If I'd fed her whenever she thought she should be fed I'd have been feeding her all day. Young Joe enjoyed being the big brother for a short time but then the novelty wore off and he'd busy himself with his toys. When my mother left I was totally at the beck and call of a very demanding baby. If only I could have put her in the pram and walked down the street, met some other young mothers, exchanged notes, I'm sure it wouldn't have been so bad. Instead I'd leave her out in the garden to scream. I knew there was nothing wrong with her, and I had a little boy who needed attention too, so I wheeled her outside and left her to it, to give myself a break. Looking back I'd describe her as a classic colicky baby. At the time, though, I had no idea about colic. By Christmas a more settled and contented baby was the best Christmas present I received that year.

With two children I very rarely went to Picton. If I needed stores urgently I had them delivered on the twice-weekly mail boat. Otherwise I phoned through my order when I knew Joe was going to town. Often I thought I'd like to go, just to have a change of scenery and to talk to other people, but the effort involved with the children put me off.

Out of the blue one night Joe said, "I've been thinking. We hardly use the speedboat now as it's too small. If we sell it, and with what we've saved, we'd have enough to put towards a new boat. I'm sure we'd be able to get a loan." Coming from a 40-hour-a-week wage-earning family as I did, the amount he mentioned horrified me. But he'd decided it was his time to go it alone so he commissioned D F Robb Ltd, boatbuilders in Timaru, to build us a 38-foot wooden-hulled fishing vessel which was launched in March 1966 in Timaru.

I left Helen with friends as she was only five months old, but I took Young Joe, 22 months. Joe's parents flew down for the launching, too, and after her sea trials Joe, Charlie and two crewmen left for Okukari in the *Heather*. The name was Joe's idea. He said it was so I couldn't growl when he spent a lot of time away on her, fishing. "You see," was his smart comment, "when I'm not with Heather, I'll be on *Heather*."

As the *Heather* steamed out of the harbour I told myself that if we ever got another boat built, and it was at all possible, I'd be aboard for the trip up the coast. Meanwhile Ruby and I brought our car back to Picton and hired a boat to bring us to Okukari.

Her maiden voyage took 34 hours and averaged 9 knots. From Kaikoura on they had run before a southerly which was quietly freshening. Memories of the night our men were caught out in the storm a year ago were still vivid in our minds and the joy when we saw the *Heather* surf into the bay overwhelmed us both. I looked at the boat and saw our whole savings plus the loan. It was a daunting thought. We had two children, we owned our car which was kept in Picton, and we had a bank balance of 25 pounds.

The *Heather* was the sixth vessel to join the small fleet of fishing craft operating from Tory Channel and based in Picton.

The first trip out Joe went on his own and came home with 55 big groper. We were delighted – it was a good omen.

"If we're going to have a family, the children may as well be close," was my reply to people when they found out I was expecting number three in August 1967. There would be 22 months between Helen and the new baby, and I thought it was great planning.

Young Joe had a bad squint which was getting worse, and a trip to Blenheim's Wairau Hospital to see the Wellington specialist sent me into a state of shock when I was told he had to be operated on as soon as possible. "The longer it's left," I was told, "the less chance he'll have of using both eyes together."

I went home and waited to hear from Wellington Hospital. Three weeks before the next baby's due date I was phoned from the hospital to inform me a bed was available for Joe in three days. "I'm worried I might have my baby in Wellington," I replied. "It's due in three weeks."

A laughing voice replied. "That's not a problem. We'll look after you if you do."

Helen stayed with Joe's parents, and Joe took Young Joe and me to Blenheim to catch the early morning flight out to Wellington. At the hospital Young Joe burst into tears. It was hard leaving an upset child in a strange place. He clung on to me so tightly I had to prise myself from his grasp. The nurses on the ward suggested I leave and he would come right. His operation was to take place the following morning and they said as it was his eyes they'd prefer it if I stayed away that day. His screams followed me out of the ward as I left with my aunt with whom I was staying out at Makara. I was obedient and didn't go in to see him the day of his operation but the hospital assured me everything had gone well and my son was fine.

That night as sleep started to take over my body I hoped my little boy was all right. I was looking forward to seeing him the next day. I never dreamt that within four hours I'd be with him in Wellington Hospital with yet another son.

Suddenly my waters broke and I went straight into labour with a vengeance. My uncle had the job of driving me into the hospital. He dropped me off and by the time he arrived back to his home in Makara my aunt was able to greet him with the news that I had a 6 lb 5 oz son.

I wouldn't have made Picton if I'd been at Okukari. This baby would have been born in Queen Charlotte Sound. So I was pleased to be in Wellington. Early next morning I was taken to the children's ward in a wheelchair and an excited little boy climbed on my lap before we were wheeled to the maternity ward so he could meet his new brother.

When I was back in the ward a stranger in a hospital uniform came up to me and started apologising. "I'm so sorry. I was the voice who persuaded you to bring your son over for his operation. I typed your admission papers this morning and I feel dreadful. No wonder you didn't want to come at this time."

"It was the best thing I could have done. I'd have had James on the boat if I'd been at home. Thank you for making me come."

Later in the day Joe arrived from Picton with my suitcase, and he was able to take Young Joe home. I just wanted to be home, too, and as soon as I could I left the hospital. My mother flew down to Wellington, and we both flew with one-week-old James across Cook Strait to Blenheim.

Our family was complete. James was a delightful baby. He cried very rarely and when he did get upset he had a brother and sister always ready to comfort him. As our family grew so did our house, and a third bedroom was added.

Somehow I didn't bounce back from his birth, and even after a good night's sleep I'd wake up still feeling tired. I'd missed my six-week check after James was born and I began imagining something was wrong with me.

"I think you should stop breast-feeding him," Joe said. "Give yourself a chance to come right."

The thought of lighting my stove to heat a bottle when I needed to feed James made that an easy decision to make. "No way. But the next time you're going to Picton I'll come and visit the doctor. Perhaps I need a tonic to give me a boost."

In the doctor's surgery I climbed up on the bed for my belated six-week check which was eight months overdue. "*Heather*, do you realise you are approximately four months pregnant?" The shock and horror didn't register for a minute or two. My reply was sheer disbelief. "I can't be. I've given away my baby things and even my maternity clothes."

"You'll have to get them back, then, because in October number four will arrive."

I walked down the street feeling much worse than I'd felt before I'd been to the doctor. By the time I met up with Joe I was feeling very sorry for myself. Joe thought something must be seriously wrong with me as I was so upset, and when I told him I was pregnant he was quite relieved. "Well, at least you know why you're feeling dreadful. You'll feel better soon." And I actually did start to feel better once I took stock of myself. I tried not to dwell on the fact that when I had this baby our eldest child was going to be only four years and four months, Helen one month off three and James 14 months. On the plus side, the children would be good playmates and once Joe started school lessons my baby days would be over and I could give him the time he'd need.

My mother told me that after this baby she'd send me a congratulatory card every year I did not become pregnant. When I was shopping in Picton an elderly lady seemed horrified to see me pregnant again, and asked how ever I was going to manage with four children. She had no reply when I asked her which of my children I should part with.

I felt an absolute fool asking for my baby things and all my maternity clothes back, but later on it was joked about. I and the woman I'd lent them to had our babies within weeks of each other, and the babies grew up good friends.

Towards the end of this pregnancy my stove often seemed to match my moods. I felt well but I lacked energy and felt lethargic. My stove wouldn't get hot. The fire sat in the grate, it wouldn't draw, and smoke belched from the stove top. I blamed the wood. "It's not the wood. The chimney probably needs cleaning," was Joe's reply after I'd abused him and the lousy wood he'd got me. A few days after this conversation I was to have the cleanest chimney I'd ever had.

The stove had been shut down most of the day and I came inside about 4.30pm to open the dampers up in readiness for cooking dinner. As usual it wouldn't draw. The grate was choked with clinkers so I lifted the hot plate to juggle the embers around with the poker. Nothing would entice it to spring into action.

I went outside to take the clothes off the line when a tremendous whoof from the chimney nearly deafened me. The fire was certainly burning well. Three feet above the chimney. Thick black smoke left the flames behind and drifted out the bay before spreading down the coast.

No fire brigade to call here. I shouted out to my mother-in-law to ask her what I should do. "You'll have to put wet sacks over the top of the chimney to smother it!" she called back as she ran over to help. I thought it'd be no trouble at all.

James, then 12 months, was dumped unceremoniously in his cot so I knew where he was. Young Joe, four, and Helen, nearly three, damped down sacks in the tubs, then passed them out through the laundry windows at the back of the lean-to where Joe's mother took them and passed them to me. By leaning over the roof edge I could take the wet sacks, carry them over the flat roof, clamber up on to the main roof and drag them up to the chimney. Dripping sacks made the steep roofing iron slippery. I felt like a spider clinging on to the roof. All arms and legs. The only difference was this spider was a very seven-months-pregnant spider.

By the time Joe arrived home I was in control of my fire. Dinner was cooking and Young Joe and Helen had learnt a new song for Dad. London's Burning.

After James's rapid entry into the world, Joe suggested I should go to Auckland a month before this baby was due and stay with my parents. Joe could keep on fishing without the constant worry that I might be in labour when he wasn't home. Three children and I flew up to Auckland to be met by my delighted parents, and I enjoyed two weeks with them before Pauline Louise arrived two weeks early and weighing in at 6 lbs 8 oz. James was still crawling when I went into hospital but he toddled to meet me when I came out four days later. Pauline was six days old when she flew home with her two brothers, sister, grandmother and mother. I was 26 years old and I had four children. This was definitely going to be our entire family.

For the first time in my life I became a sick person. We were home a week and I developed an infection in my uterus. The pain was so bad I couldn't walk to my in-laws' house to ring the doctor, and when Mum phoned him he advised me to come into Picton. That was out. I couldn't stand the bed being bumped, let alone a boat trip, so he sent medication out on a charter boat so I could receive it more quickly. We all received a shock when Mum phoned him the next morning to let him know how I was and he said, "In the olden days your daughter would have been dead." The magic of antibiotics worked wonders and in a few days Mum could leave, knowing I was coming right.

Then Pauline and I developed whooping cough. That was the worst period of my life. Besides feeling ill myself, I had to keep a constant watch on Pauline. When she started whooping she had to be picked up and the choking phlegm cleared from her throat. I took her with me in her pram to hang out the washing, to work in the garden – wherever I went, she was with me. When she whooped she'd be sick and I'd have to feed her again so she didn't become dehydrated.

James was still a baby. He was only 14 months. Joe was four and Helen just turned three, and they also needed mother-time which I struggled to find for them. Pauline was able to have her first three-in-one injection for tetanus, diphtheria and whooping cough early, which helped her immensely, and I felt better as she recovered.

I'd been to the very bottom of the pit, it seemed. There was only one way out, and by the start of 1969 I'd begun the long climb out. I had to be at the top by May. Joe would turn five and my school teaching days would begin. The responsibility began to weigh on me. Would I be good enough to teach him – to teach all four of them – so they wouldn't suffer because of where we lived?

CHAPTER FIVE

A Way of Life

A TRIP to Picton with four young children, a long list of things I must do, a long list of things I might do if I had the time, and as always that long grocery list – I suppose it was no wonder I was never very keen to make that journey. I maintained it took me three days for one day in town. A day to get organised, the day in town, and a day to recover.

With children ranging from three months to four years I told myself it would be much easier when they grew up a little. I wouldn't be lugging nappies, baby food, special toys and cuddly blankets. But I discovered that a trip to town was just as bad when ages became five to nine years. School had to be caught up on for that day in town, and four tired pupils yawned their way through lessons the next day.

I became a list lady. As I ran out of items or they became low, I added them to my grocery list. My list of things I must do usually meant a visit to the doctor for checks or injections, a dentist visit for myself and the dental nurse for the children. My list of things I might do if I had time was the longest as it kept on growing.

After a day in town it seemed that few things on the 'might do' list would be deleted whereas extras were soon added, ready for the next trip. I'd dream about what I might do, such as seeing if any nice materials had come in. They could be put away to make up when needed. Then I'd love to have time to browse around the plant shop and buy one or two new shrubs for my garden. Or visit a friend. People were always saying, "You never come and visit me when you come to town." Birthdays coming up – maybe I'd have time to find a couple of presents. The first aid kit could do with topping up and I'd dearly love to get to the library and spend an hour catching up with home-town news from the *New Zealand Herald*. But this was always impossible. There was only time to grab two or three books to take home and hope I'd choose well. The children were always needing jerseys – I'd try to get to the wool shop. I always like to have knitting on the needles.

The day following a day in town always seemed to end with one or two grocery items heading a new list. I have stood at the counter as my trolleys of groceries have been priced, with waiting customers behind me sighing, changing positions and pacifying their impatient children, making me feel quite guilty. I'd feel like saying, "Hey! I won't be back for at least a month!" Once I had the basic grocery stock built up, it was usually only replacements I needed.

But milk and bread don't keep well in fluctuating temperatures, and when we were in between house cows I had milk sent out on the mail boat twice weekly. The freight on bread was so high I'd get it only when it was absolutely necessary. This was more often than I cared to admit. Between my stove and my uncertain talents, the outcome of my breadmaking could not be guaranteed. Success was a real treat for us, and failure a real treat for the pig.

Bulk groceries were bought when our boat went to town. I'd have my list, but the basic items filled up two or more trollies before I started on everything else:

> 2 20-pound bags of flour
> 24 pounds sugar
> box tea
> 12 pounds butter
> 15 loaves bread
> 6 blocks cheese
> candles
> matches
> eggs (depending on chooks)
> crate milk
> batteries for torches and radio

Then I started on the rest. Every household needs supplies for the bathroom, laundry and general cleaning. Then there were items needed for the grocery cupboard, cordials for drinks, biscuits, treats for good kids, pencils, rubbers, glue and any other school things we might need. I did buy a lot of tinned food as I didn't have to worry that it might deteriorate and I could always make a quick meal out of something if I had to.

At the bottom of the grocery list was the butcher's list. We killed our own meat – mutton – but I longed for a nice juicy steak occasionally and always came home with sausages, mince and stewing steak. Webster's Butchery was a treat for the four children to enter. They were always presented with 'a red sausage' which disappeared as if they hadn't seen food for a week. Jack Webster always asked if their mother hadn't fed them that day. A 'no' reply gave them another saveloy.

Into the fruit and vegetable shop and four hopeful children would advise the shopkeeper that they'd had red sausages at the butcher's. Their appeals fell on deaf ears and a rather embarrassed mother would feel like dragging four children out of the shop by the scruffs of their necks.

I hated these too-packed trips to Picton and I had to keep reminding myself how the children must feel – used to the wide open spaces and tearing around all day. Now they were being carted from shop to shop. But when the 'things

I had to do' list was completed, they could have their treat. Usually they asked for an ice cream, milk shake or chips. Except for one day. By this time Pauline was four. She wanted a witch cat. "What's that?" I asked. I imagined it must be a new sort of lolly or ice block.

"No. A witch cat. You buy it at the chip shop." That was a start. We'd try there. Nothing with the name witch cat was advertised. I was stumped. "How about chips instead?" My patience was wearing thin. A tearful head shook no. Next to us an order was given. "Two hot dogs and chips."

"That's it! That's what I mean. A hot dog, Mum." The face beamed and I breathed a sigh of relief. At last I could drive to the wharf, unload the car, put everything aboard our boat and then Joe could take the car to the garage we rented a short distance up the road. All I wanted to do was sprawl out on the bunk.

James had a special teddy bear, Ted. He was his best friend and came to town with James when he was little. Joe had just arrived back at the boat after putting our car away when a tired little voice cried, "My Ted has gone."

"He must be in the car," suggested Joe. "We'll get him next time."

"No way," I said. "He's got to be found today. I can't put up with James without his Ted."

I waited on the boat with the children while Joe ran up to the garage. He arrived back without the bear. James's tears were in earnest now, so we sat down and made a list of all the shops we'd been in. Off Joe went again. At last he found Ted, sitting on a shelf with a row of brand new bears in a toy shop. James had thought Ted needed some friends. Fortunately for us no one had wanted to buy him. An exasperated Joe arrived back at the boat. "Quick. Let's get on our way before anything else is discovered missing."

On the way home in the boat the children nearly always went to sleep. We'd get back and they'd all wake up scratchy and the younger ones would be howling as they stumbled along the wharf and up to the house. I was so thankful we had this wharf. Memories of one particular pre-wharf trip from Picton were still too vivid.

Young Joe had been only six weeks old. A southerly buster came in on the way home. By the time we reached Okukari a big sea was rolling in. My parents-in-law now owned the *Midlothian*, and, after it was moored in the bay, Ruby and I were rowed ashore first. A strange phenomenon of nature sends in three big waves, a lull, then three more crash on to the beach. We bobbed around in the dinghy outside the breaking water, waited for the lull, then were quickly rowed ashore to leap out before the next wave landed in the dinghy. I couldn't imagine my first-born coming in like this, even if he was snuggled in his carrycot. I stood on the beach, bracing myself against the wind, and not noticing the cold as Joe and Charlie waited for the lull. It came, and the eight-foot pram dinghy, Joe, his father and baby all surfed ashore on the low wave. I couldn't wait to get my hands on the carrycot and get my baby up to our house.

In 33 years the only box of groceries that has ever come to grief on the way home was a carton of tinned food. As Joe lifted it off the boat and on to the wharf the bottom fell out and the contents fell into the sea. The next day when the tide was low we went down and fished the tins out. I don't think we lost anything apart from all the labels off the tins. Sitting on the wharf I had about 20 rescued cans of tinned food. Baked beans, spaghetti, pineapple, tomatoes, corn – and all were the same size. We had lucky dips. A few shakes, and we'd try to guess what we were going to eat. Pineapple or baked beans for dessert?

As I became more and more dependent on my many lists I found I was mentally slotting other aspects of my life, or the way I think about them, into groups. I didn't realise just how much our way of life has made me 'a list lady' until I began working on this book.

The many searches and rescues we've been involved in, for instance, and the tragedies and near-tragedies tend to run together in my mind. This may make it sound as if life at Okukari is one long almost Hollywood-type drama. At times it does seem like it, but mostly our days and weeks are the same blend of fishing and farm work, always ruled by the weather.

My calendar changed when I came to the island. I no longer thought of seasons. Instead I thought of mustering or lambing, tailing, shearing or dipping, and, if it was fishing, it was lining for groper and school shark, cray fishing or tuna fishing.

And I had a different time system. My battery clock hanging on the kitchen wall ticked its way through the hours but I worked on ferry time. When the first Cook Strait roll-on roll-off ferry, *Aramoana*, started running in 1962, followed by the *Aranui*, *Aratika*, *Arahunga* and *Arahura*, the 10am ferry from Wellington passed our bay at 12.10pm. If the men were out on the farm they saw her come past and knew it was lunch time. On her return journey she left Picton at 2.20pm. When she steamed past our place at 3.20pm it was afternoon tea time. In 1994, with the introduction of two fast ferries, my time system wasn't reliable any longer as the timetables kept changing.

Now there are so many crossings of Cook Strait, with one ferry sailing 24 hours a day, that I could have a ferry time to tell me when to go to bed and when to get up, if I wanted to. The ferries carry more than a million people through Tory Channel every year, and I've often wondered as I see them gliding past what the passengers think as they see our bay.

When I've been on a ferry I've enjoyed standing at the rail and listening to the comments. Our houses have been called cribs, and I've heard comments such as "Fancy being stuck out there!" "What about stores?" "What a beautiful bay!" And – that old favourite – "I wonder what they do all day?"

Photos of Okukari must be in many travellers' albums all over the world as

I've seen cameras out as we've gone past. These days the ferries have videos of the history of Tory Channel. I've enjoyed watching them and imagining myself a traveller and seeing it for the very first time, when all the while I know the history began for the Heberleys when John Guard set up a whaling station in Te Awaiti in 1827, and then when James Heberly arrived in 1830. After 169 years, today's Heberleys live within rowing distance from where my in-laws' forbears first stepped on to New Zealand soil.

It is not only on the ferry that I've heard "What do you do all day?" When people have seen me take my butcher's list out of my purse in the chemist's, or a wrong list in another shop, they've grinned as I've rummaged through my purse, and when I've tried to explain why I have so many lists the response is often, "How wonderful to live out there. But what do you do all day?" Sightseers on the mail boat ask the same question. I shrug and just tell them I manage to keep busy.

As I'd go on to my next job my mind would race as I'd think how I could best describe a week in my life. They are never the same, and in among the fishing and the farming there can be a search and rescue, an accident, a serious illness – any of these. Suddenly an ordinary day can turn into one of drama.

One such day in July 1983 began like any other day. We'd had a lot of heavy rainfalls, cold southerlies and the occasional fine day. Our ewes had to be crutched before lambing, making it easier for young lambs to find their milk supply and latch on to the bursting udders. At last three fine windy days in a row allowed the sheep to get dry. We mustered them in and organised Bluey and Alan to come down to crutch the sheep.

At 19, Young Joe had his first boat. It was 16 feet with a 90 horse-power outboard. There was no cabin, just a windscreen and two seats. It was his pride and joy and when his father suggested to him that one of the fuel tanks leaked and he should replace it, the voice of youth told his father it was fine – he filled that tank up only as far as the leak.

Bluey and Alan were going to be picked up from Picton at 11am and as the morning was fine and the sea glassy calm Young Joe was going to get them in his speedboat. The strap on his life jacket had broken and he'd brought it home for me to mend which I'd done immediately, but it'd since hung on a hook by the back door. Every time he'd be going in the boat I'd remind him to take it as it wasn't much use where it was, but still it hung there.

The bright winter's sunshine had lifted the frost where it had rolled down the sloping lawn to the front fence. The channel was a bright silver ribbon threaded between dark green hills. In the still air the drone of the outboard echoed around the bay and even after the boat had rounded Wirikarapa I could hear a faint hum. The barking of the farm dogs as Helen and her father drove sheep into the yards brought me back to the mundane things I had to do before Young Joe arrived back home with the shearers. I'd been told we'd be crutching immediately after lunch, so I wanted smoko and that night's dinner organised, and meals for tomorrow.

I was preparing the vegetables, had butter and sugar creaming in my cake mixer, a cake cooking in the electric range – thank God I didn't have to stoke it up – and at the same time I was racking my brains as to what I'd give them for lunch. I decided on a pizza. Rummaging through the cupboard for the tin I wanted, I ended up with everything falling out at my feet. The VHF and the radio, blaring, added to the clatter of all my pots and baking dishes. "Bloody hell!" I swore aloud to myself. I went to turn the VHF off, but Joe had asked me to listen for the forecast so he'd know whether or not to shed-up the sheep that night.

After a while I found some order out of my chaos, things were back in their cupboard with the door slammed tightly shut and the promise I'd tidy it up after sheep work was finished, one cake was baked and I had my pizza and another cake in the oven. On the radio the gravelly voice of Rod Stewart was singing Sailing, and I wished I was doing just that.

Suddenly words on the VHF radio made me stop everything. "Yeah. He was right in front of me. Explosion. He passed me coming out of Many Coves. Was just a huge bang and flames leaping off the sea. It's either young Fishburn or Heberley. Both their boats look the same."

My world stopped. I knew it was my son. He'd told me he would go into Gem Resort, in the Bay of Many Coves, for fuel. At this time our VHF only received so I couldn't call up and find out more. I flung open the window and screamed out to Joe who was still in the yards. He told me later he knew from the sound of my voice there was something wrong.

Joe was catching his breath as I told him what I'd heard. "I don't know who was calling – the name of the boat, or how far away they were from the explosion!" I cried. "What do we do?"

"I'll ring Don Jamison. He'll be able to find out what's going on."

Don, Picton's harbourmaster, hadn't heard anything but he promised Joe he'd find out and get back to us as soon as possible. This was a different type of rescue for us. We weren't involved in any search but it was the most desperate we'd ever had anything to do with. Every second pressed on my heart.

Then the shrill ring of the phone in the silence nearly made my heart stop. Joe answered it and I clung to the receiver with Joe, straining to hear Don's voice.

"It's your Joe. I don't know the extent of his injuries but he's been picked up by Richard Todd in the *Rongo*. It seems he saw it happen. He was steaming up behind Joe. I do know he was in the water about 15 minutes. Sounds a lucky lad to me."

The next message told us the float plane had been diverted and had picked Joe up off the *Rongo* as he was suffering from hyperthemia. That was it. We were off – sheep work forgotten and promises from Helen to take the last of my baking out of the oven.

The *Fugitive* was driven hard all the way to Picton. It must have been the fastest trip I'd ever had on her, and we were in Picton in an hour. Joe had been taken to the doctor's surgery by ambulance. When his temperature had come back to an acceptable level he'd rung Maureen Stewart. She'd collected him, and was now mothering my son. He said he still felt very cold but his temperature was rising. His hair was singed and his face looked as if he'd been lying in the sun for three or four hours.

"I don't know why I took my life jacket," he told us. "As I ran out the door I saw it hanging there and something made me flick it off the hook and take it. I'd be dead if I hadn't had it."

What a fragile hold we have on life.

"My fuel tank must have leaked into the bilge," he went on. "The boat stopped, water mixed with petrol surged under the floor boards, and when I started her again there was this explosion," he said. He'd turned around and flames were leaping off the petrol tanks in the stern. He grabbed the fire extinguisher and leaped up on the forward deck where he started to put on his life jacket. "She went up and I was in the water. It was the strangest thing. I was in this circle of flames on the water. I could feel the heat off them on my face. They were burning all around me." He struggled to kick off his thigh-gumboots that were dragging him down. The life jacket gave him extra buoyancy so he could keep his head above the water. His Swanndri and woollen jersey were heavy.

He couldn't remember his plane ride. Fifteen minutes in July's water in the Sounds, with shock, brings on hyperthermia rapidly. How thankful I was that Picton had Float Air. Our son might have died from the cold if he hadn't been brought in by plane. Bruce Fulton owned Float Air at this time and I remembered reading in the *Marlborough Express* of his incredible list of mishaps. A few months after his take-over from Russell and Flora Smith, the Cessna smashed against their floating jetty and broke a wing. He bought a new aircraft but it sank at its moorings. Eighteen months later a replacement overturned on its moorings and was written off.

Today Float Air still operates out of Picton, giving visitors a chance to view the Marlborough Sounds from the air, and it runs flights daily between Porirua and Picton with stops at holiday resorts or private homes in the Sounds. In an emergency it can be the difference between life and death for those of us who are isolated.

On the way home later that day we called in to Curious Cove. The remains of Joe's boat had been towed into the bay and pulled up on the beach. I couldn't believe that the black heap in front of my eyes was the boat I'd watched skimming up the channel less than seven hours ago. It had burnt to the water line. We recognised the twisted remains of the fire extinguisher that must have dropped back into the boat as Joe was thrown out. Everything else was gone.

We steamed over the area where the boat had exploded and the flames had burnt so fiercely on the surface of the sea. Everything was still, and not one piece of debris was in sight. The sea had taken it all.

The next day crutching began at 7.30am. The day before was now only a memory, and a lesson well learnt on safety at sea.

Reading Joe's mind is a feat I have always been expected to accomplish. Just as, for instance, I've worked out a complicated knitting pattern and at last am seeing its results as the ball of wool grows smaller, Joe may arrive inside and I'm supposed to know if it's a cup of tea or an early lunch he wants before the men set off crayfishing again. The crayfishing grounds at the channel entrance, where they start pulling their pots, are only five minutes from home, and the men will often come home for a quick meal or drink while they wait for the tide to slacken and the gear to come up to the surface.

And when I'm up to the most exciting part of a book and am thinking I'll just have time to finish it, Joe's likely to come in with, "Didn't you hear us coming?" I can never claim life is predictable.

Ordinary days sometimes find me being a plumber. Heavy rain washes out the hose which carries the water from the creek to the tank, or the hose blocks up with small stones which wash down the creek. Stock can break the joins in the hose where it lies on the ground between the water tank and the house. As I've trudged up the hill behind our house to see why we haven't any water I've often turned around and walked up backwards so I can drink in the beauty before my eyes. The best times can be in the early mornings when the sun hasn't reached the gullies, and only the higher ridges are lit up with the first rays. The sea, still uncaught by the sun, is purple in the early light, and the ferry coming up the channel at 6.40am, bound for Wellington, adds another dimension to my marvellous painting.

In December the Royal Port Nicholson Yacht Club holds its annual yacht race across Cook Strait and once again my painting changes when it becomes filled with the vibrant colours of the spinnakers and headsails as the yachts race through the channel entrance to the finish line off Te Awaiti. They haven't always raced in. Some years we've watched as they've drifted in on the tide, the wind gone, and then the tide has changed and they've slowly drifted out.

How can I be lonely in a place I share, from a distance, with so many people? The beauty and different way of living it gives, even if I do have to live by my lists, makes up for its isolation. And as each day grows into weeks and they become years, the ordinary days are hard to remember as the eventful ones crowd my mind.

CHAPTER SIX

The Correspondence Years

YOUNG JOE became one of New Zealand's 1613 green envelope children on 11 May 1969 when he joined the Correspondence School. Besides being mother and often father, certainly nurse and playmate, I became a teacher. This was to be my most challenging role yet. I was going to be responsible for my children's education. Their whole future was in my hands. I really found this daunting, something that weighed on me from the first day until the last day. It was 13 years of stress and constantly asking myself if I was giving them my best.

Excitement was high when Joe's first parcel arrived from the Correspondence School. There was equipment to be used for mathematics, cakes of paint, art paper, buttons, coloured paper, paint brushes and thick crayons. A treasure trove for any child and a new school pupil, a great way to build up anticipation of school.

The following mail day the hallmark of the Correspondence School arrived, three green canvas envelopes, each one bulging with 10 days of lessons which make up one set, a separate book for the supervisor, lots of first reading books and the first letter from Joe's teacher. It was a letter written especially to him and there was also one for me. We immediately felt we belonged to this school, and a warm friendship soon developed between faraway teacher and pupil.

In our little house Joe sat at the kitchen table for his lessons. I sat with him, guiding, one eye on Pauline as she crawled around the floor, or on James as he played outside, and four-year-old Helen who wanted to do school the same as her brother. The first months were like any school – not a great deal of work and lots of enjoyment in what was done. The learning was subtle and gradually the lessons took more time to complete. The fun started to go out of it when Joe realised he couldn't go out and play when he wanted to. School came first.

I made myself strict rules. I had to. All this responsibility for their future – was I really up to it? It would have been so easy to say, "Let's skip school today. We'll do it tomorrow." In all my teaching years I never made this excuse to myself. That's something I'm proud of, because I most certainly was tempted.

School started at 9am, morning tea break at 10am and at 10.30 we'd start again. Lunch was at noon till 1pm and then we worked until the day's lessons were completed. As more of the family came on the roll my time became more stretched and the day's lessons sometimes didn't finish until after 5pm. Admittedly these were the bad days when I wasn't happy with the standard of work and I'd make them do it again.

One such night Joe arrived in from fishing and one stubborn child was still sitting at the table. The others had been playing up all day and I was close to tears. "Speak to your kids," I growled at Joe. "Hi kids," was his reply. I could have murdered him. I always felt I was the ogre during school, and Joe was this wonderful man who came in after lessons and never had to do the stern speaking that I did. It really came home one night when I was putting Pauline to bed. It was the first holidays since she had started school. Two little arms wrapped themselves tightly around my neck and she whispered in my ear, "I love you in the holidays, Mum." It struck home. I paid a price for my strict rules.

At the end of one particularly bad day of school I needed to be away from four children for a while, and no doubt four children needed space from their mother. It was too wet for them to be outside so I donned my coat and told them I was going to Grandma's for afternoon tea and I'd be back soon.

The quiet in my mother-in-law's house, and the talking over of my problems while we had a cup of tea, always served in a nice fine bone china teacup, made me feel much better. I'd think that Ruby must have had problems like mine and if she could look as young as she did, then somehow I could survive this school teaching.

This particular day I'd run home and opened the door to get in out of the rain before I took off my coat. My hand was still on the door handle when a voice shouted from the kitchen, "Don't slam the door! We've something in the oven."

I'd always vowed my children would all learn to cook, partly because I've a husband who when I married him, would meet me after a day in town with, "What have you brought home to eat?"

So I felt a warm glow. They must have a sponge in the oven, I thought to myself. The good kids. They're learning. In the kitchen my eyes swept over the pile of dirty dishes on the bench but I wasn't going to growl. Somehow it didn't look as if a sponge had been prepared.

"It's fudge," James whispered. "In the oven."

Trying to keep a straight face I explained that fudge should be cooked on the top of the stove. Of all the cake tins to choose from they had used my expanding tin. When I opened the oven door to remove the fudge and put it into a saucepan, I found the fudge had leaked from its tin. It ran out the oven door and down the front of my coal range, baking on hard. I had to let the fire out before I could clean the oven and stove front, but first, to keep the peace, a pot of fudge had to be made.

James was eager to start school because, he told me, then he'd learn how to write his name and could write cheques. But I was worried. When he was little he sucked his third and fourth fingers. All the time. From the days he started to talk his fingers were constantly in his mouth. I believe he never learnt to use his tongue. The other children could understand what he was saying. Somehow I never had enough time to stand and listen and when he asked me something and I didn't know what he wanted, the other children would tell me.

As his school days drew closer I worried, so I took him to a speech therapist in Blenheim.

"I don't know why you're concerned," I was abruptly told. "Once he starts school he'll soon learn to talk when he mixes with all the other children."

The therapist didn't seem to understand that's why I was worried. He'd be on correspondence lessons. There wasn't going to be a playground full of children. I was told to go to our doctor and check that he wasn't tongue-tied.

There was nothing wrong with James's tongue. He just didn't use it. I rang Errol McConnell, the resident teacher, and he contacted the Correspondence School for me and explained my concern for James.

Today all pupils are sent a portable tape recorder if there isn't one in the home but when James was five they were not in use. But I was sent one, along with special speech books for James. He had to make hundreds of sounds on the tape, then send it to his teacher. It was made into a game for him even though the extra hour it took me daily once school was finished didn't seem like a game to me. But within a year his speech was as good, if not better than, his peers', and we were able to pack up the tape recorder and send it back to the school.

On fine days during school breaks the beach became a real attraction. I'd watch from my picture window and see deep holes being dug in the sand. After a storm any kelp washed up on the beach was soon buried, and the rotting kelp made the sand black. I found out only recently that the holes were being dug in earnest. The children were digging to China which they had learned was on the other side of the world. Once they reached the black sand they were positive China must be getting close but the clock always beat them and it would be school time again.

Helen and Joe began their school life around the kitchen table. When James turned five, three on the roll meant huge amounts of school materials had to be stored. The old sets of lessons had to be kept, and by now I had boxes of them. Then there were the sets they were working on, and the sets still to be done – we always had a month's work in advance – and all the other school requisites. The Correspondence School system gives its pupils the same opportunities as a normal school gives. Our children worked with the same things as any child in the country and they read the same books. When they did get into a classroom situation they were familiar with the work but not with the volume of noise generated by 30-odd children, and they found this hard to cope with during our special 'school weeks'.

Once a year a 'school week' was organised in Blenheim by Errol McConnell, the resident teacher in Marlborough. But I never sent the children through to Blenheim as they knew no one there. Instead they stayed with friends of ours in Picton, and attended the small St Joseph's School. They coped far better in a smaller classroom situation. I don't know if the children really enjoyed the times there but I certainly enjoyed the break from lessons.

In 1973 my Okukari school roll climbed to four children with Pauline. For the next two years I became totally absorbed in school lessons. When new sets arrived in the mail I read them through to familiarise myself with them, especially the lessons for the older two. I had to work hard to remain a jump ahead of them.

Now I had to be really organised. My mornings started at 6am. Joe and his crew man left much earlier. I started our generator and in the three hours before 9am we fitted in breakfast and anything I needed electricity for. I had to have my house tidy and then I could give all my time to lessons. If the children wanted to start lessons earlier they could, but doing only the work they could do on their own. They knew, when the power went off, that my time was theirs. I had knitting, sewing, letter writing or accounts to do while I supervised school. By the time Pauline began school Joe and Helen worked a lot on their own but some help was usually needed at some stage during the day. Days five and ten always had spelling tests and maths tests. Nature studies and social studies were added along with science. New maths came in while I taught, so I learnt as the children learnt.

After a week at St Joseph's, as well as keeping up with their counterparts in town as far as lessons went, they'd come home with all sorts of tricks and ditties. Perhaps the phone would ring, I'd go off to answer it, and I'd hear the giggling as I spoke to the caller. A loud roar would go up, then crying. I'd race in the schoolroom to find rulers being hidden, pieces of paper around the room, and someone in tears. I remember doing the same thing and pinging bits of paper off a bent ruler when I was at school and the teacher out of the way.

Shortly after one such annual school week we were out mustering. My mother-in-law and I were on the top beat with James and Pauline. James went through bush in case any sheep were hiding. Supple-jack grew thickly and the long vines hanging overhead made wonderful swings. A little voice wafted out:

"Tarzan swings. Tarzan falls.
Tarzan hurts his hairy balls."
"What did I hear?" asked my very surprised mother-in-law.
"Exactly what you thought you heard." That's what he'd learned by going to school in town.

July meant the Winter Party. Correspondence School children and families from all over Marlborough gathered in the Blenheim RSA clubrooms for the day. For us it meant leaving home about 7am if we were to arrive in Blenheim by 10am. The Owen family from the whaling station combined with us and we travelled to Picton in one boat. As they didn't have a car I offered them a ride to Blenheim. It was the days before seat belt awareness and we all piled into our car. Eight children and two adults. As usual, time was tight and lunches still had to be bought. As everyone crammed into the car I piled all the bags in the boot. Every inch of space was precious. In Blenheim I parked the car and reached for my handbag to find the key to open the boot. The handbag was in the boot.

"The garage will have a key to open it," I calmly told eight 'now what do we do?' kids.

"Sorry, ma'am," I was told. We can't help you there but I can get in through the back seat if you like."

"That'd be great, thanks. C'mon kids. Out." Eight kids and Mary Owen oozed out from the car. I felt so embarrassed but worse was to come. Years of lolly papers, the famous TT2 ice block papers, dried pieces of discarded fruit and their skins – it seemed as if the back of the seat had become our children's rubbish dump. The garage attendant reached the bags and I showed him which one held the key. I opened it. I couldn't see it. I tipped the contents out but there still wasn't a key. My hand went to my mouth and I cringed in shame. I remembered, now, that I'd carefully put the key in the glove box just so it wouldn't get locked in the boot.

The garage man stood patiently by the door, his arms leaning on the car roof. If only he'd walk away, I thought, I could get the key from the glove box and pretend it had been in the bag all the time. But no. I had to come clean and admit my stupid mistake. He cracked up, and when I asked the cost I was told it was nothing. It had made his day. Once again eight kids and Mary squeezed back into the car and I heard laughter coming from the garage. No doubt my mishap was being told around the workshop. I eased my conscience slightly by giving the office girl money for a 'shout' for the man who had helped me.

Things never seemed so difficult after I was able to talk with other correspondence mothers at the annual party. Their problems were the same as mine, except for the key episode. I'd kept quiet about that but eight little mouths had worked overtime telling their friends about it.

A teacher would come from Wellington to work with the children. They were taken to places like the fire station or police station. Team games were a highlight, and just mixing with other children doing the same style of school work always brought a new rush of enthusiasm in the next few days of lessons.

Miss Hilda Wise, head of the Correspondence School's junior department, broadcast to the children every Tuesday morning at 9.30. We listened in on our transistor radio, and everyone buzzed with excitement when a poem or story was read out followed by Joe's, Helen's, James's or Pauline's name. That link was vital, and I know it made the children strive harder to achieve more things to be acknowledged over the radio.

From the age of seven, or standard one, Marlborough pupils of the Correspondence School were eligible to attend the five-day camp at Lake Rotoiti in the Nelson Lakes. This took place during the first week in December. The first year that Joe went I took him to Blenheim where we met up with the other families and children who were going. We enviously waved to more than 40 children, supervisor Errol McConnell and some camp parents as they drove off on the 90-minute journey. Two or three of the children's teachers followed in a private car. On Friday afternoon the same people gathered once more to wait for their return. Happy but very exhausted children and adults staggered off the bus. They were wonderful camps.

I didn't really appreciate them or realise how hard the camp parents worked until 1975 when Pauline was old enough to go. James was going too, but Helen and Young Joe were with the older children at Massey University with the Correspondence Residential School, so Joe and I became camp parents at Rotoiti. I learned, first hand, the effort put into the week by the teachers, and I was glad to have had that chance. Mornings started with a wake-up call at 7.30. Dormitories were tidied before breakfast, ready for inspection. This became a strong competition and the winning group was announced on the last day. The day's activities began at 9am with the older children hiking for the day, some canoeing on the lake under the supervision of the park ranger, and the younger ones spending more time in the lodge doing creative work, lots of singing and games and shorter walks in the area. On the last day our pupils challenged the local school pupils at a sports afternoon. This was followed in the evening by a concert, and everyone had to perform in some way. Not even parents could worm their way out. The natural talent of some of the children amazed me but through one little boy in particular I learned what a marvellous medium music can be.

He was so shy. A little dark head appeared over the servery counter each meal time. Two brown hands clutched his plate. As he slid it along the bench I'd question him. Peas? A barely perceptible nod. Potatoes? A nod. Meat? Nod again. Every meal was the same. Never a word spoken. He sat on his own but didn't appear to be unhappy. He never joined in games willingly but if music was involved his face lit up and he radiated joy. I played the piano for the singing and a brown head bobbed with the beat of the music harder than any other.

After all the items were finished at the concert Errol asked if anyone had anything else to offer. A quiet voice startled us all.

"If the lights are turned off and Mrs Heberley plays for me I'll sing Amazing Grace." In the stunned silence I fumbled for the keys. The purest voice sang all the verses and I was glad of the darkness as I felt tears running down my face. This child had overcome his shyness through music and at last he was one of the whole group.

On Friday morning we packed up the camp. Lost and found belongings were sorted out, and, with promises to write and "See you at the picnic in February" ringing out, we made our farewells.

The picnic was held on the Picton Foreshore. Many of the further-away families never came, but when our four children were on the roll there were 14 children living in Tory Channel alone, so we made a good number without anyone else. Once again it was a chance for the children to mix socially. With running races, swimming, lolly scrambles and a catch-up about what we'd done at Christmas, it was a fun day.

The biggest event in the school year for the older children was the residential school. This had been run since 1949 when it was held for boy pupils and then alternated with girls. When our children attended, both boys and girls from 11 years up could go. When Massey University students finished for the year, young voices took over the campus for a month. Our children were flown from Blenheim (one year we waved goodbye to 22 Marlborough children), met at Wellington Airport, and then taken by bus to Palmerston North. They lived in the hostels at the university, and were taken to research farms, factories (often with an eye to future work), and many other places of interest and fun. Our children arrived home absolutely exhausted after their times at Massey but always having loved every minute of it.

During the years I taught our children I took them over to Wellington to meet their teachers. Pauline was a year old and Young Joe was in his first school year the first time I took them. I was on my way to visit my parents in Auckland. Joe's teacher met us when we arrived in Wellington on the ferry. She took us to the school and whisked Joe away to talk 'school' while the other three children and I were given a general look around the school. Before leaving we were taken to meet the headmaster, Mr McVeagh.

We were booked on the 3.30pm train and I was starting to get anxious by 2pm.

"I'll ring for a taxi for you."

"That'd be lovely," I replied. I sat up when I heard Mr McVeagh ordering a taxi to take me to the airport.

"No. It's the railway station I'm going to."

He found it hard to believe I was travelling on the train to Auckland with four young children.

"I guess a sleeper wouldn't be so bad," was his comment.

"No way. I couldn't bear to be cooped up in one of those with four children all night."

He was horrified when I told him I wasn't travelling first-class either, and that I was travelling second-class because there was no third. "It was women like you who helped us win the war," he said. I saw it as being practical.

The school holidays were special. I'd hear town mothers complain about having their children home and how they'd be driven mad. I looked forward to the holidays when I'd become a mother instead of a teacher and have time to enjoy my children.

One of the hardest things I found when teaching school was having to bring myself down to my children's level all the time. Days when Joe would leave home before the children were up and not arrive home until they were asleep at night made me long for someone of my age group to talk to. Those days I'd have bouts of thinking 'if only...'

If only I didn't live on an island and I could jump in the car and go and visit someone. Just get away, anywhere, as long as I could talk to someone older than my children.

Days when I wanted to give it all away. Leave the bay. If only I could have jumped in the car and shot home to Mum and Dad. But real life didn't work like it did in the movies. I'd visualise arriving at my parents' doorstep, my four children's clothes and their favourite toys packed in a suitcase and my clothes in another. Worn out. In the movies the woman was beautifully made up, well dressed and swept gracefully into her parents' arms as they welcomed her back. I knew my parents wouldn't welcome me if I was running away without good reason. My father had told me that I would be welcomed home any time if ever I was mis-treated, but not just if the going got tough. So I stayed where I was and was usually glad to wake up in Okukari the next morning.

Often the only warning I'd get that Joe was going to town was when he'd race up to the house for a quick cup of tea and with the words, "I'm off into Picton. We'll leave in half an hour. Are you coming?" I'd realise how badly I wanted to come. But half an hour! I couldn't pack up school and have four children ready by the time Joe wanted to go. Frustration and the deep-down tiredness that seemed to be my constant companion – I was having medical problems in those years – soon had me in tears of anger because I couldn't get organised, and many times Joe left with me yelling at him how much I hated this place and having to teach his children school while he could go out and enjoy himself. I easily overlooked the fact that he was going to Picton usually on business, and my tears of self-pity flowed as I watched the boat get smaller as it steamed down the channel.

Four concerned faces staring at their mother would always bring me back to reality and I'd turn my back on my painting and go back into the schoolroom and get on with the lessons.

Once school was finished for the day and I became a "mother" instead of a "teacher" I'd start to feel better. By the time Joe arrived home it was usually late in the day and I'd feel quite smug that I wasn't arriving home from town so late with tired children and the thought of having to catch up school the following day.

A girlfriend who'd lived next door to me in Auckland was married and now lived in Christchurch. Her son, Mike, was James's age, and they got on well together. As teenagers they both loved pig hunting and they'd spend all their holidays climbing the bush-clad hills at the back of Okukari in search of the Captain Cookers. Mike would travel back to Christchurch with his pack bulging with wild pork and the jaws for his trophy cabinet. Diane, his mother, told me not long ago that every time she said her goodbyes to her son she thought it would be for the last time. She imagined him being gored by wild pigs or crashing down over the steep cliffs to his death.

Maureen Stewart's son, Greg, also used to spend holidays hunting with James. They started very young and would go out goat hunting. One afternoon I watched the two hunters return. They'd told me they would catch a wild goat for the dogs to eat, and true to their word they had one. Two smart nine-year-olds had run the goat down, caught it, taken off their belts and were now leading it home. It was actually leading them. They'd decided it was easier than killing it out on the hill and bringing it home dead.

The years passed, school holidays came and went, and my pupil numbers gradually declined as college age and boarding school loomed. I still seemed as busy with only three or two on the roll. Then I was left with only one. My days changed. That constant demand on my time was gone. One year after James started college it was Pauline's turn to go. Joe worried I might be bored with empty days so he bought me a spinning wheel. I'd often said I'd like to have a go at spinning when I had the time. I haven't had the time to master it yet. Perhaps when I finish writing this book.

As I packed Pauline's final set of lessons to be sent in to the school I felt that old heavy load lifting from my shoulders. I'd undertaken a massive responsibility – as every Correspondence School mother does – but I'd had no other choice unless I'd moved to Picton. I knew I'd done my very best and I hoped I'd guided them wisely. Only the years ahead would give me my answer.

The Correspondence School is a marvellous way of education. It has come a long way since its opening in 1922 when one teacher, Miss Janet Mackenzie, hand-wrote all the lessons for 100 isolated primary school pupils. It is demanding on any family involved and I felt I did not enjoy the experience at the time. The responsibility was always with me. Looking back, I can now say I did enjoy those years, but I didn't realise this until they were over.

A close relationship with each child formed during this time, and the loving bonds among all family members have remained firmly in place. If a mother is prepared to accept the responsibility and is prepared to put in the essential hours, then the children will do well.

For quite a lot of the Correspondence School years with four children, I'd had a fifth in my classroom or hovering outside. The children always had pets and sometimes they joined us at lessons. But this one was special.

He arrived in Joe's shirt pocket. "We killed the mother. We didn't know she had babies. Thought the kids would like it." It was in Joe's palm. I had no idea of the troubles I'd let myself in for when I scratched its trembling body and fell in love with its little pink trotters, twitching nose, tightly curled tail and the few sparse hairs covering its body.

"He's a real Captain Cooker. See his long nose and already you can see he'll be black and tan."

A box with the hot water bottle and old woollen jerseys was soon in front of the coal range with one warm piglet curled up in it. Once his outer comforts had been seen to, his inner comforts needed attention and he let us know with disgustingly loud squeals from such a tiny being. "You'll have to feed him that colostrum milk you make up for the lambs," I was told. "He's too young for cow's milk."

Wrapped in a cloth, the piglet was fed his mixture of cow's milk, sugar, egg and cod liver oil with an eye dropper. During the next week he was demand-fed. The children would look into his makeshift bed, see a twitching nose and feed the pig. While our household slept I'd be fumbling around in the dark to light a candle and feed the pig. Everyone, except me, said he was far too little to sleep out in the woodshed but I appeared to be the only one who heard his nocturnal squeals.

Then at last I saw his eyes were opening. I'd feed him to shut him up, growl at him, and lids with curling lashes immediately closed over his eyes, but not before I'd seen a cunning glint. I made my stand. "That pig sleeps out in the shed from now on. I'm not getting out of my bed to feed a pig again." While being told I was cruel, mean, horrible and it'd be dead in the morning, I refilled his hot water bottle, covered him up and he was put out of the house. I had a dreadful night's sleep although I never let on to anyone. I was up to him more than if he'd been inside, checking him to make sure he was still alive. In the morning I was pleased to be woken by the most heart-rending squeals of hunger coming from the shed.

He couldn't be called 'it' or 'him' all the time, so he became Charlie Brown. Soon he was only in his box at night and he'd spend the day free-ranging. He'd wait outside the door hoping someone would come out and play races on the lawn with him. As he moved out of childhood he discovered the power of his nose. My garden didn't need his kind of digging up, and so Charlie Brown was made to take up residence in a dried-up concrete dam built on the hillside behind our house. His house was a 44-gallon drum with a wooden floor. He spent the first day rooting up the dirt and rolling his drum around and when he'd organised his house to his liking he sprawled over the drum and lapped up the sunshine.

He was a marvellous garbage disposal unit and ate all the scraps from the two houses in the bay. I still remembered Isabelle and her dislike of flopped steam pudding, so I was selective about the flops I gave Charlie Brown. I wasn't going to give him the chance to refuse a steamed pudding.

The highlight of his day was to be let out of his pen. He'd tear down the hill with the children, tossing his head as he ran, bunting into the backs of their knees. Then he'd slobber over their faces if he got them down. I'd hear shrieks of laughter mixed with squeals of pig's delight.

He loved the beach. As soon as he hit the sand his snout would drop and he'd run the length of the beach, leaving a deep furrow behind. Then he'd turn around and run back along his furrow, eating the sand hoppers as they jumped out of the freshly turned sand.

With Charlie Brown in our household, summertime lazing on the beach and swims were never the same. The pig had to come too. School completed for the day, I'd take the children for their promised swim. I'd stretch out on the sand and make myself comfortable, ready to admire the swimmers' latest skills. The pig, tired after his usual run along the beach, would flop alongside me. He'd lie on his stomach, wriggle down into the sand, and with his head on his front trotters he'd lie and stare at me through sand-coated eyelashes. If I moved he'd glare at me, heave a sigh and move closer, his wet sand-coated body pushing hard against mine.

We'd had days of heavy rain. The pig relished the bog and wallowed to his heart's content. But we'd forgotten the origins of the pig house. I took his breakfast up as usual and the dam was doing the job it had been built for. It was half-full with rain water which had run off the hill, and one pig was floating around on the 44-gallon drum. There were no squeals of delight when I dragged him out. He took off down the hill and into the woodshed, the safe warm home he remembered from his younger days.

"Take him down to the woolshed. He can go out into the yards and run in the woolshed for shelter," Joe told me. This suited the pig down to the ground and now he could jump over the fences when he felt like company.

Not long after Charlie Brown's change in living accommodation, Joe and I were in town. The older children had stayed with Joe's parents for the day. No school and the sound of playing children invited the pig over the fences to keep them company. He knew there were pet lambs to be fed and loved trotting along to lick the dribbling milk from their faces. This time no one told him off when he followed the children home to wash out the lambs' bottles. He smelt the large bag of milk powder inside the back door. He wasn't missed when he later sneaked away back to our house, and found the half-full bag of lambs' milk powder. When he had eaten the contents he pulled at the bag, shook it, and ran through the house with it, leaving the evidence of his escapade in every room.

My mother-in-law spent a lot of time in her vegetable garden. On this later occasion it was December and the garden was at its best. Green tomatoes with their first hint of colour hung in clusters off lush green bushes, and lettuces were hearting off. Vegetables grew in perfect rows, not a weed to be seen, and in the evenings everything enjoyed the light rain when the sprinkler was turned on.

The dreadful screams brought me running from the house. I thought Ruby was badly hurt. In the middle of her garden, stretched out to his full length, was Charlie Brown. He must have thought he'd died and gone to heaven. He'd made a glorious wallow. It was probably the best one he'd ever made. He didn't even have to root up the dirt. It was already dug, warm from the hot sun earlier in the day. Delicious lettuces were on each side of him waiting to be eaten, he didn't mind that the tomatoes were green, and with the gentle rain falling on his face a pig couldn't ask for anything else. Sharp jabs in his rump from Ruby's rake cut short his dreams of heaven, and a muddy pig chased by my enraged mother-in-law tore out the front gate.

He had to be re-sited. Somewhere he could not escape from. He was a large animal now, and at times I was scared of him. I'd always thought of pigs as dirty animals until I'd had them as pets. I was amazed at their clean habits. They always relieved themselves in the same place in their sty and kept themselves clean. They ate with gusto and their food went all over the place but it was cleaned up after they'd eaten, with the flat nose snuffling over the ground to find any remaining scraps to gulp down. To describe an untidy room as a pig sty is simply not right.

For a special treat we'd allow the pig inside. He'd race through the kitchen, turn to go into the lounge and find that four trotters couldn't get a grip on the smooth floor. He'd be running flat out on the same spot. Then he'd slowly pick up speed again and hit the lounge carpet, and then up on to the couch. All the cushions were pushed off. If an unsuspecting visitor was sitting on the couch, the pig kept on pushing until the cushions and the person were removed. He'd heap the cushions up on the floor, his natural instincts making him want to build a high bed of fern or bracken, and then lie on top. His front and back legs stretched out, he'd rub his belly on the chintz covers, gaze at us all through his long lashes, then quickly roll over and wait for his belly to be scratched.

Friends from Christchurch had come to stay, and of course the pig had to be introduced the minute they'd arrived. In he came and did his usual act. The seven-year-old Christchurch child couldn't believe it. As Charlie Brown whipped by, Anna ran her fingers along the pig's back, looked at them, then smelt them. Her face told us her thoughts. It can't be real – can it?

But when he wanted a mate, he was mean. Friendly eyes became cunning. He no longer came inside. We built his new house next to the chook-house. He had a huge area to run in among trees and old logs, and I often didn't see him for two or three days.

One day Joe had the two boys out fishing. Helen and Pauline were at home with me. We went to feed the chooks. Helen and I were in the chook-house collecting the eggs while Pauline gathered sow-thistle for the chooks. Charlie Brown was in a bad mood and he stalked up and down the fence-line, charging it to attract our attention. A gust of wind slammed the door shut and the latch fell into the slot. I was locked in the chook-house with Helen, and three-year-old Pauline was outside. No one else was at home in the bay, nor would they be for at least another eight hours. The only way out of the chook-house was through a small hole – chook size.

"Pauline," I called through the wire netting in the front of the chook-house. "You'll have to open the door."

"Can't reach," the little voice piped out. I could hear the pig and he sounded mean. People around and no food, I imagined him thinking. There was a concrete wall alongside the door.

"Pauline, you'll have to listen carefully. Climb up on the wall, reach across and lift the latch."

"Can't."

Now I had visions of her running off down to the beach or the dip. But Helen and I heard scrabbles outside and lots of puffing as Pauline climbed the wall and reached across to lift the latch. We were free. The pig still patrolled the fence-line.

He finally became too much of a liability. "One of the kids'll get hurt by him. He'll have to go. We'll get him made into bacon." Howls met Joe's words. I certainly couldn't eat a close family member. So Charlie Brown was caught, bundled into a woolpack and taken for a boat ride to Wellington Bay. No doubt he is the grandfather of many of the wild pigs that grace our table today. And yes, I'm always being asked how I cook wild pork. It isn't really a recipe. All I do is cover the pork with vinegar, pat brown sugar over the top side and cover it with cooking foil before cooking it slowly. Many people eating wild pork for the first time have been amazed by how delicious it is.

But Charlie Brown, no. Never could he become bacon or wild pork – not in the Heberley household.

Brownie was a pony. He was the most cantankerous, cunning piece of horseflesh I've ever known although the only horse I'd had anything to do with previously was Mr Ed, television's talking horse.

Eight-year-old Helen wanted a horse. Most of her books were about horses. Black Beauty was a favourite, and she'd pleaded with Joe and finally worn him down until at last he promised he'd think about it.

Papers were pored over after mail day but by the time we read the 'horses for sale' column, they'd been sold. Helen asked Maureen Stewart if she could watch out for a horse for sale and check the local paper each day.

At last Maureen phoned with the news she'd found a pony we might be interested in for Helen. He was quiet, and would be suitable for a learner, she'd been told. In retrospect, none of us knew much about horses. He looked a nice little horse, I said, until Helen rather disdainfully told me he was a pony – not a horse. He seemed quiet, and he'd let Helen walk him around Maureen's back yard with his halter on. I watched as my young daughter scratched his head, rubbed her hand down his mane and over his wither and spoke loving horse talk, and I knew we'd have an addition to the family.

It was the Christmas holidays so Helen stayed with Maureen until the barge could be organised to bring Brownie to Okukari. Grazing was found and in the next few days Helen and Brownie were to get used to each other. Horse experts had told us he was grossly overweight, so he was kept tethered.

The day Brownie stepped foot on Okukari we began to wonder if we'd been had. Helen took his halter off and, we believe, for the first time in his life he found he could run free. The problem was he couldn't be caught. He'd charge round and round the paddock with Helen trying to throw the bridle over his head to catch him. He'd toss his head to flick it off, roll his eyes to show the whites, and gallop off.

"Be brave," a very unbrave Joe around horses, told Helen. "Look. I'll show you."

While Helen and Joe were being brave, three children and I would watch from the other side of the fence. Joe caught him and at last Helen could ride her horse. My visions of her falling off and breaking her neck were quickly gone. Brownie had two speeds. Stop and slow, although later he always galloped from the woolshed up to our house. No doubt he knew it was the end of the ride for him and he could laze the rest of the day away.

In his 16 years at Okukari Helen very rarely got him to gallop. He controlled her totally and he did nothing except what he wanted to do.

When it came time to cut his toe nails, as I put it, Joe was called on. Helen tied up Brownie and once she'd coaxed him to lift a foot up on the slab of pine, Joe with chisel and hammer started to trim the thick horny growth. Brownie didn't like it and sank his teeth into Joe's shoulder. This was too much for an already nervous Joe so he lifted the hammer and whanged it down on Brownie's nose. They were enemies for life.

His 'nails' did finally get cut with Helen holding his head away from her father and after that she'd wait until someone was down who knew about horses, and he'd get the job.

Brownie's worst fault we were to find out during our next lambing. We'd noticed a few new lambs with no tails and presumed the ewes were licking them off when they cleaned their lambs. It wasn't until Charlie was checking the sheep and came across Brownie with a lamb that we found out. He was licking a new lamb and had actually licked so hard he'd skinned it and it was dead. Charlie caught him and tied the dead lamb around Brownie's neck to teach him not to do it again.

As the lamb rotted we hoped it was teaching the horse a lesson and for a few years we believed it did, although we tried to keep him away from any lambs. Then he started again. This time it was the ears he seemed to like. One of these lambs survived to become a pet. He was named The Fonz. As he was pulled out of the catching pen by an unsuspecting shearer and sat against his legs before starting up the shearing machine, the look of amazement on the face of the shearer as he pushed the sheep's head to one side to shear the wool off its face had us in fits. Joe liked to tell them we were trying to breed a new sheep. No ears.

Brownie survived because he was kept away from the sheep at lambing. But he never became Helen's joy and she never experienced the thrill of jumping over fences and riding with the wind through her hair as they did in her storybooks.

Joe decided it was time the horse earned his keep. The Stewart family were staying with us and Joe and Cedric had planned a pig hunt on the Cook Strait side of the farm. "I'm not walking all that distance," Joe said. "I'll ride Brownie to the top of the hill and pick him up on the way back."

Maureen and I couldn't believe that Joe was serious. He hated the horse as much as the horse appeared to hate him and we watched in silence as Joe saddled him up. What we didn't know and Joe didn't know was that he put the girth of the saddle around Brownie's flanks. We learned much later that this is what they do in rodeos on the bronco horses. Cedric set off up the hill with an "I'll catch you up," from Joe. From the kitchen window we saw Cedric disappear over the brow of the hill as Joe came into view. Brownie pig-jumped, bucked and snorted and Joe hit him with a stick, yelled, and kicked him in the flanks. In the kitchen Maureen and I were doubled up with laughter. I phoned Joe's mother. "You've got to come and see this. Your son's being a stockman." She came up with her binoculars and joined in our laughter.

It all got too much for Joe. Cedric was well gone and he was left way behind. We saw him jump angrily off the horse and look down towards the house. I ran outside and heard him tell us to get Helen to come up and pick up her damned horse. So Brownie was tied to a fence and when Helen brought him back to the flats I'll swear his head was held higher, his steps lighter, and his eyes shone with the light of victory as he passed our house.

It was old age that killed Brownie. He lay in his grave until Pauline, in her third year at Massey, wanted a skeleton of a horse. He was brought to the shed in boxes where he was unpacked. I looked at his remains and thought at last he had something to give, even if it was two years after his death.

One of the great days in the correspondence years came early on, when I was already finding that the constant pressure of teaching one child, while looking after three others, was stretching my sanity to the limit. It seemed I was always talking to children. With the oldest five years, and the youngest 12 months, I felt my conversation skills were being smothered and my only reading books seemed to be Young Joe's little reader books. We had gone through the red ones, yellow, green and blue. I knew *Grandma Comes To Stay*, where she arrived in a Viscount, off by heart, and whenever it was read to me my mind would drift on another tangent and I'd be wishing it was as easy as that for my children's grandma to come and stay.

My social time began every weekday at 2pm. Doreen of 2ZB came into my kitchen. This was my time, my link with the outside world. It helped keep me sane. She spoke of happenings, gave recipes and advice and had guest speakers in the studio. After the death of Aunt Daisy with her nationwide 9am weekday slot it must have been a hard act to follow, but it was a totally different format. Today when I listen to talkback shows on air I realise Doreen's programme must have been the forerunner.

One afternoon after listening to one of her guest speakers, I wrote to tell Doreen how much I enjoyed her show and tried to explain why it meant so much to me. A few weeks later I received a letter inviting me to go over to Wellington and join her in the studio with five other listeners, and speak on air. The show was a birthday celebration and they wanted it to be different.

My first reaction was excitement. How I wanted to go, but how could I with four children? Besides, how could I get to Picton in time to catch the 10am ferry as I knew Joe would want to go fishing. He wouldn't take me up. No, I couldn't go, I told myself, but it was wonderful to have been asked. Then I thought, even if I could go, how could I speak on a radio station when there were hundreds of people listening? My small world I'd grown into couldn't cope with that.

When Joe came home and read the letter I was told I was going. "It'll do you good," I was told.

My excuses of "I can't. I've got school. Four children. And how can I get to town?" were met with answers. So I found myself on the ferry to Wellington. Joe's mother had four children for the day, Joe took me in to Picton and I was on my own – the very first time without the responsibility of children since the day Young Joe was born.

I sat on the ferry completely lost. As we passed Okukari I came out on the deck and waved, feeling homesick when I saw the bonfire that had been lit for me to see. I had no one to point out the sea birds that swooped down on the ferry. I stood on the deck and watched in a lonely silence as dolphins played around the boat, and wished that I could share these things with four wide-eyed children.

Once in Wellington and I'd met Doreen at 2ZB, home was forgotten. Five other listeners, all nervous, laughed and joked. Doreen spoke with each of us and I found when it was my time to talk on air with her I felt completely relaxed. I wasn't worried if there were hundreds of people listening in and hearing about our lifestyle. As Doreen said, I had something to tell.

After the interviews with the six of us, listeners were invited to phone in and ask questions. I was grateful to learn that I could still talk, and the experience gave my self-confidence the boost it needed. Then we enjoyed afternoon tea with a birthday cake and before I left I was taken to meet another person I loved to listen to. It was just on 4pm. Time for John Gordon's programme of classical music on National Radio. The red light was showing above the door when we reached John's studio and we waited outside until he'd finished introducing his programme for the afternoon and his first piece of music was playing. The quietly spoken person I met was as pleasant off air as on, and over the next years I enjoyed his programmes even more as I pictured him in my mind.

Too soon my fairytale day ended and I was on the ferry once more. Joe met me in Picton. But even if I felt like Cinderella as I changed out of my town clothes back to Okukari clothes once more, I was so happy to be home.

CHAPTER SEVEN

New House, New Boat

WE OUTGREW our house soon after Young Joe began Correspondence School. The farm-sized kitchen and living area were fine. We needed a schoolroom even though our one-bedroomed house had grown to a three-bedroomed house. Bunks in the two additions made the rooms big enough but storage space was limited. Before summer I'd sort through the children's clothes and pack the winter ones in boxes so their summer clothes were in drawers. Our bedroom sported a pile of cartons in the corner but at least it kept their rooms tidy. In winter the process was reversed. Besides being too small the house needed a lot of money spent on it if we were to stay on.

The roof leaked. When it rained the persistent dripping of water was heard in quite a few rooms. I lay at night and listened to it over our bed.

"Imagination," I was told. "It's not that bad. You just want your new house."

I noticed a bulge appearing in the ceiling above the bed. Now I was seeing things, I was told. Days of heavy rain and the weight of accumulated water in the ceiling finally proved too much. Mushy gibralter board and cold, foul-smelling water landed on top of us. We both leaped out of bed, trying to find candles and matches. The bed was uninhabitable so the rest of the night we spent on the floor. But even in the dark it had been frightening. I couldn't help feeling smug. It wasn't my imagination and I hadn't been seeing things. The discomfort we felt and the mess I cleaned up were worth it when Joe said, "That's it. We'll build."

Books, plans, bits of paper with sketches and ideas cluttered up any remaining space in our house. We spoke to builders, saw houses they'd built in town, received quotes, changed plans and finally decided on what we wanted. The choice of a big plain house, with a laundry with a large catchment area for all the clothes I had to deal with, and a large area inside the back door to pile everything inside after a day in town, won over a smaller, fancier house.

The final quote was above our budget so it was agreed we'd build the terrace and put in the septic tank ourselves. In the contract we had to put all the materials on the site. The builders organised the sub-contractors.

At different times of the day and on windy days we took our plan all over the farm, looking for the best place to build. We could have shelter but not a lot of sun, or have wind with the sun and a view. The view won. I still had my painting.

Gilbert Perano brought his bulldozer over from Whekenui and levelled off

Joe and I on the night of our engagement.

On my wedding day, with my father and mother.

My parents-in-law, Charlie and Ruby Heberley.

Joe at the wheel of the Heather.

First formal portrait, taken in Auckland in 1969. Joe aged five, Pauline one, James two and Helen just four.

Lucky pursues me into the pantry for his vanilla wine biscuit.

Rough weather at Perano Head, at the start of the Cook Strait Surf Lifeboat Race.

Our two boats, the Fugitive *(left) and* Te Wai.

Paul Palmer photographer.

The Fish Hanging Party under way.

Picton friends Cedric and Maureen Stewart.

The Dominion.

Our fishing boat, the Fugitive, tows four of the lifeboats of the Mikhail Lermontov to Picton.

Where the power lines cross Tory Channel from Arapawa Island.

Paul Palmer photographer.

Taking school shark from the freezer, ready to unload.

Throwing a fleece.

Pauline at her clinic.

Marlborough Express.

Sea-Tow's scrap metal barge in our bay.

After a southerly, a raft of pine logs is washed ashore in our bay.

Pulling the boat in to the wharf.

Paul Palmer photographer.

James and Joe pull up a crayfish pot, and re-set the pot.

Paul Palmer photographer.

Tennis students form a guard of honour at the wedding of Dene and Pauline.

Wedding Arapawa Island-style, with the stretch limousine, overlooking Tory Channel entrance.

the site. Ours would be the third house at Okukari, furthest up the hill from the beach and the last house before Cook Strait, or the first on Arapawa Island in Tory Channel.

In one afternoon our green sloping land became hard shiny clay, waiting for the first pick-axe to break its surface. Until power was on the site nothing could happen. Over Christmas 1971 we built a shed for our new seven-kilowatt generator. It was brought out on the barge and its arrival time in the bay had to coincide with high water. This made it easier to slide the generator on to the waiting sledge on the wharf. I watched its slow progress as the tractor ground its way up the rough track from the beach. At every bump I expected to see it roll off. I wished I was in town and all I had to do was phone the power board and they would come and put a wire on a pole.

On 2 March 1972 the barge arrived with the first house-load, mainly builders' equipment. Our house had begun. On Monday mornings Joe met the builders in Picton at 7.30. They stayed in our house all week and returned at 3.30pm on Fridays. Four men came in the first few weeks. Bodies squeezed into our little house. The four children slept on the floor on makeshift beds. Joe's crew man boarded with us, bringing our numbers to 11 at the start. Numbers working on the house varied. At times there were six extra men, and when we couldn't fit another body into our house my in-laws found themselves with extras.

This year, 1972, was Census Year. We carefully filled the form out:

Square footage of building	800 sq feet
Number of rooms (we even counted the toilet)	6
Method of cooking	Woodstove
Method of heating	Woodstove
Number occupying dwelling on Census Night	13

We wondered if this was some sort of record.

For the next three and a half months I was perpetual motion. Joe and his crew started each day off with their breakfast about 5am before going fishing. Next sitting was at 7am. The builders started work at 7.30. School began at 9. Joe aged seven and Helen aged six needed lots of supervision with their lessons while James at four, and Pauline at three, just needed supervision. All the time.

School lessons and afternoon tea over, the remainder of the day disappeared in dinner preparations and housework. By the end of the first week our house had foundations. I stood inside them, saw myself in the finished rooms, and dreamt.

The truck that came to Picton and collected the men on Fridays always brought a load of gear down for Joe to bring back home. He never arrived home before 8pm and we'd spend the next hour lifting the gear off the boat to stack on to the tractor and drive it up to the site, ready for Monday morning.

A massive quantity of gravel for the foundations was brought up on the barge. It was shovelled into a wheelbarrow, then pushed along a plank lying between the barge and the trailer, three hours of shovelling at a stretch. The only other time we used the barge was to bring down the gold Summerhill Stone bricks. They were already stacked on pallets so we hired a forklift to use at our end. This was going to be easy. The thrust of the forks to pick up the first pallet wiped the smug grins of our faces. Our forks were too narrow. Spare timber quickly turned into two new pallets to fit our forklift. Each brick had to be reloaded on to the new pallets, taken up the hill and unloaded until we'd shifted them all. It was all hands and the cook. No one had any skin left on fingertips that night. We could have committed any burglary without leaving clues.

Weekends were busy. School lessons usually had to be caught up, cake tins filled and, as the house grew, I painted inside the cupboards. When Joe came in from fishing he tidied around the section. He dug the hole for our septic tank. Instead of making boxing for it, we used steel shutters the plumber had lent us. We mixed the cement to line it and were delighted with our success.

Joe and I were in the hole, struggling to remove the shutters, when Helen poked her head over the top and yelled to us. "A boat's coming into the wharf! We've got visitors."

"You'd better go and tell them we're up here, please."

Down she raced and couldn't wait to blurt out, "Mum and Dad are in the septic tank. They said to come up."

The septic tank became the biggest problem in Okukari. There were 72 feet between the house and the tank, and the drain was built with too little fall. The pipe always blocked at the entrance of the tank and always it seemed it happened when we had visitors. As they were leaving and farewells were being said, such as "Loved having you. Come again", I was thinking of what we had to do when we got back to the house. Often they would be still steaming out of the bay when Joe and I had the cover off the tank to syphon it out. So regularly did this happen that we kept our black polythene hose especially for the job. The exact length, it reached the tap on the front of the house, from which I'd fill it with water, run across the lawn, then throw my end over the steep bank into the creek that ran up the side of our section. Joe pushed his end into the offending tank. We became sick of being "shit stirrers" and within a couple of years made some alterations to the plumbing ourselves. Now we keep a careful watch on what goes down the kitchen sink, and we have had 'town sewerage' for years.

If you can't make fun out of these situations, you're the wrong type to be in a place like Okukari. I remember one shearing time. We had four shearers in the house and it rained so they were waiting for the sheep to dry. Our old problem recurred. No waste drained from the house at all. Hard-case guys, these shearers. One of them had the solution.

"Get out that fire pump of yours, Joe. The water she pushes out must clear it."

"Yeah. Probably would. Might cause a blow-back, too."

"No, come on mate. Let's give it a go."

All the experts helped set it up. I heard them laughing and giving advice to each other. I'd teach them a lesson.

There were two sausages in the fridge so I carefully placed them in the bath. With the addition of wet toilet paper and curry powder it certainly looked like something regurgitated from the septic tank. Outside the pump started up. Loud noises reverberated through the drains, then gurgled as the unblocked drain sucked the build-up back into the septic tank.

Everyone coming inside was taking the credit. "That made it easy." "Better than syphoning." "Great way to do it." I waited in the lounge while they went to wash. Silent laughter waited to explode.

"Jesus bloody Christ! Come here. My God, it's come up the drain! Shit, Joe!"

I followed them in – five grown men gazing in silent awe at the phenomenon before their eyes. I couldn't trap my laughter any longer. The spell broke.

"You didn't fool us," Blue laughed. "But God I hope it's not sausages for tea."

Harry, Joe's crew man, had a house near Dieffenbach. On days when Joe worked on the house or bad weather kept them from fishing he'd putter home in his dinghy with outboard attached. He rang one Thursday evening.

"Mind if I hitch a ride into Picton with you tomorrow, Joe? I'll meet you at Dieffenbach in my dinghy."

"That's fine, Harry. We'll be going past about 4.30pm."

All the men were keen card players and as soon as the boat left Okukari the cards came out for a game of five hundred. The auto pilot was on, and Joe kept checking on its course every few minutes. Engrossed in the game, he forgot all about Harry. The next time he jumped up to see that no boats were coming, he happened to glance down and saw sinewy fingers frantically clawing along the side of the boat. Harry, waiting in the dinghy, had expected Joe to stop. Right in the boat's path he realised too late that he wasn't being picked up, and made a lunge for the boat as it went past. He did come back to work for Joe, but only for a short time.

There have been ever-increasing goats on Arapawa Island since they were introduced by Captain Cook. They destroy the native bush, but they used to be kept under control when a bounty was paid on them. For every tail presented, three shillings was paid plus three rounds of .303 ammunition. Joe nailed his tails on the woolshed door. When that was covered, the walls sported drying tails. With his bounty money we paid for floor coverings throughout our house except for the schoolroom. Three hundred goats later, that room too was carpeted.

Once the house was finished, all I wanted to do was move in.

"No," Joe said. "We'll lay some paths first or we'll just be tramping mud inside."

This was sensible as our house now sat in a sea of yellow clay. We also had to erect a fence on the edge of the steep bank of the creek. When school and fishing finished, each day we'd mix enough cement for two or three sections of the path and work on the fence. Soon there was no reason not to move in.

Weather permitting we would move in on Saturday. Our original little house had become quite empty. After school the children and I shifted whatever we could carry. Old cupboards became empty as the new cupboards filled up. It got to the stage when if Joe wanted something and couldn't find it I'd answer, "It's up in the new house."

House moving was accomplished in one day. Everything except for my piano. That was too heavy for us to carry. I'd had to wait patiently for it to get into the little house. Now I had to wait until some visitors arrived so we could reverse the process of getting it out through the door, and all of us bring it home. This time there wasn't anyone to raise a flag on the lookout, and our new house had a ranch-slider to bring the piano through.

Money was tight but we had our house. A lounge suite was a luxury we didn't need immediately. After all we had our soft goat-tail carpet to loll around on. Today we still prefer to sit on the floor, ignoring our comfortable chairs and couch.

Four young children, a fisherman husband and one crew make a lot of washing. A clothes line in a windy sunny position was a top priority. I fought with my old line every day. I carried the washing across the back lawn, up a steep bank and over a wire fence. To hang it out I tied the line down to stop it whizzing round in the wind. Sheets flattened by the wind against the wires bent the centre pole. The arms turned upwards till they looked like the spokes of an umbrella blown inside out. If the clothes stayed on the line long enough they dried quickly. I told Joe, "When I'm too old to get to the clothes line it's time to leave Okukari."

Nature took a hand before that happened. Metal fatigue occurred. The centre pole snapped, and my washing, still on the line, bowled along the ground until it came to rest in a patch of gorse. The twisted remains of the lines are still there. They are my reminder that man proposes but God disposes. There was a bonus. The pet goat would no longer be able to dispose of my washing. I'd had to be very careful how I hung my washing on the line, and I still carried the picture in my mind of shirts with short sleeves, shortened long trousers and jerseys with pruned sleeves. The goat had stood under the clothes line and eaten everything within reach.

The children thought they shouldn't be the only ones in a new house.

"Please build a new chook house, Dad."

Helen and James pestered their father until our eight fowls had smart new living quarters behind our shed.

Passing it on his way home for a cup of tea, Joe went in to collect the eggs. A Canadian goose had moved in. It sat, sprawled over the nest, and its baleful look backed Joe out in a hurry. He shut the door, came inside and told me, then said to James, "I noticed the chook house door shut. There'll be no eggs in the nests if the chooks can't get in. How about opening it, son?"

We waited for the roar.

"Done it. Can I have a biscuit now?" as he raced inside.

"He must have seen it," Joe said as he went to see for himself.

The goose was still on the nest. He managed to get Helen and Joe in there for other reasons. No one saw the thing and his joke fell flat until Pauline importantly went out with her basket at feeding time.

"Don't forget to give them fresh water."

Soon an angry ball of energy burst through the kitchen door.

"A father chook's in there. He hissed at me."

Next morning the Canadian goose was gone and chook house life returned to normal. Pauline wouldn't go near the chook house for a month.

Salt setting on the roof after a southerly means we can't collect the rain water off it so water for our house comes from a creek to a holding tank. After heavy rain we always have problems. The pipe washes out of the creek, stones block it, and silt slowly builds up in the holding tank until our water stops running altogether. We discovered town water systems didn't work in our situation. Ball-cock valves kept blocking with small gravel and we'd find ourselves with no water. Joe drilled a bigger hole in the toilet system and fixed that, but the header tank in the ceiling gave us no end of trouble. With the water coming straight in from outside, any debris from the creek immediately jammed in the valve. Joe used a thick darning needle to clear it. Then I'd hear him giving the ball-cock and pipe a good shake.

Of course the time had to come, on my birthday of all days, when it blocked and Joe had left home early. I had a fair idea what he did, so four kids pushed their mother through the manhole. One evening when I was young I'd been attacked by a man in Auckland, and since then I've a fear of the dark. Enclosed spaces make it worse. The torch's feeble beam wasn't much comfort as I crawled over ceiling joists to the tank. Cobwebs clutched at my hair. I was sure I heard mice scurrying away and probably there were rats lurking in the dark corners. Perspiration ran down my back and I felt my hair clinging to my forehead. Balancing the torch on the edge of the tank I tried to clear the valve with the needle. No water. I shook the ball-cock. Still nothing happened. I shook harder. The torch fell in the tank and my light died. My mouth went dry. My heart pounded in my throat and it was hard to breathe. I couldn't stay up here any longer, but I gave the ball-cock one last frantic shake. Suddenly the whole thing ended up in my hand. Now I had plenty of water, but it couldn't be stopped. I scrambled to the square of light, thankful for an excuse for my hurried exit, then down the hole to turn off the main supply outside. Luckily for me Joe had to go to Picton later that day, because we needed a new ball-cock.

When he arrived home he gave me my birthday present.

"Happy birthday, love. Sorry I didn't have it for you this morning." It was one of the nicest wrapped gifts he'd ever given me with a beautiful big red bow on the top. Inside was a new ball-cock.

A house needs lawns and gardens. We fenced off the section and concentrated on our lawns. The top soil we'd removed was wheel-barrowed back. A 12-gallon drum filled with concrete made a wonderful roller and by Christmas we almost had a lawn. If you lay down and looked across it you could see some green. This lovely green struggled to survive over summer, and during its first winter the southerlies kept burning it off. By next spring we had a lush green lawn but with no shelter. Anything I tried to grow in the garden died. Salt spray blown in with a southerly wind burnt everything except the hard shiny-foliaged shrubs I was growing. The northerly wind roaring down the gully usually blew anything left in the garden out of the bay. I'd watch in tears as my hard work disintegrated before me.

"Right," said Joe. "Next trip to town we'll get some shelter trees."

So we started from the outside in and planted pine trees down the southern side of our section. A friend in Queen Charlotte Sound told us we must grow she-oaks. His grew so thick and fast he had to keep chopping them back. That seemed just what we needed so we planted 100. Today only seven are left. Our conditions wiped them out in the first six months. Oh those people who plan and plant and end up with perfect *House and Garden* displays! I try not to be envious, and anyway envy doesn't help. The fact is that Okukari would challenge any fulltime gardener, and I was far from being fulltime.

But we kept at it. Next we built a wooden fence, and gradually I filled in my garden. Close planting means shrub protects shrub. The weather is a selective pruner, and many things don't grow at all or remain stunted until I get rid of them myself. I no longer attempt a winter garden. It just isn't worth it. In any case it makes me appreciate the spring flowers all the more. Summer grows a wonderful garden, and it lets me forgive the winter.

For months after we moved I'd wake up in the night after having dreadful nightmares. They were always the same. Our house had burnt down. Still caught in my dream, I knew I couldn't go through those three and a half months again, of too many people in too small a space, not being sure where everything was, and sheer hard unremitting work. Seeing the familiar shadows of our new bedroom calmed me and I'd drift into sleep again. I knew the hard work was behind us.

There was, and still is, intense satisfaction in knowing that every single item that went into building our house was something we had personally handled. And not just once. Often three or four times. Then there were the distances our boat had covered between Picton and Okukari. At least 60 trips – 120 hours' travelling time. I can think back over the 100 pounds of flour I'd made into scones and pikelets for the men's morning and afternoon teas. And how clearly I can see the 2600 bricks we'd had to lift on to pallets – and yes, in the new lounge and kitchen I still have my painting. But now it is much larger. Now if I open our bedroom curtains I have the same picture. Another day to enjoy our home.

We hadn't been in our new house a year when I noticed Joe sitting over a cup of tea and staring out the window. I knew something was on his mind, and before long I was told. "You know, love, I'm sick of the long hours I have to put in steaming just to reach the fishing grounds." I knew what he was going to tell me. "We need a different type of fishing boat."

I couldn't complain. I had my new house. Joe would have his new boat.

The *Heather* was sold and a 40-foot hard-chine wooden vessel designed by Colin Neill was built by Morgan's Boat Yard, Picton. In April 1974, Helen cracked a bottle of champagne over her bow and the *Fugitive* rumbled down the rails to meet the sea.

That week before her launching was to be the biggest test of Maureen Stewart's and my friendship. The month before the new boat's launching Joe had been staying in Picton with Maureen and Cedric. When Maureen phoned and suggested I came up and stayed with them the week before the boat was launched, and the four children could go to St Joseph's School, I jumped at the invitation. I was sick of my own company, and fed up with trying to teach four children who were all wildly excited about the new boat and wanted to talk about nothing else. I felt school was getting nowhere.

Six Heberleys made the Stewarts' home bulge. Four extra beds were made up on the floor and Joe and I took over the lounge. Our bed was able to be left made up, and everyone used the family room for the week. I loved the peace that settled on the house every morning once my four and Maureen's two boys had left for school and we were left with Jane, Maureen's pre-schooler.

By mid-week the usual launching crisis had developed. It always happens. Everyone decides the boat won't be ready. The paintwork will be soft. The engineering won't be finished, nor will the auto-electrical work. They all know they should be launching her the following week – not in a couple of days. But that wouldn't make any difference. Whatever date is decided on for a launching there is always that mad panic at the end.

Joe had his long list – he'd learnt about lists – and Maureen and I were going to Blenheim to get his shopping. After the mad scramble of getting six children aged from ten years down to five years to school on time, I was exhausted and intended to have a quick bath before we left for Blenheim.

I put in the plug, turned on both taps and found there was no water. Surely this sort of thing happens only at Okukari, I thought as I went through the house to ask Maureen if she knew the reason. In the paper we read the council announcement that the water would be turned off.

In Blenheim Joe's list steadily got shorter, and by lunch time there were only two things missing. I couldn't buy exactly what he wanted. "They'll be home for lunch," Maureen said. "Go and ring them up."

As I waited for the rings to be answered I had time to think what a lovely morning I'd had. No mad panic to get Joe's shopping and I'd even had time to window shop. It was ages before the phone was picked up and the voice that roared down the line when I asked to speak to Joe made me wish it had been left unanswered.

"Who the hell left the taps running and the plug still in the bath?" I was stunned. I couldn't speak. "I've had to sweep the water out the doors." And I was told Joe was off to the boat yard getting a large drill to drill holes in the floor to let the water drain away.

I ran back to where I'd left Maureen. "Maureen," I gulped. "Something awful's happened."

When I told her I'd flooded her house I burst into tears. I'll never forget Maureen's reply. "Is that all? I thought someone must have died or there's been an accident."

We forgot Joe's list and arrived in Picton just as Cedric was ripping up the last of the carpet, leaving Maureen to pacify an irate insurance company. Later we found out that the water had come back on at 10am. For two hours the taps had poured water throughout the house. All the beds on the floor were wet. The blankets on Joe's and my bed hung down each side of our bed and had acted like giant blotting paper, sucking up the water and saturating our bed. And it was raining.

At the time there was an electricity shortage, and hot water cylinders were being turned off during the day. Cold Water Surf had become very popular as more and more people used it to wash, and it was hard to buy.

I went to the grocer whom I always phoned for stores and he managed to sell me two packets of this cold water washing powder. The blankets were sent to the local laundry with the promise we'd have them returned that evening. Thank goodness we still had electricity, and by breaking all the rules about excessive use of heaters and clothes dryers we managed to have dry beds by bedtime.

Picton is a small town and news travels. The next day I was in a shop when

I overheard one person asking another if she'd heard about the lass flooding Stewarts' house. "Actually," I said. "I'm that lass."

They were embarrassed, but we all laughed.

The insurance company laid new carpet throughout Maureen's and Cedric's house. The house was on the market at that time and I'm sure the carpet helped it sell.

We are still friends, we stay with them when we are in Picton, and I am allowed to have a bath.

But back to that week. Having the *Fugitive* built and launched in our home town was exciting, and having our friends around us helped make it so much fun.

"Let's hire the back bar of Oxley's and have a launching party in the evening," Joe suggested. This was a great idea. Friends helped to make supper so it wasn't much work for anyone. A friend from Auckland who was in Picton for the launching had been staying with us at Okukari. "Which dress will I wear?" she asked me after seeing my one and only dress which was suitable for evening and which was hanging in lonely splendour. "You're so lucky, Heather, not having to make such a decision."

I grinned to myself, remembering those words, as I dressed for our night out. I'd rather have our new boat than a wardrobe full of dresses. The song My Old Man's A Dustman had just hit the charts and with a bit of cribbing here and there we composed a launching song. To the same tune we gaily sang:

My old man's a fisherman
He owns the *Fugitive*.
He catches lots of fish you know
So that we can live.

He sometimes stinks of fish bait
And wears a yellow smockie
We may sling off about his smell
But thank God he's not a cockie.

The verses went one and on and everyone knew them very well by the end of the evening.

Back home again and crayfishing was in full swing. The new boat was performing better than Joe had ever imagined. She was fast – about 18 knots – and they could work more gear as they could get around faster. After the round-bilged *Heather* her manoeuvrability in the water was amazing.

My nephew Tom from Auckland was fishing for us at the time and they were pulling their gear around The Brothers. The wind was strong nor'west. The engine coughed, spluttered and died. Tom tore up the bow, heaved the

79

anchor overboard and just stopped them from crashing into the sheer cliffs. In the engine room Joe quickly found out that the fuel line was blocked. He managed to fix it well enough to get the engine started again, and limp home. During the building something had got in the tank and blocked the line where it came out of the fuel tank. A new verse was added to our song:

Once out by The Brothers
In a nor'west gale
The engine of the boat stopped
And Tom and Dad turned pale.

Mackerel are used for groper bait. They are a pelagic fish of coastal waters, distantly related to the tuna. They are a beautiful fish to eat smoked, but apart from using them as bait there wasn't a market for mackerel, and the fishermen at that time received only 2.5-3 cents a pound for them. The dark flesh and high fat content seems to deter the New Zealand housewife from buying them. Canning now seems to get some of these fish on to the international market.

In the winter months mackerel come in Tory Channel to spawn. Any time from Queen's Birthday Weekend on we could expect them to show up in our bay. We'd see bubbling greasy patches in the bay and nets would be out and run into dinghies, all ready. Competition is fierce and many hot arguments are won and lost among the local fishermen trying to catch their winter's bait. The men use a drag net, and once the shoal is encircled and the fish trapped the net is towed out to the waiting boats and the mackerel scooped out on to the decks.

Three or four boats had a good haul late one afternoon. It was going to be five or six hours before the net was cleared. Joe rowed ashore and asked if I could heat up some soup and bring it out for everyone. The little dinghy was on the beach and when I'd organised my pot of soup I carried it down to the beach, carefully placed the pot on the seat and rowed out to the boats. I shouted but everyone was flat out and no one seemed to notice a little dinghy alongside a boat with me in it, trying to balance my soup and tie up the dinghy at the same time. I stood up to lift my soup on board. The dinghy lurched and the pot fell off the seat. At last they heard me. "If anyone wants soup they'll have to bale it from the bottom of the dinghy." No one took up the offer. Even though soup was off the menu, my mishap seemed to cheer the fishermen up and loud laughter echoed around the bay.

CHAPTER EIGHT

Life and Death

I KNOW that if I had lived in Auckland, in Bluff or in a remote country township, bringing up a family would always have had times of anxiety, especially if there were sickness or accident. But an island in the Marlborough Sounds, when a boat takes the place of a motor car and the 'road' is governed completely by the weather, made this expected anxiety so much greater.

When I knew I was going to be making my home on an island and that the nearest doctor was a sea journey away, I'd gone to two courses run by the St John Ambulance Association in Auckland. I came away with certificates in nursing and first aid. Much later I had to up-date my first aid, but it was something I enjoyed learning. Certainly I made good use of it when bringing up the children, all of whom were happier out roaming the farm than sitting down to do school work.

Whether it was the genes, the life style or plain luck, our family has been blessed with fairly good health. Of course there were the childhood sicknesses that all children get, even on an island, but the worst of these had to be the time Pauline had whooping cough. This made me realise how lucky we are to have the benefits of vaccinations.

Young Joe seemed to go through his childhood determined to kill bees either by standing or sitting on them. Every bee sting to his foot would swell his leg up and he seemed to get more stings than anyone else. One summer he'd had three or four stings in as many days. He was outside playing with his cousins from Nelson and he sat on a bee. Thin cotton shorts didn't stop an angry bee pumping its venom into soft buttocks and he tore inside screaming that a bee had got him again. I had become an expert at pacifying him after a bee sting and within minutes he was outside playing.

"Auntie Heather, Auntie Heather!" "Mum, come quick! Joe's funny." I heard the shouts and flew out the door. Joe had been led home. Tears squeezed from two slits and rolled down his face. A grubby fist rubbed at his swollen lips and he told me his tongue felt funny.

"Get Grandma! Quick!" I yelled to the frightened children. I ran the bath to the top with lukewarm water and once Joe was in I gradually replaced the warmer water with cold. Joe's mother took one look at her grandson and rang the doctor. She had some anti-histamine tablets and was told to give Joe one of them and get him to Picton as soon as possible. In the meantime I was told to keep Joe in the bath with the water up to his neck, to reduce the swelling.

All the men were out mustering but we could hear them coming. One of the older children ran to meet them. Joe, with Jim Shallcrass who was fishing with Joe at the time and who had a speedboat, left the muster and dashed home to take Young Joe to the doctor.

His allergy was kept under control with anti-histamines, he was made to wear shoes, and Joe's parents got rid of their beehives.

James developed asthma when he was six years old. I had no idea that his persistent cough was a warning sign. He'd come inside on a cold day when he'd been running around outside during a break from school, sit at his desk, and cough and cough. Nothing I gave him stopped it.

One night Joe was still away fishing, and was due home about 11pm. We'd had a freezing winter's day, and sitting around the fire that night James developed his cough. I didn't take a lot of notice at first as I'd heard it all before, but then I noticed his breathing was laboured and he was sitting bolt upright in his chair, chest pushed right out. Every breath was a struggle. He walked over to the mantelpiece and put his arms up on it. His own body, although none of us were aware of this at the time, told him that by lifting his arms on to the high mantelpiece he was expanding his chest and making it easier to expel air from his lungs and take it in again.

I thought he must be coming down with a bad cold or a dose of flu so I took his temperature. It was normal, and in fact he seemed very healthy except for the fact he struggled with every breath. Joe's parents were overseas so I couldn't call on them for advice, but I knew this was when I needed to talk to a doctor.

Dr Ron Mills was the doctor in Picton and when I phoned and explained James's symptoms he asked, "Has anyone asthma in your family?"

Asthma? I was stunned. "No!"

"What about parents? Yours or Joe's?"

"No."

"Okay. How about grandparents?"

The realisation hit me. "My grandfather."

"I'm not saying it is asthma but it seems possible. Keep an eye on him tonight and bring him in as soon as you can," was his reply when I told him Joe wasn't coming home until later.

As their bedtimes came, Young Joe, Helen and Pauline were sent to bed. James I kept up. I was terrified to put him to bed in case he became worse or stopped breathing. When I heard the boat come in the bay and knew Joe was home I breathed a sigh of relief. I needed Joe to be home and share my anxiety. James's breathing had got easier as the night wore on and I felt more at ease when he went to bed once his father was home. Neither Joe nor I slept that night. We lay in our bed listening for any change in our younger son's breathing pattern. It was a relief to get out of bed in the morning and go into Picton with

James, although he woke feeling fine and had no sign of any breathing difficulties.

Dr Mills was right. James had asthma and was put on medication immediately. He also had an inhaler to use when he felt his chest getting tight or he had an attack. I made a bag for it which he wore around his neck, and when he went out climbing the hills or mustering he managed well. On the few times he had to use the inhaler on the hills, I noticed he'd sit down for only a few minutes, then he'd be off again.

Only once did the inhaler became a worry and then it was the lack of it. James had taken it off his neck and left it lying outside where the pig found and munched on it. Fortunately it was a mail day, and I was able to get a replacement inhaler that same day. This addition to the pig's diet had no effect on him, although I could have killed him when I realised what he'd done – and we've never eaten one of our pet pigs yet. They are either given away or we liberate them.

Our trips to Picton because of accidents have far outnumbered trips when there's been sickness. Heberley men, these strong, tough fishermen and farmers, faint at the sight of blood. I couldn't believe my own eyes when my father-in-law cut his hand on the circular saw. The sight of his own blood made him legless. A weta had been crawling on the bench, and, when he'd brushed it away, the teeth of the saw grabbed his hand. He staggered inside and Ruby got him into the bathroom where he fainted. Joe wasn't home but hearing her screams for help I ran over. I propped Charlie up while Ruby washed and bandaged his hand.

This was in the whaling days when the chasers meant a trip to Picton took less than an hour, and within minutes of a phone call to Gilbert Perano he was at the beach to pick up my in-laws and take them to Picton, where Charlie's hand was stitched.

Not long after Joe and his father began fishing in the *Midlothian*, I was to discover Joe was as bad as his father at the sight of blood. They were cutting up bait and his finger got in the way of the knife. A white face passed my kitchen window and I knew something had happened. I met him at the door. His hand wrapped in a tea-towel, blood already seeping through, he collapsed in a chair at the kitchen table. When I unwrapped the wound he was quite unable to look. It was a clean diagonal cut across the middle joint of his forefinger, and once it was bathed and dried it could be easily pulled together with plaster butterfly clips. With the wound covered, and after a sweetened cup of tea, Joe was fit to go fishing again.

When a dog bit Joe's backside he nearly fainted, not from the wound or the sight of blood, but from my treatment. Boss was a black and white beardie. With his untidy hair hanging around his face and over his eyes you couldn't help but love him, and he always appeared to have a grin on his face. Whenever the tractor started he'd become wildly excited, charge around, and bark and jump at the tyres, frantically trying to bite them. This day the batteries were flat and the tractor wouldn't start with the key. Joe was cranking it when Boss flew at the front wheel, missed, and sank sharp canine teeth into Joe.

The wound was bleeding profusely when Joe arrived at the house, roaring like a bull. I could count how many teeth Boss had by looking at the bite. Some looked very deep punctures and others weren't so deep. "I'll have to clean it. Goodness knows what he's been eating."

"Just pour some Dettol or something on it. I've gotta go."

Rocks in Auckland are covered with rock oysters, and in the yacht of my childhood there was always iodine in the first aid kit. An oyster cut never became infected when it had been treated with iodine. The pain of the treatment probably prevented any infection. The oyster treatment was clearly needed for this dog bite.

"Bend over." I thought my sergeant-major's voice might have made him ask what I was going to do. The orange liquid ran into the open puncture holes and dribbled over his skin.

"God Almighty! What's that?" Joe leapt up and pulled up his trousers, dog bite forgotten in the agony of the cure. I knew it would sting, but not as much as it obviously did.

I was in big trouble and it was a long time before I was allowed to get near Joe when he needed first aid, but, all the same, the dog bite healed beautifully without a trace of infection. No doubt it was the result of the iodine.

Bikes have been the cause of most of the accidents that have meant a trip to Picton. Before the motorised bikes came to Okukari, Young Joe managed to tangle his big toe in the front wheel of a tricycle while we were at a children's birthday party at the home of Janice and Harold Saunders, in Jacksons Bay.

Joe was in Picton with the boat on the slip, and the children and I had been picked up by another family in their boat. Fourteen children, ages ranging from eight to a few months, and their parents were celebrating the birthday. The older children were outside, riding bikes down the sloping front path. They were ordering the younger children to push them, and they'd fly down the slope, feet off pedals. When they had to slow down before reaching the end of the path, feet would feel for the free-wheeling pedals, and halt the moving bike once feet had caught up with them.

Young Joe missed the pedals and his foot dug into the spokes, ripping his big toe in half across the base of his nail. I was tuned to my children's screams. I knew when screams meant real pain. It was hardly bleeding but, when I moved his toe, deep red blood oozed from the cut. I felt his pain as I carried my first-born inside where I checked him out before ringing the local doctor. As it was a Saturday, I was told to take Joe to Picton Hospital when I arrived, and the doctor would see him there.

84

I couldn't get hold of Joe before I left Jacksons Bay with Harold in his trawler *Narina*, so I left the rest of my family with Janice and her assurance she'd keep trying to find Joe, and let him know we were on our way to town. The two-hour trip seemed to take forever. Every cry told me that the way we lived, in isolation, was causing my son pain, pain he wouldn't have had to bear if we hadn't chosen to live in the Sounds.

Janice had tracked Joe down and when I saw him on the wharf waiting with the car I felt some of the tension leave my body. We were both here for our son. My responsibility was halved.

Joe carried him into the hospital where the doctor was waiting. When he saw the cut he warned us it was going to be very painful to stitch as the base of the nail is hard to anaesthetise. "It would help if you hold him," Joe and I were told.

All I wanted to do was hold our son and comfort him. I had forgotten my strapping husband's reaction to blood, made worse when it was his own son's, until I saw him staggering towards the door and fresh air. Later he admitted it was worse sitting outside and listening to Young Joe's screams and knowing he was unable to help.

It was made even worse for Joe when he brought us back down to Harold's boat, and I had to prise a clinging child from his father. Joe had to stay in Picton to work on our boat so he could bring it home as soon as possible, and I had to get back to the Saunders' to pick up our other three children and get home to Okukari.

With my father-in-law's dire words of warning about motorbikes ringing in our ears, the first two-wheeler farm bike arrived in 1979. Joe was motorised. He'd never ridden a motorbike before and we spent many entertaining hours watching him gather up numerous bruises and grazes. He persevered, and mustering on Okukari changed forever. Joe's father shook his head and muttered about the "bloody dangerous things".

Then came the day when Joe was riding down a steep ridge. A stick jammed in the front wheel, causing it to lock, and he was tossed over the handlebars. He'd hurt his ankle and by the time he arrived home it was very swollen. Next morning it was worse and we wondered if it could be broken and needed an X-ray. But the next block had to be mustered or the sheep would all run back and the first muster would have been in vain.

This was our first November shearing since Joe and I had taken over the farm, and my father-in-law had come over from Nelson to help us out.

"We'll have to go and bring in that next block, son. Ring the float plane at first light and get that foot seen to," was Charlie's advice to Joe as we set off mustering.

This service had been operating out of Picton since 1973, and in times of emergencies a trip to Picton in the float plane meant only five minutes in the air. Although this wasn't an emergency, or not as we defined emergencies, there was no other way Joe could get himself to town, hobbled as he was. When we reached the top of the hill I was relieved to hear the float plane's engines as it landed in the bay to pick him up.

Charlie, four children and I managed our muster very well and we had our mob home by mid-afternoon. I phoned Joe and heard he had to stay in Picton until the next day when another X-ray would be taken on a slightly less swollen foot. Then he'd come back down with our shearers. In the meantime any daggy ewes had to be put across the board and cleaned up before shearing.

Joe's father was crutching. Helen pulled out a sheep to drag it across the board for him. I bent down to pick up some wool at the same time as Helen's sheep reared up on its back legs. She fell against the door and my head collided with it when it flew open.

Later I was told, "You were home, but your lights were out." This time it was my first-born who took me to town and medical help, in the *Fugitive*. Joe met us, and he's never forgotten how I greeted him with the words, "If you can't beat 'em, join 'em."

I don't remember saying this. In fact I remember very little of the first two days of our first shearing, days I spent in hospital. Joe, still hobbling, supervised from a seat on a box in the woolshed and his sister Jocelyn came over from Nelson and ran my kitchen. Certainly it was a shearing I won't forget even if I can't remember all of it.

The next serious bike accident made me thankful again for Picton's float plane. I'd been home from hospital for just two days, after major surgery. It was the school holidays and Pauline, James and Helen were home from boarding school. They were all up the flats teaching Pauline how to ride a motorbike. I was sitting at my kitchen table. The 11 o'clock sunshine was streaming in on my back as I stared out the window watching the ever-changing patterns the wind drew on the dark blue sea. The freshness took my breath away after I'd spent the last fortnight cooped up in a hospital ward.

I heard the bike arrive at the house, and clattering as the bike riders came inside. The bath was being run – I guessed they must have managed to get bogged. Helen burst through the door. "We've had an accident. They're fainting."

Forgetting my fragile body I rushed to the bathroom. James was perched on the bench of the vanity unit, his hand under water that was rapidly turning red. Pauline was sitting on the edge of the bath, holding her head which had an egg already bulging on the side. From the colour of the bath water, she was obviously cut somewhere. Both were in a semi-conscious state.

Trying to be strong for them, I checked out their injuries. Helen filled me in on how it had happened. James was sitting on the carrier, telling Pauline what to do. She'd lost control and the bike had spun out. James's thumb went in the back sprocket. Now his thumb looked like a half-peeled banana with the skin dangling around the base of the thumb. Pauline had a gash on the sole of her heel, and a sprained ankle, as well as her injured head.

The fishermen weren't due home until later in the day and I knew Pauline and James needed more medical attention than anything I could give them. I phoned the doctor, and the float plane was at the bay to collect my children within 10 minutes. There was no way I could go with them, much as I wanted to. It was too soon after my own surgery and so Helen was to accompany them on the plane and my friend, Maureen Stewart, was going to meet them when they arrived in Picton and take them to the doctor.

The pilot understood my anguish when I asked him to take special care as he had three-quarters of my family in his plane.

I sat on a log on the beach, watching the plane taxi out the bay before taking off and heading towards Picton. I felt hot tears washing my face, and, uncaring, I rubbed my running nose with the back of my hand. I picked up handfuls of sand and let it trickle through my fingers. Its warm caress somehow eased the pain in my chest. When the plane was no longer in sight or sound I slowly walked back to my empty house, to wait for Maureen's call to let me know what was happening in the place I wanted to be.

I imagined the very worst. James's thumb would have to be amputated, and Pauline probably had severe concussion, a cracked skull and a broken foot. When the phone rang I picked it up before all the rings were completed, forgetting it might be for someone else on our party line. Maureen's voice reassured me. The children were fine. James had his thumb stitched up and Pauline had stitches in her heel, and her ankle had been strapped. No bones were broken, and the bump on her head looked worse that it was.

Later in the day Joe went up on the *Fugitive* and brought home two rather subdued, sore children, together with Helen. I was just happy to have them back with us but their father gave James and Pauline the dressing-down they deserved. Now they'd be in no doubt about what to wear when they next tried cross-country bike riding.

Those first few weeks after I had my hysterectomy were some of the worst in my life. While in hospital I'd developed an abscess in the wound and this turned my week in hospital into two weeks. I wanted to come home where my family was, but no surgeon was letting me out of hospital to go back to an island in the Marlborough Sounds. This didn't help the healing process and I was told to go to the occupational therapy ward and find something completely different to do.

I discovered great pleasure in making a big teddy-bear. He kept me sane. The smiling face I gave him with his bright beady eyes helped me over the days until I was allowed home.

Once at home all I wanted to feel was well again, and the slow process made me frustrated. Then another infection developed in the wound and I had to be taken in to Picton for daily dressings. For me it was hell but looking back I must have been hell to live with. I knew I had to go and have the wound dressed but I remember sitting on the kitchen floor and howling because I didn't want to go in to Picton. I couldn't face the boat trip, or the doctor, and then making up school lessons that were getting behind. I was a mess.

But then slowly I started to feel better. Things were no longer crowding in on top of me. School wasn't so bad, the doctor had been kind, Picton is a nice place, and best of all, I'd live.

About this time I discovered I was the only person in the bay who couldn't ride a motorbike. The truth was I was scared of these heavy two-wheelers but I longed to experience the freedom of movement around the farm that they offered. So whenever I found myself on my own I'd sneak out to the shed, push the huge thing outside, and try to recall the ease with which everyone climbed on, and how they started it. I managed to cruise slowly down the hill from our shed, across in front of the woolshed and into the bottom paddock. As the days went by I started to feel more confident but I kept my secret. One day I'd give Joe this wonderful surprise and I imagined his look when he saw his capable wife speeding up the paddock on his bike.

The day came when Joe poked his head in the door to shout, "I'm just going to shift the ewes from the bottom to the top paddock. Coming?"

"Are you taking the bike?"

"No."

In my mind I was already driving up the paddock to meet Joe when he was on his way home. "No thanks. I've a bit to do here."

Adrenalin was pumping through my body as I pushed the bike around and out of the shed, jumped on, kick-started it, and began my ride to surprise Joe. It was a glorious day. The wind blew my hair off my face. I gripped the handlebars tightly as I rode through the first gate and prepared myself to drive through the stony creek bed. Suddenly my visions of a capable wife riding to meet her husband were shattered. However did it happen? I was in the creek with the bike on top of me.

The water was cold and my thigh was hurting like hell. In fact my whole leg hurt. I eased myself out from under the bike, heaved it up and pushed it out of the creek bed and on to the grass. My leg was so sore I couldn't make it move to kick-start the bike and all I wanted to do was get home and lick my wounds before Joe found me. But I had to wait. My leg wasn't going to let me go anywhere.

When Joe came across me and asked me what the hell did I think I was doing, the taps turned on, and I couldn't speak for tears and pain. He started the bike and took me home in an angry silence.

"Get in and have a shower. You're soaking wet," I was told.

Until then I hadn't looked at my leg. I presumed I'd have a mighty bruise forming by now. When I peeled off my tracksuit pants and saw what I'd done, the pain felt much worse. A great wide gash spread across my knee cap. After my shower I came into the kitchen.

"Feel better?" Joe asked.

I lifted my skirt. "You'll have to take me to town. This needs stitches."

Joe took one look at it and fetched the first aid box from the bathroom. Head averted, he passed it to me. "Sorry, love. You'll have to wrap it up. I can't."

While I attended to myself Joe brought in the boat. Motorbikes were off my list of accomplishments for now, so I hobbled down to the wharf and clambered on to the boat. Eight stitches later we arrived home, and I was told I was banned from bikes.

I had no desire to ride one until Joe decided to change from two wheels to four. I was elated. I knew I could keep four wheels on the ground and so at last I've found the freedom a motor bike can give even if I've agreed to certain conditions. Anyway I have no desire to ride up the side of a hill. There are plenty of farm roads and flats to drive on.

Stories of bike misadventures could go on for ever, but one accident comes to mind whenever yarns are being told over a few drinks. It was a Sunday and we were all going to the Fishburns in Dryden Bay in Queen Charlotte Sound, for a church service. Joe wanted to go over the hill to Wharehunga first as he needed to check a fence before we shifted stock. As James and his father went out the door Joe said, "We'll be home for lunch and we'll leave at 1pm. You must be ready."

Lunchtime passed. By 1.30 I was worried. Joe is never late. Something must have happened. I felt it as I stood at our window, focusing binoculars on an empty clay road that wound down the side of the hills from Wharehunga. At last I saw the blue four-wheeled motorbike being driven slowly across the flat. It crawled to the house and two dejected people walked inside. They were covered in scratches and grazes. Their dishevelled clothes were full of gorse and dried sticks.

I'd been so worried that all I could do was growl. "What the hell've you done? We'll be late."

"We're lucky to be here at all," was Joe's reply and when they told me the story I knew how lucky I was to still have a husband and son.

"We'd fixed the fence and had the coil of netting we didn't use on the back of the bike. James spotted a fly-blown sheep so we stopped and caught it and after tying its legs we put it on the front carrier and headed for home. You know where the road comes out of the gully and around that point where the telegraph pole is?" I nodded, and visualised the steep drop there, of five or six hundred feet. "As we came round that corner the sheep struggled and its back legs hit the throttle. We roared off the road and were airborne."

James interrupted his father. "All I could see was the pole coming at us. I thought we'd hit that."

"I heard James's voice saying, 'Shit, Dad, shit'. The roll of netting held him tightly against me. About a chain down the hill we hit the ground. Both of us were thrown off and the bike kept bouncing end over end until it reached the bottom."

"What about the sheep?"

"God knows. It came off the bike somewhere on the way down. We didn't see it."

"But I saw you come home on the bike?" I was still trying to put this story together in my mind.

The two of them burst into hysterical laughter and I realised they were suffering from shock even though they didn't know they were.

"You should have seen Dad, Mum. We got to the bike, stood it up, straightened the handlebars and when I suggested we ride it out of the scrub and out on to the flat Dad refused. But it started first go and once I was in the clear Dad climbed on."

We did get to the church service, a little late, but thankfully my family was still intact. Before we'd left, I wondered why Joe was taking so long in the shower. I imagined him in the shower, probably in a dead faint from delayed shock, and I ran in to see if he was all right. I heard laughter from the bedroom and when I opened the door, there was my Joe gazing out the window. Between his outbursts all he could say was, "Look where we came from. God, we were lucky. Look at it." He was definitely in shock but after I'd looked up the hill and re-lived the experience with Joe, he calmed down and we walked out of the room together, thankful we still had each other. As we walked down the passage I'm sure I heard Charlie's words when we bought the first bike. "Bloody dangerous things."

The story didn't end there. We claimed insurance as the bike was in a sorry state with broken headlights, bent carriers, and bits broken off it everywhere. A claim form arrived in the mail and to our astonishment we were asked to draw a picture of the scene of the accident. I hoped the insurance company appreciated my picture of one four-wheeled motorbike tumbling down a steep hill, two stick figures high in the air as they were thrown off the bike, together with a coil of wire netting and one trussed-up sheep.

Not all accidents involved bikes. Years later Pauline, our youngest, was visiting our older daughter Helen, who was by then married and living at Dryden Bay. The phone rang and the words that I heard made me grow cold. "Mum. It's Helen. Don't panic. Pauline's fallen off the roof. She was fixing the TV aerial."

Don't panic. "Is she okay?"

"She's unconscious. There's no one home in our bay. Can you ring the doctor and organise the float plane? Ring me back."

God. Don't panic, I'm told, and my baby is lying unconscious after falling off a roof. I opened the front window and roared out to Joe. He knew there was something seriously wrong by the tone of my voice.

I phoned the float plane and the doctor, and in minutes I was able to call Helen back and tell her to keep Pauline warm and not move her. While Joe put the speedboat in the water I phoned Maureen who said she'd go down and meet the float plane and see how Pauline was.

My practical side told me to pack an overnight bag, but apart from thinking of a toothbrush, my mind wouldn't function. The mother in me just wanted to be with Pauline. I remembered to grab our car keys as I raced out the door and down to the wharf to jump into the already running speedboat.

As we turned out of Tory Channel into Queen Charlotte Sound the float plane flew over us. I knew Helen was in the plane with her sister and I felt her anguish and wondered how she was feeling watching her sister strapped in the stretcher, her injuries unknown. Maureen met us in Picton and told us the doctor had met the plane, examined Pauline briefly, and sent her straight through to Blenheim's Wairau Hospital for X-rays, with Helen in the ambulance with her. Maureen cheered me up when she said Pauline had greeted her with a smile and a "Hello, Mrs Stewart."

By the time Joe and I had got our town-based car and arrived at the hospital, Pauline was having X-rays taken and her first words made me cry in sheer relief. "They've cut off my best jeans, Mum. They're ruined." My lovely darling, I thought as I hugged her as close as I could. What's a silly pair of jeans. There's plenty more where they came from.

The X-rays showed that Pauline's 15-foot fall on to concrete hadn't broken one bone in her body. She'd hit her head on a concrete curb, resulting in unconciousness, and she was kept in hospital for 24 hours' observation. Pauline was told her escape was because she was so fit. When she'd landed on her feet, her legs were able to take the weight of her fall.

I felt Helen suffered the most because she'd seen her young sister lying on the concrete path, not able to speak, and my grown-up daughter found out that day that you're never too old to have a mother's arms wrapped around you and have a good cry.

On the afternoon of Friday, 19 August 1977, I lost the joy of having my own mother's arms wrapped around me in love. My mother and father were in a car crash. Mum died before reaching hospital. Dad needed surgery before being in the intensive care unit at Auckland's Middlemore Hospital.

That day remains as vivid in my memory as if it was only yesterday. We had left Okukari in a heavy frost to get to Picton early, as stores had to be bought, Joe had a fishermen's meeting to attend, I was to meet my nephew who was flying down to Blenheim from Auckland for the school holidays, and best of all it was school holiday time, no more lessons for two weeks and Young Joe would be home from boarding school.

Why didn't I feel something as we steamed into Picton that day? Picton Harbour was like a painting. Frost lay on the shore to the water's edge. Tentacles of fog lifted off the water and wound their way up through the bush which looked black on the shadowed side of the harbour. When my eyes lifted to the skyline, a brilliant winter's morning sun drove its rays through any gaps in the high trees. Boats on their moorings had their mirror images shining back at them. The world was still, as the ripples we'd created could be heard slapping the shingle as we steamed slowly past the Queen Charlotte Yacht Club building before reaching Picton to tie up at the wharf, ready for another madly rushed town day.

My day changed at 4.30pm. Betty, my sister, knew we were in Picton, and so she phoned Maureen Stewart and told her about my mother's death. It was left to Maureen to find Joe and give him the news. When Joe took me aside to tell me, I didn't believe him at first. Then with the realisation that Mum was dead and Dad was in intensive care, all I wanted to do was get to Auckland.

First we had to get back to Okukari with the children. My in-laws suddenly found their family increased by five as I now had my nephew with me but I somehow got myself organised, and bags packed. A faster boat than ours had been ordered and was coming to Okukari shortly to pick up Joe and me. We had plane tickets booked for late evening but for me all track of time had gone. On the way back to Picton my amazement at seeing the ferries still running gave me the jolt I needed to bring me back to reality. The world hadn't stopped. Only mine had for a short time.

In Auckland I gained comfort from my father and he slowly recovered, although he wasn't able to attend Mum's funeral. My Scottish mother was so fey, and I was angry that she hadn't let me know her time of death. Why hadn't I felt her presence? Then, in conversation with Betty, she told me the hospital rang her at 3.20pm. Suddenly I remembered how, on that day, I'd picked up Young Joe from his school hostel, Innes House, and we'd stopped on the way out of Blenheim to buy honey from an apiary. An awful feeling had washed over me. It had left me with the shakes and a deep apprehension that I couldn't understand. Young Joe had asked me if I felt all right. "You're sure you're okay to drive, Mum? You look dreadful."

"I feel ghastly. Don't know why."

All this had been forgotten after I'd arrived back in Picton and spoken to Joe. But now, after hearing all this from Betty, I wondered, and when I returned from Auckland I couldn't wait to talk to Young Joe.

I asked him if he remembered what time it was when we'd stopped off to buy the honey, the day his grandmother was killed.

"It must have been just after 3.20pm. Remember we passed all the girls biking out of college and they finish at 3.20pm."

I knew. My mother hadn't left me without a thought. She was concerned that my sister would have to carry all the weight when she was told. Somehow our mother had been able to let my sister and me share the burden.

But her death was so unexpected that it hit me with the sickness of despair. I sank so low into the black hole that I couldn't climb out. Bedtime became a nightmare. Every night I'd sleep for about one hour and then I'd wake up screaming for Joe. Mum would be standing by me but when I reached out my trembling hand there was only the blackness. I became too scared to go to bed. Joe would stop the generator and he'd plead with me to come to bed. I couldn't sleep because I knew I'd soon be awake, terrified of the presence standing beside me. What if it reached out and took me with it? So I'd pace up and down our lounge in the dark. I'd see a cold moon laying an inhospitable pathway down the channel, black forbidding hills standing out against a black sky, and even the stars looked dull. I lost two stone in weight and at last Joe spoke sternly to me. "I'm taking you to the doctor today," and when I protested he answered, "Well, if you don't need to go, I soon will. This can't go on."

For the first time in my life I found myself on medication when I didn't believe I was sick. My doctor put me on amitriptyline. I worried that I'd become addicted but Dr Mills said I was to regard it as a temporary crutch, and I did. Looking back, I can now understand how ill I was, and how lucky I was to have an understanding doctor and supportive family and friends. The pit I'd got down into was deep but once at the bottom I learned there was only one way out. Up.

A few months after my father was discharged from hospital he had a stroke. It brought a proud independent man to his knees. He wanted to learn to be well again but the stroke left him paralysed down his left side, shuffling with a quad stick, and dependent on others.

Joe and I had been up visiting him for a week and it shattered me to see this shell of a man whom I recognised only by his features. His bright personality and the happiness that had radiated from him were gone. He blamed himself for my mother's death and I knew he wanted release from his body. The day we left Auckland and I waved goodbye to my father standing at his front door, I said to Joe that I would never see him again.

The following evening the phone rang and Joe answered it. It was Betty. Dad had died. He'd put a hose from the exhaust of the car he'd bought soon after he'd come out of hospital. My nephew heard the car running in the garage, opened the door, and found Dad. He was unable to be revived but Betty and I believe he wouldn't have wanted to be.

This time the tears were able to flow and in my sorrow I felt the waves of relief wash over me. My father was free of the body that had held him captive after his stroke. The shock was there but this time when I arrived home I didn't let myself sink into the pit. Instead, I let Okukari heal me – the beach where I'd taken so many troubles to before, the view from the high hills where I'd sobbed into the ground in the first months of my married life, and the joy my painting gave me as I sat over many cups of tea at the table and looked out the window. My mood matched some of Chopin's sombre music but it acted as a release. I'd play through tears and know that this time my mind was being healed through the love of the place I'd made my home.

CHAPTER NINE

Mayday Mayday Mayday

THREE WORDS crackling over the VHF (very high frequency) marine radio in our kitchen bring everything to a halt. In the tense silence we wait for the next part of the Mayday message, most importantly the position of the caller.

Sad to say, some people abuse this service. Hoax calls claiming they're sinking, on fire or needing immediate aid are sometimes made. We've heard children's voices screaming a Mayday and then silence. An adult's voice will occasionally come on the VHF and apologise for their child using the radio, but it does mean that one day there might be a genuine Mayday call by a child and the radio operator couldn't be blamed for ignoring it. These calls are a waste of everyone's time and energies, and there is always the chance a real emergency could happen while the airways and people are tied up with the hoax call.

No one really knows if a call is genuine or not, and it is like playing God, trying to make the decision whether or not to go and search. Joe has spent hours searching after hoax calls. He says the hardest thing is turning back when there is always the chance that the call could have been genuine. It is hard to leave the empty expanse of sea, wondering if there is someone drifting in a life raft or floating in a life jacket.

Once the searchers get home, and the hours grow into a day, and the days into weeks, the realisation that it must have been a hoax call comes, and then the anger sets in. Anger that there are such stupid, irresponsible idiots around, who get their thrills by such childish behaviour.

For genuine callers Mayday means instant contact and assured help as soon as possible. In the Marlborough Sounds four VHF marine radio repeaters cover the region, and boats can usually call out from anywhere by changing radio channels to trigger the appropriate repeater.

Joe is the fire officer and head of civil defence for our area, as well as being the search and rescue co-odinator. His local knowledge, against a background of his years of fishing in Cook Strait, is invaluable in an emergency. Marine radios have greatly improved with the introduction of the VHF. These radios, plus electricity, have brought seafarers right into our kitchen. In earlier years the famous Sylvia Kenny of Red Funnel Launches maintained a radio watch called Picton Association Radio. Either she or the Picton Police informed us of emergencies via the phone.

When he's been crayfishing up the coast from Tory Channel to Cape

Koamaru, Joe has often been right on the spot when Mayday calls have been sent, and can give help quickly. There was the yacht whose engine had broken down off Koamaru, and the tide was pulling it on to the rocks. Another time a runabout piled up with camping gear after a holiday in the Sounds, and, with a family on board, lost its bottom out near The Brothers.

Two canoeists were pleased to see our boat after they had become swamped and washed up on the rocks near Wellington Head. Joe had no idea there was anyone attempting to paddle across Cook Strait that day, and on board the *Fugitive* our men had a shock to see two people waving for help. After drying out, the pair set off for Wellington again, this time with more success.

Very few rescues take place in daylight. Some years ago, after a call from Picton's harbourmaster at 11pm, Joe and the boys set off to search for a yacht whose engine had broken down. They were told it had rounded Cape Campbell and was near the White Bluffs. Joe said they imagined the yachties must have lost the mast or have broken rigging, as well as a broken-down engine. When the searchers finally located the boat they discovered the sails down, for no reason at all, and that the crew were merely waiting for a tow.

In my kitchen I was tuned in to the VHF. I knew something was up by the tone of Joe's voice when he called up Don Jamison, the harbourmaster, and told him they'd found the boat. When Don asked Joe what the conditions were, Joe's voice, "It's a wonderful night for sailing," said it all.

I went to bed, and it was 5am when the rumbling of the *Fugitive's* motor steaming into the bay woke me up. There was no time for sleeping for our family – crayfish pots had to be pulled up – but over a quick breakfast I heard the rest of the story.

After giving the yacht the tow line and ensuring it was secure, Joe said he put the throttle down and headed for home. Flat tack. "You have no idea how angry I was," Joe told me. I'd known by the tone of his voice when I'd heard him on the VHF but I didn't mention that.

"Then, to top it all off, when we came in the bay he wanted me to tow him to Picton." Joe said he'd pointed down the channel and told him Picton was in that direction.

The parting shot from the owner, as he at last got ready to use his sails, made Joe explode. "Thanks, mate. I'm in Picton over Christmas. If I see you around I'll shout you a jug."

It was too much for a tired man. "You don't drive a six-cylinder GM all night on a jug of beer. You'll pay me for the fuel." This was interspersed with quite a few unrepeatables, James told me later.

We did get something for this rescue and it was more than the promised jug of beer, but selfishness and irresponsibility stick in the craw.

Over the years there have been many genuine emergency call-outs. Several stand out in my mind because of particular disaster, because of their magnitude, because we knew the people, or because of the sheer stupidity of those involved.

In 1970 Joe was alerted. Two paua divers, father and son, were a day overdue. The wife and mother, Mrs Harley, was emphatic something was seriously wrong as they were due to go to Christchurch to a church conference. All the information she had was that they were diving outside Tory Channel in Cook Strait. The police requested Joe to search south of the channel entrance to Rununder Point, five miles down the coast. An extensive search found nothing and a southerly gale drove them home but not before they'd lost the gas bottle which was stored on the wheelhouse roof as the *Heather* pitched and rolled in the seas that built up with the wind. Searchers up the northern coast also failed to find any sign.

The following day the runabout was found abandoned, but anchored in Wellington Bay one mile north of the channel. A picture was put together from the known facts. The runabout had broken down. The anchor had been dropped but couldn't reach the bottom and they'd drifted out to sea. With the tide change the boat had drifted back in shore. This was why the first search up the northern coast had failed to find any sign of the boat. When it reached the shallow water the dangling anchor had hooked. It was common practice to use rubber car tubes with a net slung over them to hold the paua before offloading them to their bigger boat. But these were missing and it was presumed the two men had decided to swim ashore in their diving suits, using the tubes for flotation. Now the search was concentrated on the eastern coast of Arapawa Island. The lighthouse tender *Enterprise* brought down a search and rescue team from Picton and dropped them off at Okukari Bay to search the coast. Then she continued out to The Brothers to drop off supplies and mail to the lighthouse keepers stationed there. There was no sign of the Harleys, and the searchers returned to Picton with the *Enterprise*.

But first, while they were waiting for the *Enterprise* to come and pick them up, they came inside for a hot drink, and one of the men in particular took time out to talk with my children. And this was how, as long ago as 1970, I met the people who were to become our close friends. This man, whose name was Cedric Stewart, looked at my children and said, "Heather, what on earth do you do with them when you come into Picton? It must be hard if you've got any appointments." I'd gathered his name was Cedric and I told him I very rarely went to Picton for that very reason.

"Well, we've got three kids. Similar ages to yours. Next time you're in town, come up. Maureen would love to meet you. Leave the kids. She'd love it."

What an offer. The husband whom I'd just met was telling me his wife would love to mind my children and she didn't even know me. How wonderful to go to town, have someone to visit and have a cup of tea with. To be with another woman with children like mine.

"Don't forget, Heather. I'll tell Maureen to expect you," Cedric called as he walked out the door.

Meanwhile I was alone in the bay. My in-laws were away. The following evening I went over to their generator shed to start up the power. The dogs were barking frantically, not the barks reserved for the lighting plant, and I felt something was wrong. A stranger, whom I immediately knew was one of the missing divers, staggered through the back gate alongside the shed. He was dressed in a wetsuit which was torn off his body in parts, and he had a piece of manuka sticking through his ear lobe. He cried out. "My son is out there! Please do something!" I helped him home, rang the police – we had the phone switched to our house when Joe's parents were away – and organised him into a bath.

Four children all with eyes as big as saucers watched as I helped a strange man into a hot bath full of the usual rusty water as I'd had the coal range stoked up all day. I tried to be very efficient as I helped him off with his wet suit, and act as if I did this sort of thing every day. I could see he must have had a bad fall – there was a large gaping wound on his back. I couldn't cover it until he got out of the bath, and then I put him into our bed. Constable Matt Lindsay had assured me he would be here as soon as possible from Picton with Dr John Buckner in a hired boat.

"We'll try and get Buddy Baxter's *Sea-Bud*. She'll have us at Okukari in just under an hour," were Matt's words.

I wiped the condensation off the window pane and stared at the water, longing for their boat to appear. I'd done all I could for Mr Harley but I knew he needed a doctor, and he was desperate for a search to get underway for his son.

"Please hurry home," I whispered under my breath. Joe was out once again, still searching the coastline.

A group of volunteers from the religious group Mr Harley belonged to had been combing the southern coast. They received word Mr Harley had arrived at Okukari so they came to our bay. Suddenly I had 15 wet and cold men crammed into the kitchen of our little house. Swanndries and jerseys were stripped off and hung dripping from the lines Joe had put up in the kitchen for my washing. The sweet smell of the bush hung thickly in the room. At last I heard the engine of the *Heather* slowing down as she came into the mooring, and I breathed a sigh of relief.

Pauline, swinging on my legs and telling me she was hungry, reminded me it was teatime. "What the hell do I feed this crowd with?" I thought. My mind raced as I mentally went over what I had stored in Joe's parents' freezer. One pound of sausages, one pound of mince, some chops and some saveloys. It would be some meal, I thought. With Joe's parents away, my back-up was gone. The phone rang. "Gil here, Heather. Could you use some help? I'll bring

Nan over." I'm sure my sigh of relief would have reached him even without the phone line. "She'll have a scratch around in the freezer and bring over some sausages or something. See what she finds." Nan Perano arrived with a big pot of soup, sausages from her freezer and extra bread, and after a quick search through ours we produced quite a banquet for cold, hungry people.

Joe talked to Mr Harley who was still in shock. He gave vague replies, but from them his story unfolded. They had been diving north of the channel. The engine broke down, the anchor wouldn't hold, and they drifted away from the coast. They were fearful of drifting too far from land so decided to swim for the shore, using their inner tubes as swimming aids. They climbed the steep cliff and began the long walk to Okukari. Some time during the first night the boy slipped and fell 20 feet. The father climbed down, covered him and left him there to go for help. The boy obviously had a compound fracture of his femur as his thigh bone was sticking through his skin. The father, too, had fallen in this precipitous country, and it had taken him more than 36 hours to struggle out.

Joe, with Gilbert and Nan's son, Adrian, set off to see if they could locate the son before darkness fell. Some of the church people also went. Joe and Adrian covered distances fast. They thought they knew from Mr Harley's description where the son might be but they searched the area without any trace. With the darkness came freshening southerlies and rain. Coming back over the top of the hill before dropping down to the homes in our bay, Joe met up with one of the church searchers. No more than 19, he was exhausted and freezing cold, and told Joe he couldn't make it back to the house. Between cajoling, pushing and half-carrying him, in a bid to make conversation Joe asked him what he did for a crust.

"I'm training for the mission fields," was the quiet reply.

Most definitely not the right person in the right place in the right job at the right time. Matt Lindsay and Dr Buckner had arrived, and when the boy also arrived in our house he was treated for hyperthermia and later taken back to Picton with Mr Harley, in the doctor's care. Everyone else went back to Picton too, except Matt Lindsay who stayed to co-ordinate the search next day.

The weather in the morning was a little better. The *Enterprise* skippered by Captain Brian Pickering arrived at daylight. On board was a radio operator from Blenheim who set up a base radio in our kitchen, using 12-volt batteries. A carton of food containing bacon, eggs, flour, sugar, raisins, butter, soup mixes, fresh fruit and cheese arrived from the police and I vowed to myself that I would never be in a situation again without a large stock of food on hand to use in an emergency.

Following further questioning of Mr Harley it was decided they had looked in the wrong place for his son. He was above a small island.

"He must be above Wellington Head," (now Perano Head), Joe said. "Let's go. I doubt if we'll be able to get a dinghy ashore out there. This southerly has hung on and there'll be a huge sea running."

The *Enterprise* left, the radio operator tuned in, and all we could do was wait.

I learned later what happened.

The strait was rough. Very rough. Swells that had begun their relentless journey far out to sea curled up six feet high before crashing on the rocks. Spume, blown off the tops of waves, landed high in the scrub and clung to branches of dead bushes that had long given up the struggle for survival.

"A dinghy can't go ashore in this. She'd be matchwood in five minutes," Brian Pickering told the men already scanning the cliffs for the boy. Everyone felt heartsick.

"We must get ashore."

"No dinghy. It's ridiculous."

"Okay, we'll swim."

Chris Brown, Colin Norton and Joe pulled on wetsuits and, with a life-line each, swam through the churning seas to be dumped high on the beach with the other flotsam. They climbed up Wellington Head. The boy wasn't there. As they clung to the face of the cliff the helicopter in the search party hovered over them. Joe waved it away and the pilot thought he was directing him closer. Stones loosened in the wind created by the rotating blades pelted the three men as they pressed their bodies into the cliff face until it flew off and they were able to slide down the steep face to the beach. There were no lines to help them out to the waiting *Enterprise*. They had to swim through the breakers to reach the dinghy that had been tied to a long line and now floated outside the turbulent breaking seas. They climbed in and were pulled back to the boat.

At Okukari base, the message came through from the *Enterprise* to Matt Lindsay, the field controller, telling him there was no sign of the boy on Wellington Head. It was then decided to request that Mr Harley be discharged from Wairau Hospital. Using the helicopter, they'd fly him to the scene of the accident to see if he could pinpoint the exact position he'd left his son.

He was discharged under the supervision of a doctor who was dropped off at our place before the helicopter continued its flight to take Mr Harley out to the search area. As usual our children were charging around and the doctor asked me if she could leave her pack in a safe place. "There's plasma in it. If the boy's alive he'll need it."

A hard lump built up in my stomach. I knew from conversations with him that Mr Harley's religious beliefs would not permit any blood to be given to his son. I knew that was his belief, but I felt angry that my husband, the father of our four children, was risking his own life out there, and the life he was risking it for could die if he didn't receive blood. And Joe wasn't the only one. There were the crew of the *Enterprise*, and the pilot of the helicopter, and a team from the air force base at Woodbourne, led by Frank Burns, was coming overland from East Bay on the opposite side of the island in case a rescue could not take place from the coast. All these lives at risk – and quite likely for nothing. Why? I kept asking myself this all day.

From the helicopter Mr Harley located the place. His "island" was March Rock, not far from Wellington Head. From the *Enterprise* they saw the boy. He had fallen further down the cliff from where his father had left him. It was impossible to reach him from the shore. The overland team reached the edge of the cliff and a man was lowered to the boy. He was dead.

By then the sea had gone down enough to get the dinghy ashore, and the body and all the men were brought out on the *Enterprise* as they arrived on the beach. The operation was over, 52 hours after the alarm had been raised.

The next time I went to Picton I visited Maureen Stewart. In a short time I felt I'd known her all my life, and an abiding friendship began. She has been there for me so often over the years. My children loved meeting and playing with Maureen's. Today they are firm friends.

The memory of the Harley search is still with me whenever I am shopping for groceries. I am careful to buy those extras – just in case.

A phone call just on 6pm one cold winter's evening made me feel sick. A passenger on board the Cook Strait ferry had seen a woman leaping off the top deck just outside Tory Channel. The Picton police asked Joe if he would go out in the *Fugitive* and search.

Ten minutes later I heard the motor start up, then gradually grow quiet as the boat steamed out the bay before it disappeared around the point.

This was a call-out when for once I held no fears for my family. Instead I sat in the quiet of my lounge and let my thoughts drift back to my father's death, and then to the woman's family. I knew what they'd feel when they received the news. I could feel their pain. Why? They'd keep asking themselves. Why? Was there anything we could have done?

All the questions that had gone through my mind after Dad's death raced through my mind now. I thought of the person who'd jumped. She might be found. And then I wondered, if she'd been so determined to die, would she thank her rescuers?

That ferry had left Wellington at 4pm. All that time had she been plucking up the courage to jump, and only been able to just before the ship entered the calmer waters of the Sounds? What must have been going through her mind for all that time, and why didn't any of the other passengers notice her distress?

As time passed and there were still no sightings of her I knew she couldn't still be alive. The water temperature would be so cold. Just sitting at the window had made me cold and I wrapped my arms across my chest in an effort to keep warm. I closed my eyes and tried to imagine my own body falling through space. I hoped when her body hit the water that she was knocked unconscious before the coldness closed over her.

The search covered the area as far south as Jordy Rocks. It was called off after five hours. Her body was never found.

We've even had our own relatives giving out a Mayday. Easter Saturday 1990 was a beautiful fine day and all the men were out, fishing for groper somewhere in the strait.

"Mayday Mayday Mayday!" blasted through the kitchen. I knew that voice. It was Rex Guard, Joe's uncle. I heard him say he'd hit the rocks outside Tory Channel entrance and was trying to make it in to Okukari.

I tore outside and ran down to the beach. Rex's boat was steaming into the bay flat out and I could see immediately she was making water. She was listing heavily and very low in the water. Rex kept her coming and drove her straight up on to our beach where she lay on her side. The galley with its oven was on the high side, and sea water was now pouring out the oven door. I could see a large hole in the bow.

Rex said the steering went and before he could do a thing the tide had slammed the boat against the rocks. Water was washing over the stern of the boat with the rising tide.

"If I could get the fire pump going, that'd keep the water from rising and doing any more damage," I suggested to Rex. "Surely between us we can get it going."

As Joe is the fire officer for our area, I'd helped drag the fire equipment out of the fireshed heaps of times when Joe had been called out to a fire. This time I was on my own and my eyes boggled when I saw all the different parts and all the hoses that were stacked in the shed. It was by good luck rather than good management that the right pieces arrived down on the beach and we were able to assemble the pump, prime it, and keep the water level down in Rex's boat until the tide started to drop, leaving his boat high and dry.

Out fishing Joe had heard the Mayday and he too recognised Rex's voice. By the time they got back to our bay a local boatbuilder had arrived and patched the hole. He was waiting for the water to rise around the boat to float her off the beach before beginning the tow in to Picton for slipping.

I wish all Mayday calls happened on days like that, with no loss of life, but it is usually because of the weather that a Mayday is given. That, or a life-threatening situation.

We'd watched a yacht sail into Tory Channel. She was struggling to make headway in the gale-force northerly winds. The marine radio weather forecasts were predicting a wind change for later in the day with south-easterly gales.

"I'm glad he's coming into the channel with that forecast," Joe said as he watched the yacht's slow progress. The crew seemed to have trouble getting the anchor to hold and it took quite a few attempts before they were secure. Joe's comment, "I hope they've got a good anchor and chain," reminded me of my father's words of wisdom: "Your anchor's only as good as the weakest link."

True to the forecast the southerly ripped in the bay just on dark, and the sound of wind lashing against the windows made me breathe a sigh of relief that the yacht we'd seen earlier in the day had indeed been coming into Tory Channel – not going out.

We went to bed. Long-short-short. I heard the telephone rings on the party line. Through a mind still wanting to stay asleep. Long-short-short.

"Joe! Joe! Phone!" With me prodding him in the ribs and yelling in his ear he was out of bed like a shot and ran into the office to answer it. I could hear his side of the conversation. A boat was in trouble. No wonder my mind was wanting to stay asleep, I thought, when I partly opened one eye to see what the time was. It was only a quarter to eleven.

I couldn't help but be wide awake when Joe yelled out to wake up the boys as he dressed. I dreaded my family's having to go out in the storm that was still raging. "I'd say it's that yacht we saw earlier. She's broken adrift and run ashore on rocks three miles down the channel."

From the house I could hear the seas, built up from winds of 50-60 knots, crashing on the beach. My stomach churned with anxiety as my mind ran with Joe and the two boys down to the beach, pulled the dinghy down and waited for that lull in the seas to launch it, before all piled in and rowed out to the boat moored in the corner of the bay. The sound of the motor starting was like music in my ears. They'd made it.

I watched their lights until they were swallowed up in the rain and spray, and listened to Joe's conversation on the VHF with the stricken boat . Because it was so close I could tune in to their working frequency and know what was happening.

Joe was right. It was the yacht we'd seen earlier. I heard them telling Joe that their anchor had dragged and their motor wasn't powerful enough to keep them from being blown ashore. The boat was pounding on the rocks.

Joe told me later that when they arrived at the scene he knew he couldn't get our boat close enough to them to offer assistance as the water was too shallow and the wind was driving straight into the bay, pushing the yacht harder against the rocks. While Joe kept the *Fugitive* in deeper water, Young Joe and James tied a light line to one of the 60-inch diameter red plastic floats they used at the end of the lines when fishing for shark and groper, and then fastened that to the tow-line. The wind blew the float alongside the yacht and the men aboard were able to pull it aboard and then pull in the tow-line.

At my end of the radio I breathed a sigh of relief when I heard voices telling

Joe that their end was fast, and to start towing. I stopped worrying. The boat was going to be all right. It wasn't until Joe arrived home three hours later that I heard that their troubles had been far from over.

Joe said they'd towed the yacht out into deeper water and waited while the crew checked to make sure she wasn't leaking. But then they had to find somewhere to moor her. The southerly whistled over the hills, and willy-waws racing over the sea made it impossible to moor her in close by. They ended by towing her up into Ngaruru Bay, seven miles further down the channel from our bay.

The storm raged for two more days before the yacht was able to let go of her moorings and head to Picton.

There have been so many different calls for help on the sea. For Joe and our sons it is part of a long family tradition. As long as a Heberley lives at the entrance of Tory Channel I know they'll give freely of their time and knowledge in any emergency.

So often it's a southerly that's responsible for Joe's being called out. Sometimes plain commonsense could have averted a distress call.

In one such incident two men in their 23-foot fishing boat could have drowned. This boat was on its way from D'Urville Island, heading to Port Underwood. They passed the northern entrance to Queen Charlotte Sound and instead of running for shelter in the strong southerly winds they kept on steaming down the outside coast.

Their distress call was sent out just before 6pm. The boat's engine had broken down and they were now caught in the rip at Wellington Head. Once again I kept my lonely vigil by my window. This was a time I'm glad I didn't know how extreme the conditions were, not until our boat arrived home.

Seas in Cook Strait can be ferocious in any gale, but at Wellington Head when a strong flood tide meets a southerly gale face to face, the rip generated can send rogue waves leaping out of nowhere, and then just as quickly disappear, leaving deep holes that a boat can slide down, to let the following wave pour over the deck. The most experienced fishermen will steam around, rather than go through such severe conditions.

Joe told me that when they reached the boat she was 300 yards off the rocks, wallowing in waves that were at least 12 feet high. They had an anchor out but, Joe said, they were in "severe difficulty". When the boat was finally taken under tow, two brand-new tow-lines were broken in the heavy seas before she was towed to safety in our bay.

My three Heberley men sat around the kitchen table, talking about that evening's experience. I sensed a need for them to get it out of their systems. I was told that standing on the stern deck of our boat, watching the boat at the end of the tow-line in a trough of a wave as our boat reached the crest, was like sitting on the highest part of our roof and looking down on the lawn.

I understood how serious it must have been out there when Joe quietly admitted to doing one wrong thing. "I should have insisted the boys wore life jackets while working on the deck."

Of course our boat carries life-jackets so I asked Joe, "Why? Why didn't you make them?" He said he just didn't think of it at the time. "But," he said, "they'd be too bulky to work in. They're more for surviving long periods in the sea."

There was a happy ending to this rescue for us. The Marlborough Coastguard donated a new towing line and two life-jackets, easy to work in, that automatically inflate if the wearer falls into the sea. This meant that in future rescues my men would be safer as long as the life-jackets were on their backs, and not shut away in a cupboard.

The sea drama that really shattered our small community happened on 10 June 1974. It was such a lovely day – fine, clear and calm. Perfect for fishing in Cook Strait. Dig (nicknamed because he was born on Anzac Day) Thacker and his crew man, 23-year-old Malcolm Kirk, left Te Iro Bay at the Dieffenbach end of Tory Channel in the 36-foot *Tory*. They fished for groper and school shark on a spot seven miles off The Brothers' light, and they were winching up their last line for the day.

At home in Te Iro Bay, Hilary, Dig's wife, tuned in as usual, ready to listen to the marine radio weather forecast issued at 3pm. Dig always called her immediately after the weather to let her know what time he'd be in from fishing. Dave Fishburn, a commercial fisherman on his *San Pietro*, was fishing outside the *Tory*. He noticed a Korean fishing boat heading through the strait. This wasn't unusual. After refuelling in Wellington this was their route back out to sea.

Soon afterwards he saw that the *Tory* was listing, and that the Korean boat was nearby. At once he realised the implications. The *Tory* had been rammed. Dig and Malcolm had been tossed into the sea on impact. Dave Fishburn tried to contact Wellington Radio but could not raise them as they were broadcasting the weather. Beacon Hill Radio Station cut in at 3.10pm when Wellington Radio had completed the forecast, and told Wellington Radio there was a call for them. They then called Dave back, and he reported the accident.

Alone in her kitchen, Hilary heard this message. She had only a receiver so she couldn't transmit. She had no contact with any boats so she couldn't find out exactly what had happened. She didn't know Dave had steamed over and found that Dig had been plucked from the sea by the Koreans and was aboard their boat. There was no sign of Malcolm.

Dig jumped aboard the *San Pietro* and a rope was fastened across to the forward bollard of the *Tory* to prevent her sinking. The *Enterprise* was an hour away but when Brian Pickering heard Dave's call he steamed to the area where he took over the *Tory's* line from Dave, and with Dig on board – Dig was in shock – he set off through the northern entrance of Queen Charlotte Sound headed for Picton. An extensive search was mounted for Malcolm until darkness fell, but he was never found.

Joe was on his way home from Picton when he heard the message on his radio telephone. He steamed towards the northern entrance of Queen Charlotte Sound and picked Dig Thacker up from the *Enterprise* to get him home faster to Hilary, who was a registered nurse. He knew Dig had a heart condition, and by this time he was in extreme shock. The *Enterprise* continued her slow progress towards Picton with the now semi-submerged *Tory*.

Malcolm Kirk had been a lighthouse keeper before becoming a fisherman. His parents, Mary and Ian Kirk, lived in Deep Bay on Arapawa Island, four miles down Tory Channel from our bay. Malcolm had done what our boys always said they wanted to do when they grew up, so they looked up to him. We had spent many happy times with Hilary and Dig at their home, too, and Malcolm, who lived with them, always had time to spend with our children if he wasn't working. His death was our children's first experience of death within their world.

Young Joe and Helen became quite paranoid about their father out at sea. "Will he drown like Malcolm did, Mum?" I was asked whenever Joe went fishing. Pauline became scared of the water, scared of the cracks in the wharf, and refused to go swimming for more than a year. "I might drown like Malcolm."

James jealously guarded a toy car garage Malcolm had made and given to him a few days before the tragedy.

Eleven days later, Dig Thacker died at his home. The stress and shock following the accident had been too much. Two deaths in such a short period totally numbed our small community.

After Dig's funeral service in Picton, followed by a service in Christchurch, everyone gathered once again for Malcolm's memorial service at his parents' home in Deep Bay. More than 200 people, mostly casually dressed, arrived by boat and float plane. I sat on the hillside, grieving for Malcolm, and with my mother's heart aching for Mary.

I felt the peace seeping in from the tranquil scene below me. Forty boats and a float plane lay at anchor. Close to the shore the hills' shadows made the water black, but out in the middle of the bay the sun shone on glinting green water, and I could see by the lighter shade where the water became shallow towards the head of the bay. In the wintery afternoon sun the green hills with shadowed gullies hid grazing sheep from view. The 2.20pm ferry en route from Picton to Wellington slowed in deference to the occasion and the flotilla of craft in the bay.

I listened to the words spoken about Malcolm by men who tomorrow would once again be out on the sea working. They gave me a sense of human frailty against this mighty sea. The lump in my throat wouldn't let me sing. My voice wasn't missed. Men's voices, unaccompanied, echoed around the hills. I saw weatherbeaten faces with rivulets of tears sliding down the wrinkles come from many years of working on the sea.

Positive voices never broke as they sang For Those In Peril On The Sea. When the last verse of the hymn was sung, I found my peace.

> O Trinity of love and power
> Our brethren shield in danger's hour;
> From rock and tempest, fire and foe
> Protect them whereso'er they go;
> And let there ever rise to thee
> Glad hymns of praise from land and sea.

The sea had claimed another life, but people who have learnt respect and discipline can still rejoice in their love of the sea.

Hilary Clere, the widow of Dig Thacker, asked me if I would include here the findings of the *Tory* inquest, to exonerate her husband from all blame for the tragedy:

Calm seas, a light swell and bright weather conditions prevailed.

The Korean vessel was on automatic pilot.

There was no one on the bridge keeping a lookout.

The Korean boat had no radio, and its radar and depth-finding gear were faulty.

There is no need to say more.

CHAPTER TEN

Life After Correspondence

WHEN our youngest, Pauline, began her secondary education in 1982, she boarded at Innes House in Blenheim and attended Marlborough Girls' College with Helen while the boys were at Marlborough Boys'.

I counted up. I had lived and breathed teaching for approximately 4745 days. Now I had five or six hours to spare every day. The hardest decision to make was what I'd do first in my spare time.

Cleaning out the schoolroom and school cupboard was the first thing on my list. I'd have a spare bedroom. I visualised two beds with a set of drawers between. A bedside light on the drawers. New quilts and curtains.

No more desks with rulers, pens and pencils waiting for reluctant pupils to pick up. For the last time I'd be school cleaner, and clean up all the drawing pins and bits of chewed-up rubbers, the paper bullets flicked off a bent ruler when I was out of the room, the shavings from a pencil sharpener and the fragments off a rubber when a mistake had been rubbed out.

The school cupboard was built from floor to ceiling and its 10-foot length was the width of the room. The shelves were packed with 39 terms of school sets. They represented years of hard work mixed with laughter and frustration and the joy of achievement. I sat in the quiet room going through old school sets, shelf by shelf. Sets from the first days of school, each set comprising 10 days' work. I couldn't part with everything. It had been my life for so long.

The first work ever done by each child was called 'My Very First Set'. The front page of James's first set was beautifully coloured with a red horse, green cat with a yellow front leg, a blue tree and a red dog with a black head. On the first page there was a car and a garage, and a horse and a stable. The pupil was asked where the horse was going and where the car was going. He had to make a path with a pencil or crayon to show the car going into the garage and the horse going into the stable. I remembered how each of the children held the pencil so tightly and pressed so heavily that the line was visible through the next few pages and how proud they were of their work, rushing to show it to Joe when he came in at night. The story of The Little Brown Hen was in the first set. They all loved this and by the time Pauline came to it I was nearly word perfect with the story. Special sets like these I kept to give to each child one day.

In the art corner of the cupboard were the paintings. There were too many to keep but I found myself putting aside those that Helen and Pauline had created showing themselves as brides with red dresses covered with yellow daisies, and blue and green bridesmaids' dresses. Then there were the paintings Joe and James had worked on after they'd been fishing with their father. They were clad in yellow smockies with a huge fish in their hands and a boat stacked up with crayfish pots. There were blue boats on a red sea but all of them had smiling yellow suns.

I spent days in this room cleaning it up. I was glad my days of teaching school were over, but now there was a huge void in my life. I felt I lacked direction. When I'd taught school I'd made myself rush around in the mornings and have all my housework finished by 9am. Then I'd become a teacher until the lessons were completed. Now I had the whole day to myself. After April, when the electricity was switched on to Arapawa Island, I had even less reason to rush as I didn't have to hurry and switch the generator off. I could do housework all day if I wanted to. The constant thump of the lighting plant, reminding me how much diesel I was burning to do my washing and ironing, was no longer there to drive me. I seemed to live in a permanent muddle.

I missed the children. I'd dreamed of the time when I wouldn't be teaching school but now I longed to have them around me again. I lived for the weekends when they were able to get home.

"Come fishing. Better than moping here," Joe kept suggesting.

"When I've caught up with everything I will," I'd tell myself as well as Joe. One of the things that kept me home was the luxury of having electricity in our house. I'd get up in the morning and cook breakfast for the fishermen but then I didn't have to go out and stop the generator, and I could leap back into bed with a book and stay there until I wanted to get up again. It was a luxury I'd never had since being married, and I revelled in it.

Joe felt I didn't like his Christmas gift of a spinning wheel, and I knew I had to try to master it. The tangles I got myself into and all the snarl-ups were more frustrating than teaching some of the mathematics that I'd struggled with myself. I had no idea how to work the wheel but with a few helpful tips via the telephone I managed to get some hard stringy thread on two bobbins. It certainly was not wool suitable for baby garments.

"You don't knit that. It has to be plyed," the experts told me. My book of directions informed me that 'plying gives wool added strength, bulk, texture and variety'. My first attempt left me with a thread that unravelled as soon as I drew it out to admire my efforts. Then I found out it had to be plyed the opposite way from how it had been spun. At last I had a ball of wool to hold in my hands while I felt the satisfaction of the fruits of my labour. Wool from our sheep – I was a pioneer. I tried not to think that it would have been much quicker if I'd gone to Picton and back twice, and bought some wool.

My finished yarn was not unlike my gravy. Thick, thin or lumpy. With this I made my one and only garment from my own spun wool.

The boys like to wear woollen Johnny hats when they're out fishing. There's always a need for these hats as they are forever being lost overboard and they shrink with the salt spray fishermen expect most days. Joe had given me my spinning wheel, so he should have the first thing it produced, I decided. I'd knit him a hat.

The finished hat was heavy, thick, and somehow with lots of pieces of sticks, seed heads and prickles in it. It also smelt of sheep because my direction book said the lanoline 'turns' wind and rain, so I didn't wash the wool. This was a hat for rugged outdoor use.

The hat went fishing. I was told what happened. It was an extremely rough day. As they went steaming into the seas to gaff the craypots, sheets of spray were shovelled over the boat, keeping the crew and the hat wet. The weight of the water stretched the hat and blocked Joe's vision. He rolled up the band and it felt snug again. More water, and more hat fell over his eyes. Joe kept rolling up the hat and soon had quite a thick band of excess hat around his head. Another sheet of water and he took another turn, only to find there wasn't any more hat. The hat was now a sweatband serving a purpose. No salt water ran down into Joe's eyes.

I'd sewn it up with my thinner spun wool so I could pull it through my knitting, and it couldn't take the weight of the water. The stitching gave way. But one day I'll try again.

My piano had become lonely as I became more and more involved in school lessons. To keep one jump ahead of the children and appear as if I knew what I was talking about, I often studied their work the night before. I had no time to spend with the music I'd loved. But I knew I'd have to keep at my music or lose it, and when at last I had the time to sit down at the piano and enjoy it, I realised I had lots of hard work in front of me in relearning.

Maureen Stewart suggested I phone Mrs Doris Rockliff, a nearly retired Picton music teacher. I did, and my life took a new turn.

From the age of nine, she had learnt the piano for three or four years and in this time had sat a music exam each year. Then her parents moved and the piano she'd loved stayed behind. She was one of a family of seven, and her parents never knew of her love of music that was slowly buried. Numbness had enveloped her when she thought her piano playing days were over.

It was to be 33 years before she began to learn again, and taught herself Grade 8. A teacher friend heard the music she made and suggested to Doris Rockliff that she sit the exam. She passed it and then set her sights on her diploma for her ATCL. On her third attempt, and when she was 52, she gained her letters.

I too had been away from music for so long. It was a love in my life that had been swallowed up in a growing family and school lessons. Doris Rockliff's ability and understanding helped me find it again.

I rediscovered Mozart and Chopin. We played duets, and some days we'd just talk music and composers. Mrs Rockliff would sort through her music, hunting out pieces she thought I'd like to play. She'd play them for me and make me want to play them too. My lessons were very spasmodic. In a year I might have only eight or ten lessons, and six of these could have been spaced within six weeks. I went to music lessons when my time allowed and when it was convenient for my teacher. Slowly my confidence returned and all the spare time I promised myself disappeared at my piano.

The first year back into music I worked so hard. My fingers had become lazy. They had to learn to feel the keys again. Playing for sing-songs and songs for the children to sing certainly hadn't extended my music skills. I practised for hours, and the sense of satisfaction in being able to play pieces I used to play drove me to learn harder music.

Then our Sounds neighbour, Ian Kirk, died suddenly at his home in Deep Bay in 1982. I went there to stay with Mary Kirk until her sons arrived, and while Ian was being carried for the last time down the track to the beach and out to the waiting float plane, we sat in the same place we'd sat the day of Malcolm's memorial service. The mid-morning sun shone in our faces as we watched the float plane skim out of the bay on the flat calm sea and lift over the hills before heading to Picton. The noise of its engines rumbled around the bay, the waves it generated slapped lightly on the stony beach below us, and in the following silence Mary's quiet voice sounded loud. "Ian loved to hear you play. Would you play for him at his funeral, please?"

My arms were wrapped around Mary as I swallowed my doubts and told her it would be an honour.

Once I arrived home and started to sort through suitable music and find the hymns I'd be playing, I started to feel scared. More than that. I felt terrified.

"Don't be stupid," said my dear Joe, so confident in my music ability, but tone deaf. "You can play those. No trouble."

"Yes. But this is a pipe organ and I've never set eyes on it before. I don't even know how many keyboards it's got."

As usual, with Joe nothing was insurmountable. "I'll take you to Picton early and you can practise on the organ. You'll be fine."

He was right. I was very nervous but I played for Ian and the singing was so loud that no one would have heard any mistakes I made. But before the last hymn was sung I had a panic attack. I suddenly imagined I didn't know the last hymn. My fingers would never hit the right notes, I thought. They were wet and slippery with nervous perspiration. My whole body shook. I was back in time listening to the children's stories on the radio and remembering Sparky and his talking piano. He'd thought he could play until he woke up and found himself dreaming. His mother was calling out, "Play, Sparky. Play!" His fingers fumbled for the keys but he couldn't play.

I was Sparky. It was for Ian, but I wouldn't be able to play For Those In Peril On The Sea. My fingers wouldn't find the right keys.

I took three deep breaths and placed my trembling fingers over the keys ready to play the opening bar as soon as the vicar, Fred Grieg, announced it. The first chord was right, the introduction was completed without any mistakes, and then Ian's and Mary's friends took over in the singing.

After the service Fred Grieg came up to me. "We're needing another organist. It would be great if you could come and play at Sunday services."

I was floored. "Fred, how could I come in on a regular basis? I couldn't use the fishing boat. And even if I was able to borrow Young Joe's speedboat the weather wouldn't let it be regular."

Fred wouldn't give up. "Just occasionally, then. Once a month?"

"I'll talk about it with Joe and give it some thought," I said.

I'd fallen in love with the pipe organ in Picton's Holy Trinity Anglican Church and I desperately wanted to be able to play at some services.

"As far as getting there, Mum, I can take you up if I'm going out on a Saturday night, and if you can't hitch a ride home with someone else on the Sunday afternoon I'll come and get you."

"There will be days you can't get up because of the weather. I hope Fred realises this," Joe said.

When Fred rang to ask if I'd made my decision I had my answer ready. "If I can organise a ride to Picton, weather permitting I'll play once a month."

The months flew by and have become years. I miss the occasional Sunday because of bad weather or when farm work keeps me at Okukari. There is a new dimension in my music now and I have learned some of Bach's fugues and his famous Arioso and Air (G String) organ music. I have played for our four children's weddings, as well as weddings of friends or other family. I've played at the funerals of people who were special to me or our family. The medium of music has consoled me and helped my grieving.

At the same time as these changes were happening in my life, it was becoming obvious changes would have to be made in the fishing industry to halt our dwindling New Zealand fish stocks. In 1986 the government introduced the ITQ (Individual Transferable Quota) scheme as of 1 October. At the same time GST was introduced. The paper work increased 200 percent, our toll account doubled with the SOS calls I made to the Ministry of Agriculture and Fisheries in Nelson when trying to work out the quota system, and I knew our accountant's telephone number off by heart. It became my worst nightmare. It was worse than teaching four reluctant children. Sitting in the office one day trying to work out the mess, I jotted down my feelings and sent off my effort to the *Commercial Fisherman*, the magazine published by the Federation of Commercial Fishermen.

23rd Psalm for Fishermen

GST is my nightmare; it will consume me.
It makes me want to lie down in the office
It steers me into the roughest waters
It troubles my soul, it leads me into a deeper maze of paperwork than ever
before.

Yea though I struggle through this whole mess and confusion
I will try not to be destroyed.
All other fishermen must be in the same boat.
We will meet together, they will comfort me.

The Inland Revenue Department preparest our numbers
They wait grinning for our returns.
We must deliver them all into the presence of our enemies.
If late or wrong – $15,000.

Surely one day organisation and sanity will come to me.
Or will I have to keep digging myself
Out of this quagmire forever?

As I became more familiar with the system, organisation and sanity did come to me. I kept reminding myself that every other fisherman's wife in the country must be going through the same thing.

"If we bought another boat we'd be able to catch our cray quota faster and get rid of them while the prices are high, earlier in the season. Once Australia and South America flood the live market, you know how our prices drop." My heart stopped too when I heard this. I knew it made good sense, and Young Joe and James were fishing with us now, but the idea of another loan didn't thrill me. Joe's reasoning won and on 18 September 1990 we became a two-boat family with the addition of the *Tineke*. Another Morgan boat, she was a sister ship to the *Fugitive* but only 38 feet long. Anyone who knows boats will know what I mean when I say she was a pretty boat.

I was keen to sail aboard *Tineke* but I choose my fishing days carefully. After a few days of settled weather and the prospect of a lot of groper being caught I find myself making a bold statement. I tell Joe I'm coming fishing the next day. This is after I've listened to three or four marine weather forecasts on the VHF and studied the weather map on television. But as I shut the back door on a warm house and comfortable bed, and step into a cold, early-morning darkness, I find myself questioning my sanity.

Down at the wharf on this occasion, the *Tineke* with Joe and James aboard, and the *Fugitive* with Young Joe and his crew aboard, were tied each side of the wharf which was lit up from the bright lights on their back decks. As I jumped aboard the *Tineke*, my boat for the day, I could see hundreds of mullet as they shoaled in a mad frenzy in the circle of light.

"Got your seasick pills?" someone shouted.

"No. It's going to be fine." I'd never been seasick and I knew they all waited for the day when I would be. Before I'd come down to the boat I'd listened to the 5.30am forecast and I felt pretty confident that today wouldn't be the day.

Everyone worked in a companionable silence and the only sound was the rhythmic bang, bang, bang, as the knife cut the mackerel. I watched as James filleted a fish before cutting each fillet into three or four pieces. Soon a heap of cut bait was stacked on the bait table and Joe brought out the groper drags from the cabin to start baiting up. Each drag is made up with a wire backbone and this has 35 monofiliment traces each with a hook, joined to the backbone by a swivel. Today, I was told, we'd be setting groper lines and Young Joe would set the long-line. I mentally calculated that if we worked 10 lines and Young Joe the long-line with its 500 hooks, a lot of bait was going to be cut. The banging of the knife continued as darkness gave way to light and turned the water in the bay to navy blue. The northerly wind drawing down the gully whistled past the mast but wind ripples riding over the bay didn't even break its shiny surface.

With most of the hooks baited, both boats pulled away from the wharf. They were fishing in different places, and at the channel entrance Young Joe headed straight out while we headed north.

"We're on pilot and GPS. Keep a watch," I was told. "We'll finish baiting up."

The hills in Wellington Bay were still in shadow. Wellington Head stood out in relief as the sun rose above Mana Island. I could nearly follow the silver path that shimmered on the water. Over Wellington there was a thick grey cloud bank, but above that the azure sky assured me I'd chosen my fishing day well.

We were going out to the Swimming Hole today. This was the Heberleys' private name for their special fishing grounds. Last year they'd been fishing these grounds when Young Joe had fallen over the stern as he was feeding out the balloon rope. James rushed to grab him, and with an "I'm coming, Bro," he joined his brother. It was left to their father to pick up his two sons floundering around in Cook Strait. It was a story Joe loved to tell, with embellishments and great laughter.

Now James came into the wheelhouse, glanced at the Global Positioning System and showed me where we were on the screen. "It's good having the pilot running through the GPS," James said. "We've plotted in the longitude and latitude of the spot we've been catching fish, and with the GPS to navigate it'll put us right back on the same position again."

As we got closer to James's 'spot' I noticed Joe was staring at the land. At the same time as James yelled out that we were there, I saw Joe nodding his head.

"See, love," he said. "See that high peak? When that low scrubby hill in front is lined directly beneath it, we are on the grounds."

Once again I felt the conflict of old meeting new. Fishermen had made a living from the sea since before civilisation began, relying only on landmarks they'd worked out for themselves. With modern equipment, fishing grounds could now be found with the push of a knob. I felt that Joe still liked to be able to see the marks his father had handed down to him, as well as having the GPS.

No time was wasted and the first line was being set. In this process, one end of the drag is tied to a grapple which is hooked over the stern of the boat on the opposite side from where the hooks are being set. Once the drag with its 35 hooks is in the water a lead weight weighing about a kilo is tied to the top end of the drag, followed by the ropes and groper balloons, made of red plastic. These are another check that the line will be in the right place when it sinks. Then the grapple is thrown overboard, taking the line with all its hooks down to the bottom. The lines are set the last hour before the tide stops, and winching to pull them in begins at slack water.

Then the waiting begins. It isn't the relaxing wait of amateur fishermen as they wait for a bite on the end of a line. The lines must be watched. All that can be seen of them are the red balloons bobbing in the waters of Cook Strait. The small 40-inch balloon below the surface is to take the jerk out of the line if there is a swell, and the big 60- or 80-inch balloon is to mark the line's position.

I could see they were in a pattern in the water but even so I found it hard to keep track of the balloons as they lifted and sank in the swell. Joe steamed the boat down the line of floats, picked up a buoy and felt the line. "There's a few bites. Good sign." I felt the excited anticipation of every fisherman.

This was a good time to eat some lunch, and as it was calm James suggested cheese on toast. I didn't think it was calm. The sea wasn't rough but the boat was rolling in the swell. But still, if they wanted cheese on toast, I'd make it. With the boat lurching it was difficult lining up the oven tray to put it in the oven but at last the smell of toasting cheese was wafting around the deck. Just when I was thinking what a great job I was doing, the boat rolled extra heavily and the toast with runny cheese flew out the oven door and landed upside down on my gumboots. This was serious. I'd brought the food for the day with me and it was all on the floor.

I looked outside. Neither Joe nor James had heard or seen what had happened so I quickly scraped it off my boots and put it back in the oven. It tasted delicious washed down with a cup of tea as we sat out on the back deck waiting for the tide to slacken.

At last it was time to start winching the gear. The first line was hooked with the boat hook, the groper balloons pulled aboard and the line put on the winch. The balloons were untied and stacked up the side of the boat. As the rope was winched in James coiled it on his right arm. Each full coil was tied and put away, ready for the next day. Fifteen minutes later the first hooks broke the surface quickly, followed by 11 groper. These deep water fish pop to the surface, floating the line of hooks. On the boat they are stacked in ponds, made from pond boards that fit across the stern deck, dividing it into sections (ponds). Without these a boat with a load of fish could roll over if the fish all slipped to one side in a sea.

Our tally grew. When the last line came up we had 56 groper stacked on our deck, averaging about 40 lb and a good 3 feet long, and a few shark about the same weight. As we steamed home the last of the hooks on the drags were cleaned, twisted around the trace and hooked on to the wire backbone. The fish were cleaned and the cheeks and throats cut out. I knew what we'd be eating for the evening meal and my mouth watered as I thought about it.

The fish were packed away in the ice-hold and by the time we arrived back in Okukari the *Tineke* was scrubbed, with all the fishing gear stacked neatly away until tomorrow. As much as I enjoyed going fishing I love arriving home, opening the door to my kitchen and seeing my painting before me once more.

Tineke's lines were beautiful and she was a good sea boat but too small for where our men wanted to fish. I felt sad when she was sold in December 1993 to make way for the next new boat we were getting built at Gough Brothers in Invercargill. This boat was of aluminium construction and 46 feet long. Colin Neal, who had previously worked at Morgans' boatyard and who had designed the *Fugitive* and *Tineke*, designed her for us. She was launched at Bluff on 26 March 1994. Her name – *Te Wai*, the name of Worser Heberley's wife. Te Wai was married to Te Rauparaha's elder brother, Na Horua, often known as Tom Street. It was while the tribe was over in the South Island that Te Wai's husband was killed, and she met, and later married, Worser Heberley.

When *Te Wai's* sea trials and marine survey were completed I realised the dream I'd had as I'd watched the *Heather* steam out of Timaru in 1966. This was my time. Here I was, coming up the coast in *Te Wai* with Joe, James and Young Joe.

I kept a log of the trip up the coast:

Thursday 31 March 1994:
7.30am   Fueled up. Have 4700 litres of diesel aboard. After breakfast
                   went to Syncrolift wharf and Graham Gough arrived bringing

Russell Hughes, Gough's engineer, with him. Russell was coming up the coast with us as far as Port Chalmers in case we had any teething problems with the engine. Checked engine – all okay.

9.15am   Left wharf.

9.27am   Passed Stirling Head. Called Mary Lesk, the radio operator for Bluff Fishermen's Radio. Arranged to call her tonight. Wind 15 knots WSW. At 1650 revs boat speed 10.5 knots.

12.15pm   Off Curio Bay. Lunchtime – pies and tomatoes. 2-3 metre swell.

3.25pm   Off Nuggets. Speed 12.5-14 knots.

7pm   Teatime. "Seafarers' Treat" – steak, sausages, tomatoes, spuds and onions. Dunedin lights showing up on our port side. Off Tairoa Head. Easterly – 5 knots. 1.5 metre swell.

9.10pm   Arrived in Port Chalmers. Russell checked engine. Flat calm. Beautiful evening in port. Called Mary at Bluff Radio to let her know our position. Travelled 141 miles averaging 14 knots since leaving Bluff.

9.33pm   Said goodbye to Russell and Port Chalmers.

10.15pm   Tairoa light astern and set a new course for Akaroa Head – 146 miles. Joe and James turned in for four hours. Joe and I on watch.

Friday 1 April

2.15am   Boys awake. Swapped shifts.

5.30am   All up and awake. 38 miles east of Timaru. Passed five squid boats between us and land. NW 10 knots. 2 metre southerly swell. Quite sloppy.

7.15am   Wind change. Westerly mainly. Light airs. Joe's parents rang from Nelson.

10.15am   Stopped engine 6-7 miles of Akaroa Head. Checked oil. Wind now light NE.

12pm   Northerly 5-10 knots. Passing northern end of Banks Peninsula. Approximately 164 miles to Okukari and a still house.

3.45pm   Calm – sunny. Nearly to Point Gibson. I christened shower. Great.

6.30pm   Had tea. Cooked scones in oven. No complaints on results. Passing Conway River mouth. Seas smooth – slight swell. On dusk steamed through schools of dolphins playing. Beautiful evening. From Kaikoura seas gradually building up. Off Kekerangu wind northerly. 25-30 knots.

Saturday 2 April

12.15am   Abeam Cape Campbell. Engine vent on cabin top leaking. All awake while fixing the leak. Boat handled rough conditions excellently. A rough ride home but boat performed better than we ever dreamt she would.

3.20am   Tied up to wharf in Okukari Bay.

The trip took 42 hours. Every bit of it was the experience I had dreamed of for so long.

On Saturday mornings Marlborough Radio rings Joe to ask him the weather conditions at the entrance of Tory Channel. In the previous 42 hours Joe and I had had only three hours' sleep. When the phone woke me at 7.40am I sleepily picked it up. "Hello."

"Brian Palmer here for Radio Marlborough. Can I speak to Joe, please?"

I put the phone against Joe's ear. "It's for you."

"What's your weather down there this morning, Joe?"

"How the hell should I know? I'm off Lyttelton!" The silent phone was slammed down.

"Joe, that was Brian Palmer for the weather report." I was horrified. It rang again.

"Hi. It's Brian Palmer here for Radio Marlborough. Can I speak to Joe, please?"

A very apologetic Joe soon explained to Brian, and the weather for weekend boaties was broadcast as usual.

Joe had still been harping at me to do a fishing trip with him. I'd enjoyed the day trips crayfishing, or groper and shark fishing, but I had managed to talk my way out of longer trips. "All you want is a cook," was my answer when he tried to talk me into coming on numerous trips.

In January 1993 Joe decided to join the exodus of fishing vessels from Picton to Westport, and chase the tuna. This wasn't fishing, I was told – this is a sport. I'd heard stories of the bar at Westport and Greymouth so I made more excuses not to go. I'd never been seasick but I knew there was always a first time and I was scared I might find myself 50 or 60 miles out at sea and be ill. But Joe finally wore me down. I had the time, and I couldn't think of any more excuses not to go fishing with him.

Saturday 11 March 1995 was the day. I was going fishing. It was a clear day and a light air from the south-west ruffled the water in Westport Harbour as the *Te Wai* and *Fugitive* iced up. Three tonnes of flaked ice were poured into the fish freezers below the stern decks of both boats, and the hatches closed. Next time they would be opened would be to put in tuna. I had two hours to change my mind and jump ship and head back to Picton by car while Joe waited for weather faxes and latest forecasts to come through before he committed himself to set out to sea. The day before it had been very rough on the bar with a strong south-westerly blowing, and most of the boats were in port for the weekend.

At 12.35pm he turned the key to start the engine. We were on our way.

We lay in the lagoon out of the river flow while Young Joe on the *Fugitive*, and James on the *Te Wai*, let down the tuna poles which had been pulled up against a yoke fitted near the top of the mast. Now the boat had two arms reaching for the sky in a wide V shape as the tuna poles were fastened in position. Four rubbers, or overgrown thick black rubber bands, hung off each pole and I was told these acted like shock absorbers. Lines with brightly coloured lures stretched from these and when there was a strike the rubbers told the story as they stretched out from the poles. Later three lines (shorties) would be hung from the stern of the boat, all with rubbers. The middle of these three had a dive board fitted to it, and this took the lure to a depth of four or five fathoms to entice deeper fish.

Once we hit the river our speed picked up as the Buller River was running at six to seven knots that day. I was used to the beautiful colours of the sea in my painting at Okukari, and I couldn't believe the colour of the river. It had been raining heavily and logs and other debris jostled us as we sped through the dirty brown water towards the bar. James kept a watch on the leads as his father steered out past Tip Heads. It was calm today but Joe suggested I come in the wheelhouse in case a rogue sea crashed over the deck. There was no order in the waves that popped up out of nowhere, dirty brown waves with light brown foam curling over their tops. At 12.55pm we steamed out of the dirty water and into clean water. So definite was the line of colour that I expected to feel a bump. Instead we were greeted by pygmy sperms or hector dolphins.

We steered in a south-westerly direction while I waited for the calm conditions to arrive as I was having difficulty in standing up, and beginning to wonder if I wasn't feeling squeamish. Alongside us the *Fugitive* kept disappearing in the troughs of the three-metre swells but at least here I could look at the aqua-coloured sea I loved – and keep an eye on the horizon to help steady my stomach.

Cape Foulwind was my last view of land. By 2.30pm all sight of land was gone and I was totally disoriented. The water had become a deep purple and the sounder gave a reading of 120 fathoms. The swell was still making me gather bruises, so I sat carefully on the back hatch and watched as James put the lines in the water. He dropped the shorties in and I saw he had an extra one hanging from the back stay of the mast. "That's the whisky line." He must have seen my puzzlement. "It dates back to the old days. This line caught the extra fish to pay for the whisky when the fishermen arrived back in port."

At 4.20pm one of the rubbers stretched out, and the first tuna flapped on carpet laid between the pond boards on the deck. Soon there were others. The fish weighed between seven to ten kilograms and when they first came out of the water they were a brilliant blue-black and silver, but this soon dulled. That night 43 fish were stacked on ice in the fish hold, but the main thing was we were out on the fishing ground for the first light of morning.

During the night the wind and tide had carried us 10 miles. I still couldn't see land so it meant little to me. We were up before daylight and after a quick cup of tea and a slice of toast we were chasing the tuna again. At 6.55am somewhere in the Tasman, we landed our first tuna of the day. We had only 10 knots of wind from the south-west although there was still a three- to four-metre swell. I intended to land my share of fish on the boat today as I felt I now had my sea legs. Joe gave me gloves as otherwise the nylon lines would cut into my hands. I struggled to pull in the lines. The nylon slipped through my fingers. "Reach out as far as you can, grasp and pull. Big over-arm strokes!" Joe yelled over the noise of the engine and flapping fish. I managed a few but it's just as well they weren't relying on me to make money from the fish I pulled in.

We were now 50 miles from the coast and we listened to all the forecasts very closely. A low was coming down from up north and Joe was concerned that a strong northerly on top of the south-west swell could be trouble. The sky was leaden. There was an eerie light and a northerly wind was slowly freshening. For those willing to take notice, the weather was sending out warning signs. The 6pm forecast confirmed Joe's forebodings. "Pull in the gear, James. We're off. I don't like the sound of that weather report. It'll be after midnight before we reach the bar. I hope we'll be able to get in."

Back home I have the utmost confidence in Joe when we are at sea, and in the roughest weather I feel safe. Out from Westport I didn't have the same trust. It was my fear of the bar that made me nervous. It was an unknown quantity. Joe wasn't familiar with it as he was with Cook Strait.

Tonight we were lucky. The closer we got to land the calmer it became and when we crossed the bar at 12.30am it was flat calm. We unloaded because more boats were expected in, due to the predicted weather conditions. The *Fugitive* followed us in and I was awakened often during the remainder of the night as boats berthed nearby. It seemed no one was risking lives on the bar this time.

My fishing trip lasted only 36 hours. I wasn't seasick but on the first afternoon I had actually felt seasick for the first time in my life and I didn't like the feeling. But in a year or two maybe I'll remember only the good parts, and maybe I'll go again.

When I have some spare time now I spend it in my garden. Gardening used not to be a great love of mine, though I've always liked to see a garden around the house. It makes it look loved. Now as my garden has grown, so has my love for it.

New flowerbeds pop up over the lawn. Joe swears that every time he returns from a fishing trip I've made a new garden. The shrub garden around the perimeter of our front fence has at last grown into a thick windbreak. As the shrubs grow so does the garden as I have to make a wider border in front of the shrubs every year. I discovered dahlias. Tucked in front of the shrubs, sheltered from strong winds, they flourish, their masses of brilliantly coloured heads against the yellow, green and grey foliage of conifers, grevilleas, flaxes and leucadendrons giving my painting its summer and autumn look.

There is life after Correspondence School. All that is needed is the time to be able to find it.

CHAPTER ELEVEN

Shearing at Okukari

"SHEARING'S a mug's game."

Bluey Hebberd pushed the last sheep of the day out through the portholes with his foot, flicked his wrist to remove his handpiece from the down tube, straightened his aching back, walked across the board to pick up his towel, and wiped the perspiration off his face.

I've heard these words spoken by every shearer we've had on the place for 33 years but they still keep on shearing. It's their life. They are special people – they have to be special to want to drive their bodies to the limit and then a bit more.

The first time I met Bluey was in November 1963 when he came to shear the 1500 romney sheep Joe's father ran. He has seen our shearing shed move from a three-stand plant driven by a single cylinder Blackstone Lister to the four stands we have today, driven by electricity.

Six months out of the big city, I certainly was not prepared for shearing. I had never been inside a woolshed until I came to Okukari. In those first months I saw a large old corrugated iron shed sitting in the paddock overlooking the bay. I understood why it was so rusty when I saw the constant sandblasting it received when gale-force southerly winds picked up sand off the beach and hurled it against the shed. Sheets of different coloured iron which had replaced rusted or blown-away iron gave it an interesting appearance. "That green was the colour of Mum's and Dad's old roof and the red was left over when we replaced some of the iron on the little house."

The shed, inside, had a different interest. I don't believe a single thing had ever been thrown away since Charlie and Ruby had bought the farm. "It might come in handy some day," was the catch-phrase of Okukari as something was added to the pile of junk in the shed.

"Who was the bootmaker in the family?" I asked Joe when I spied the old last, sitting on the top of a wooden yoke which looked too old to carry much now.

"Dad uses the last when he puts hobnails in his boots."

The shed was a quiet place lit by shafts of light filtering through skylights. Dangling webs were home to myriads of spiders, and the grease smell of the wool from previous shearings, mixed with the smell of dust and old timber, added to the restful atmosphere – that is, until shearing began.

Nothing prepared me for the dreadful smell in the woolshed after 300 sheep had been held in it overnight. Waves of ammonia hit me at the doorway and made my eyes smart. The heat made it more overpowering. Condensation dripped off the inside of the roofing iron. It made the board where the shearers work very slippery for the shed hand who gathered up the fleeces as they came off the sheep and quickly threw them on the wool table to be skirted. I watched my father-in-law deftly skirt the perfectly-thrown fleece as it lay spread out, then throw the short and stained pieces he'd removed into a separate bin at the end of the table labelled PCS (pieces). The rolled fleece was placed in the wool press. As the press filled it was jumped down to get as many fleeces as possible in a bale.

Bluey was on the front stand. "He's the fastest so sets the pace for the others," I was told. His tall frame bent at the waist and he held the sheep tightly against his long straight legs. I watched the belly wool come off first. It was thrown aside and flicked up by the shed hand's broom and put with the other bellies. Then the wool around the crutch, the left back leg, and over the tail was shorn. Wool off the face was removed. From the clear belly Bluey ran his handpiece up the brisket to break out the neck and shear up to the ear, under the chin and over the left shoulder. He rolled the sheep to expose its back by stepping forward so he could sweep the long blows up its back, down over the right shoulder and side, and finish with the right leg. One more in the tally book for Bluey.

I thought the Lister engine was antique when I came to Okukari but it was still going when we replaced it with electricity in 1982. It was so basic that any breakdowns could be easily fixed and only once can I remember it stopping. Its one valve was stuck, but within half an hour the head of the engine was off, the carbon cleaned from the valve and shearing was in full swing again.

At the start of a run three shearers often reached the long blows all at once. The four-inch flat belt that drove the main shaft of the three shearing plants would slip, they'd get slower and slower, then stop unless one or two stopped shearing. The remedy was simple. "Run up to the house and ask Ruby for some golden syrup or honey. Please hurry." The urgency in my father-in-law's voice didn't allow me to ask why. As soon as I was back at the shed with it he spread it thickly over the belt. The golden syrup worked its magic. Shorn sheep continued to be counted and bales of pressed wool mounted in the shed.

Many years of shearing and pig hunting kept Bluey lean, and his thin greying hair gave him another name, Silver Grey. During a smoko I remember discussing dentists. I wondered which one I should go to.

"Go to mine, Heather. He's really good, never hurts, been going to him for years."

I looked at Bluey's teeth and quickly made up my mind not to go to his dentist. He had front teeth missing. The teeth still intact didn't seem too healthy-looking, either. "A man only needs a couple to hang on to a cigarette with," he added as he leant back against a bale and inhaled deeply.

I grew to enjoy the work in the woolshed but I never forgot my shock that first day I stepped into the shed. I don't know if the smell got less or if I became accustomed to it. The energy used in the shed from the 7.30am start until the 5.30pm finish amazed me. The shearers worked frantically, each trying to keep pace with the others and at the same time trying to beat their personal tally.

A certain whistle from Bluey with a "Shake'em up" and Wag, his old sheep dog, would leap over the rail into the back pens to bark more sheep into his catching pen, ready to shear.

Every fleece the shed hand threw on the wool table lay like a sheepskin rug. I was shown how to skirt it and I gingerly tried to do this the way I was shown. I was scared I might muck it up. I knew this was my in-laws' main source of income for the year, but my father-in-law guided me through that first day.

My first attempt to throw a fleece on the table ended in disaster. I'd walked into it, grasped what had been the back legs, pulled them around the heap of wool lying at the shearer's feet, and with it in my arms I'd run to the table. The throwing looked easy. Mine certainly didn't look like a sheepskin rug spread out on the table. It was upside down. I'd caught the neck wool on the end of the table and the fleece had become a pile of messed-up wool. It took me hundreds of fleeces before I felt I could do it properly.

On the dot of 9.30am Ruby arrived with smoko. Her tray groaned under the weight of scones, savouries and cream cakes. Thank God it's not me and my stove having to do this, I thought.

Work started again at 10am and by lunch time the shed was hotting up. The shearers revelled in the heat and the more sweat that poured off their bodies the faster they seemed to go. I didn't work like that. My legs ached, little cuts in my hands stung with the grease, and the wool made my body itch all over. I was glad when it was 5.30 and I could leave the shed.

If the weather stayed fine, shearing took four days. The times when wet weather stopped shearing made a lot of extra work. If the men decided to stay on it was more cooking, and if they went back to Picton it was extra boat trips.

The wool from the clip that first year I was at Okukari Charlie sent to Wellington in the *Te Aroha*, an old scow. He always sold his wool in the February sale in Wellington and this time, rather than pay freight from Okukari to Picton and then Picton to Wellington, he thought he'd try shipping it direct. The scow arrived in the early morning and ran herself aground on the incoming tide. The bales were rolled down the bank below the woolshed along planks and pushed up on to the *Te Aroha*. I was learning that everything one does down here is hard work. Once all the bales were on board it wasn't long before the tide came in enough to float her off and begin the slow trip to Wellington. It was the only year we shipped wool this way. The wool store was closed in Wellington and our wool has been sold in Christchurch ever since.

Weather plays a significant part in any shearing. It either permits it or prevents it. One bad time stands out in my mind. We had enjoyed three fine days and by lunch time the last sheep should be out of the shed. A southerly buster had been predicted. The morning grew hotter. It was airless both inside and outside the shed. Down south the sky turned a dark navy blue, and the channel water beneath it was black. Out in the paddocks newly shorn sheep ate hungrily.

"It's going to be a good one when it hits," Charlie said as he looked out the shed door. "I hope it doesn't last or it'll skittle a few sheep. It's the ones straight off the shears I'm worried about."

The wind arrived and with it came hail. Huge lumps fell and the sheep scattered. The temperature dropped rapidly.

"Knock off shearing. I'll need a hand to get the sheep in the shed."

We tried to muster in the sheep but they wouldn't move. The cold got to them and they were dying like flies. The lucky ones were those the men put on their shoulders and carried into the shed. We were fortunate the southerly blew itself out as fast as it had come in or the losses would have been far greater.

Our children were introduced to life in the woolshed at an early age. They came down first in their pram and later their highchair. As they grew older they played around the shed or on the beach where I could keep an eagle eye on them from the door. Later they all liked to help in the shed, and shearing became a family thing.

When Helen left school and was working on the farm she went to shearing school and gained her shearing certificate. She was a good little shearer and held her own with the boys.

Ruby and Charlie left the farm in 1979 and moved to Nelson. Now I was the cook at shearing time. My mother-in-law was a wonderful cook. Trying to follow in her footsteps was daunting. My smokos never came up to her standard but hungry shearers ate whatever I gave them.

One shearer, Peter, had a huge appetite. He ate until the food was gone, but the hard work kept away the fat. With a cup of tea in one hand and food lined all the way up his upturned arm he'd flop down to enjoy his feast.

I watched him in fascination. Would he eat anything? I thought I'd find out. I made lamingtons and piped cream on them – but one I made from that synthetic green stuff florists call oasis, and I hoped he'd take it. He did. I'd creamed it slightly differently from the others and I recognised it sitting on his arm. Peter picked it up and licked his lips in silent anticipation of that first bite. His teeth closed on it. "Yuk." Green oasis mixed with coconut and chocolate icing flew out of his mouth. The whole shed erupted when Peter tried to get rid of the oasis clinging to his teeth. I noticed that throughout the rest of that shearing he didn't eat another lamington.

When I had time I still worked in the shed between preparing the meals. I missed not being able to be there fulltime but when electricity came to the island it made things much easier. A new four-stand shearing plant was bought, my deep freeze now ran like any town one, and – best of all – my dream had come true. I had an electric stove. Now I could bake for shearing well in advance and spend most of my time in the shed, leaving it only to heat up meals and the smoko food.

My electric stove was installed two days before one shearing season and I was still working out how to use its various functions when we started. The first day in the shed, when I didn't race up to put the meat in the oven, Joe started worrying. "What about tea? Aren't you cooking any tonight?"

"Don't worry. It's all under control." I'd entered the electronic age and my oven was set to turn itself on without me.

"Still, I think you should check it." I was annoyed he couldn't trust my wonderful oven and walked to the door of the shed. "Mmm, I can smell it cooking." My nose can't smell 200 yards but he shut up.

At 5.30pm when the last fleece was rolled and in the press I left the shed to prepare my vegetables. They'd cook while the meat finished cooking. No smell of cooking mutton met me at the door. Running into the kitchen, I found the meat still sitting in a stone-cold oven. This was worse than the coal range days. In an hour Joe and four shearers would be up for a meal. I read the instruction book on how to cook partly in my microwave and partly in the conventional oven. I'd find out what I'd done wrong at a later date when I had more time, I promised myself.

The men consumed a few more bottles of beer than usual, and dinner was only 30 minutes late. Joe was so impressed with the ease our meal had cooked itself now we had an electric oven. I didn't tell him the truth for a few months. By then I was the boss of my stove.

Bluey still came to shear our sheep and one year his birthday fell while he was at our place. I secretly smuggled a cake with candles to the shed and lit the candles and produced it at morning tea. Bluey leaned back against a wool bale, his face lit up with surprise and delight as we all sang Happy Birthday.

He was a good shearer. Over the years our respect for him as a shearer had grown into a firm friendship. He loved telling yarns and stories over smoko – stories of happenings in other sheds he'd worked in. We often started work again still smiling from the yarn we'd just heard.

"The weather'd come in bloody shitty. The boss's boat broke its moorings and blew ashore. We all raced out the shed and down to the beach to try and help. He's Italian and the more excited he gets the harder he is to understand. He kept yelling at us to 'Lever it! Lever it!' We tore round like mad things looking for something suitable to use as a lever. I found a good strong post, heaved it along the beach and drove it into the sand and tried to lever the boat up on its keel. 'Lever it! Lever it!' he shouted again. We were bursting our guts trying to lever the damn thing. Then he shouted again, 'Lever it! Lever the bloody thing alone.' We did just that. We sat dumbfounded, wondering why the man wanted it left.

"Well, how the hell were we to know the tide was coming in and it would float off on its own in an hour or two? If he'd spoken English we'd have understood to leave it. Better than us breaking our backs trying to lever the damn thing."

Young Joe and James gave him another story to tell in another shed. One morning they'd found a penguin and put it in Bluey's tool box before he'd arrived in the shed. Penguins are cute little birds viewed from a distance, waddling on the beach or paddling in the sea. Cornered, they turn vicious.

Bluey whistled into the shed and opened his innocent-looking blue box to sort out his gear for the day ahead. It was alive with an enraged penguin. It flew at its liberator, darting in to peck angrily at his ankles before it scurried out the door, indignantly preening its ruffled feathers. Everyone enjoyed the hilarious start to the day except Bluey, but he enjoys relating the tale now over other people's smokos.

We enjoy our shearing. Most of the shearers we have had working in the shed have fitted in well and the shed's atmosphere is happy. Once we had trouble. When the only way a trouble-maker can leave is by boat it can be very awkward.

We were short of a shearer and were told of a man not long in Marlborough and looking for work. Joe was told he was a 150-a-day man – not all that fast but it meant 150 a day that Joe didn't have to shear. From the first day this man was difficult. He made little conversation and was the most ill-mannered man I've ever met.

I cooked his breakfast the first morning – bacon, eggs and tomatoes. He was late coming to the table. The others had eaten their breakfasts and gone, and when he did come his breakfast was cold, but it didn't matter.

"I never eat a cooked breakfast. I'll have fruit and cereal." Not one 'please' entered the request but that was fair enough, I thought. Not everyone likes a cooked breakfast. He sat at the table until 7.30am. I was chafing at the bit to get cleaned up as I also had to be at the shed at 7.30am to begin work. I certainly didn't want to come up to the house to set lunch with breakfast debris on the table. The other three shearers were always out of the house by 7am. I think they liked to get down to the shed and prepare themselves for the day ahead.

While he sat I managed to get everything else done, then at last I could clear the table and get it re-set for lunch. Only four days, I told myself. Don't say anything to cause trouble.

Shearing had started when I arrived at the shed. The smell, heat, condensation and the busy hum of the shearing plant greeted me but I didn't notice any of this. On the end stand was our new shearer. He was shearing with his back to everyone. He was left-handed. He was the first shearer I've seen shearing like that and we've never had a left-handed shearer since.

I knew he couldn't help being like it but it made picking up the fleeces from his sheep very difficult. The front legs of the fleece weren't lying out on the board and every time he finished a sheep he walked through the fleece, making it almost impossible to pick it up correctly. This meant it couldn't be thrown on the table so that it spread out, making it harder for the fleece-pickers to skirt. With four shearers a fleece can be expected on the table every 40-50 seconds and one messy fleece can put the fleece-pickers behind.

Before he'd started Joe had told him that if he cut off any tits when shearing the ewes he was to yell out and a shed hand would raddle the ewe. We didn't want it left in the main flock to have a lamb and not be able to feed the lamb. In the first count-out of the day Joe noticed one of his sheep bleeding badly. Both its tits had been cut off. Joe was furious and told him so. The man just shrugged his shoulders and never said a word.

During smoko everyone sits around and yarns, and laughs are the best parts of shearing. But this man always sat at the other end of the board, ignoring us all. At lunch time he arrived up at the house when everyone else had finished theirs. Lunch time became like breakfast, a last-minute scramble to clear the dishes away.

That first day after he'd showered he came into the kitchen. I was enjoying a well-deserved, long icy gin and tonic. "Scissors. Where are they?" he demanded. I couldn't believe the way he spoke to me. No one talks to me like that in my house.

"What sort of scissors?" I was very curt.

"To cut with."

"I realise that but I've my first aid scissors, as well as ones I use for sewing, in the kitchen and for cutting nails. What do you want to cut?" A thick finger with coarse black hairs and grimy broken nail was thrust under my nose.

"This."

I silently found my nail scissors and handed them to him. The others sitting around the table were horrified at his rudeness. A mutter went round the table from the other shearers and I heard someone say, "We've got a bloody Rambuka here, boys." I was glad Joe wasn't around. I'd rather keep the peace. A boat trip into town to take him back would be the last straw after a day in the shed.

Next morning Rambuka came out to breakfast, saw the fruit and cereal and demanded bacon and eggs. While I was cooking it he asked me if I had any aspirin. "I've gotta headache."

This time my tongue slipped. "Around here even the youngest learns that magic word – please. It helps, you know." I gave him the aspirin and got not one word of thanks.

128

That day went from bad to worse. He'd lost his watch and accused my James of stealing it off his arm while he slept. It was later found in his sleeping bag. There was no apology.

I heard the clothes dryer going and when I walked into the laundry the most ghastly smell of hot stale perspiration enveloped me. He had put his black woollen singlet, that he'd worn for two days' shearing, unwashed, in my dryer. The smell was putrid and it made my stomach heave. I don't mind the dryer being used to dry off clean clothes but I draw the line at what he did.

I became quite paranoid about being left in the house alone with Rambuka. His surly manner, especially with me, made me nervous. In the four days he was here we never heard one word of thanks. He didn't even say thanks when his pay check was handed to him. Only, "Give me my tally count. I want to check it out." He'd have got it anyway.

It wasn't until the end of our financial year I found out he had given me a phoney IRD number and no one had heard of him at the address he put on his tax form.

To this day the other shearers maintain that they had the last laugh. All the way to town he lay on the back deck of the boat. He wouldn't join the men in the cabin and have a beer with them. They schemed what they'd do with him when they got to Picton.

"Well, I'm buggered if he's coming through to Blenheim in my ute," said Tony, one of our other shearers.

"That's right. Let the bastard walk," said Bluey.

When Joe arrived home and told me about it he said he honestly didn't believe they would leave him behind. But when they arrived at the wharf everyone, including Rambuka, jumped off, collected their gear and threw it on to Tony's ute. He hadn't come to Picton with them but he obviously expected them to take him somewhere. Joe watched the others pile in the cab. Just before Tony climbed in he grabbed Rambuka's gear, threw it on the ground, leaped in the cab and roared off, leaving Rambuka staring in disbelief. As Joe untied the boat he watched him pick up his belongings and trudge across the road to one of the local hotels.

One shearer who had shorn here before I came to Okukari, and worked here for a few years after my arrival, certainly made an impression on me. When he was coming to the shed, so did extra beer. The rules were plain and simple. No beer. No shear. At 7.30am a crate of beer was sitting on the board by his stand before he arrived in the shed. A bottle was open all day and he'd have a drink of beer between every sheep he shore. He was a good shearer and for many years held our shed record for the highest tally shorn in a day. He died from cirrhosis of the liver.

The wharf makes shipping our wool out much easier. Weather permitting, it is stacked on the wharf ready for the barge to pick it up and take it into Picton, where it is loaded on a waiting truck to go to the wool store. We usually use the tractor to shift it from the shed to the wharf but one year the tractor had broken down so we were using our Trekker truck. Only able to shift two bales at a time, Joe was worried at the time it was taking. "The barge'll be here before we get it all down at this rate. Let's try taking three."

The third bale had to sit on top of the two stacked on the deck of the truck. "Sit on the bottom ones and hold on to the top one," I was ordered.

There wasn't room to turn easily at the shed door. After loading Joe would back down to the wharf, unload and drive back to the shed to repeat the process. As he backed down towards the wharf the bale started to move. I hung on to it as I had been told but my determined efforts were to no avail. I fell off and 350 lbs landed on top of me. It knocked the wind out of me and I hurt all over. An alarmed Joe stopped the truck and leaped out to see if I was all right. When he heard me shouting abuse at him he said he knew I was okay and I got into trouble for letting the bale fall into the wet mud. Within a few days I had an amazing body, more covered in bruises than not.

Cross-bred wool prices were dropping alarmingly. Buyers wanted fine wool and so in 1989 Joe travelled down to Central Otago, the home of the merino, to buy in some merino wethers. We weren't sure how they'd adapt to our environment so he bought only 300 the first year.

These different-looking sheep arrived on the barge, charged down the ramp on to the beach and up into the nearest paddock. In comparison with the romneys they were fine-boned and covered with a dense fleece due to the high number of wool fibres – about 50 million to the romneys' 15 million. When they hung their heads down their glistening pink noses were nearly buried in the rolls of wool that hung from their necks to their shoulders.

"They'll be bastards to shear with all those wrinkles. I might put my combs and cutters away when it's time to shear them."

They settled in well on the harsher runs on the farm and over the next few years Joe built up the flock to 1000 which we maintain today.

Shearing practices changed. "Too many bloody wrinkles for an old codger like me," Bluey told Joe when he rang him up at shearing. He came anyway and shore his way around the wrinkles.

Joe's shearing gear wasn't put away. He shore a few but found it pretty tough. He always found an excuse to leave the shed, whether to make a phone call, check a gate was open or find something to do away from the shed. Bluey came up with a new name for Joe, Abo, because he was always going walkabout.

Once while Joe was at the house ringing up, Bluey had been busy. He'd found a piece of pipe six feet long with a right angle bend about a foot long at the end. Joe burst into the shed expecting to see the shearers hard at it, the shed hands busy and the wool mounted up while he'd been away. The machines were quiet, no dogs barked to bring up the sheep, I was leaning on the wool table and Bluey stood on the board, his cheeks round with the air that he was trying to force down the pipe.

"Thought my didgeridoo music would bring the old Abo back from his walk-about," said Bluey when he got his breath back. No doubt another story to be told in another shed over smoko.

Fleece picking needed more care with the valuable harvest and it needed to be classed. A professional classer came down with the shearers. She showed us the correct way to skirt the merino fleeces and sowed a seed in my mind.

"Why don't you get your wool handling certificate? You can do it through Massey, extramurally."

I watched Karen classing the wool. I knew I'd love to do it but I wondered about learning to learn again. When she marked the bales with her professional stencil I made up my mind. I would do this same thing one day, and I could put my own stencil on our bales of wool.

My 'one day' came in 1992. I became a student and looked forward to mail day with great excitement when my marked work was due. In May I spent five days learning practical skills at Massey, with an exam on the last day. In November I found myself one of the thousands of New Zealanders sitting exams.

The night before my two exams I stayed in Picton, with Helen. I'd worried that if I stayed home I mightn't get in because of the weather. I never imagined I'd feel as nervous as I did. I was overwhelmed with fear I'd fail and my family would think I was dumb. By the time I'd dressed that morning in something comfortable I was feeling sick, and looking at myself in the mirror made me feel worse.

"For goodness sake, Mum, put on some make-up. If you look good you'll feel better."

That made up my mind. "If you want something badly enough and work at it hard, you'll get it," was the motto I'd taught our children. Getting the jitters didn't enter into it.

In the bedroom, I rummaged through my bag, found a pretty if somewhat impractical outfit, changed into it and put on make-up. I smiled as I remembered my father's affectionate teasing:

Little bits of powder
Little bits of paint
Make our little Heather
What she really ain't.

I felt much better. The exam went well and in 1993 a new nail was driven into the office wall and I proudly hung up my certificate in wool handling systems.

I still had to work for my stencil. During 1993 the merino clip and the cross-bred clip had to be inspected once it arrived in Christchurch. All the wool from our shed in that year was inspected. Alan Marshall, a wool production officer, came out to our shed when we were shearing the romneys to check on my shed management and clip preparation, and at last, in September 1994, our merino wool left Okukari with my stencil on each bale. I was a registered owner classer for fine and cross-bred wool.

CHAPTER TWELVE

Mustering the Land

THE FIRST TIME I went mustering Okukari with the men, I couldn't believe my ears. I had grown up never hearing my father swear, or nothing serious. I don't doubt that around men he was as good at swearing as anyone else but he didn't swear in the hearing of women and children, and I would have had my bottom tanned if he'd caught me at it. In less than two hours on the Okukari hills my vocabulary certainly increased as I heard my respected father-in-law yell at a dog, "You fuckin' black bastard! Jesus, I'll hammer you when I catch up with you! Get in behind!" I quickly realised this was the only language the Heberley sheepdogs understood.

Years later it was proven, beyond reasonable doubt, that it is the only language and tone of voice they know. We'd been mustering Wharehunga, the block we lease on the Queen Charlotte side of Arapawa Island. This was an all-day muster. As usual we were on top of the hill in time to watch the sun rise, and probably wouldn't arrive back with the sheep on to the flats at Okukari until the sun was setting. On this muster we'd met up with Walter and Betty Rowe who live in Aotea on the Queen Charlotte side of the island. Animal lovers rather than large-scale farmers, they'd heard we had geese on the flat and they wanted some at their place.

"C'mon get them, any time," Charlie had said. "I'd love to get rid of some. Always shitting and pulling out the grass on the flat. Make a helluva mess."

The Rowes decided to come back with us and take some geese home. We all had our muster beats and everyone was spread over the hills on the Tory Channel side of the farm as we brought the sheep down. Ruby and I were bringing our mob around the road, at the same time catching up with all the latest gossip from Walter and Betty. Across a steep gully from us, Charlie was bringing his mob down what we call the Big Ridge. It drops down into the head of the flats. Stump, his black huntaway, was exhausted and took no notice of his master's commands.

I could feel my mother-in-law cringing alongside me. Ruby Heberley, descendant of Captain Jacky Guard, not to mention wife of forthright Charlie, was no stranger to swearing. She was also ladylike. Now both of us were wondering what Walter and Betty Rowe would think when they heard Charlie working his dog. I could see Ruby was waiting for him to explode. After all, here was a dog that raced down the gully to flop in the water, then stand in it, staring back at Charlie as if he was mad. Suddenly revived, his dog was chasing all the sheep in the wrong direction, splitting the mob, then sitting on his haunches, panting, his pink tongue dripping as he waited for his next command.

"In behind, Stumpy boy. C'mon see Dad. There's a good dog."

This quiet voice speaking to Stump might as well have been in a foreign language. Stump stretched out on his stomach and slithered towards the strange voice. Ruby and I could hardly speak for laughter. The dog definitely did not understand such refined commands. Suddenly it all got too much for dog and master. Suddenly the usual lingo kept for sheepdogs broke out and Stump and Charlie brought in their sheep. What Betty and Walter thought I don't know.

Sheepdogs at Okukari have a good life. Once past the age of mustering they just retire. We've had some real characters on the place and one especially springs to mind. Born out of Queen, he was given the name of Prince. He ruled over all the dogs and what he lacked in talent as a working dog he made up for in character. At feeding time I've seen him snarling at the dogs on either side of him in their cages until they'd be too scared to go near their meat. He was like Houdini and he'd squeeze a leg through a mesh of wire separating the runs and slowly hook the meat towards him with his paw. He couldn't get it into his run, but he wouldn't let the other dogs have it either.

His brain must have had a built-in calendar. Whenever one of the Rowes' bitches came on heat, Prince knew. And this was over the hill, at least three miles away. Whenever he was needed for mustering he'd be away courting, and when Joe went and brought him home he'd be off again the minute he was let out of his kennel for a run.

One morning an exasperated-sounding Mitch Rowe rang me up. "Heather, that black dog of yours, Prince, has been over here for the last four or five nights. He's causing dog fights among our dogs."

"No. It can't be Prince. He's been in his house the last week. The only times he's been out have been in the afternoons. He's back in his house every night. In fact I can see him in it now. Must be another dog like him roaming around." I knew Prince couldn't be blamed this time.

The next morning we had a similar conversation. I walked down to the kennels and Prince was stretched out sound asleep. Poor old bugger, I thought. Fancy blaming you when you are here in your house.

The following day Joe and I were sitting at the kitchen table having our breakfast. I was watching the sun creeping down the hill when I noticed the sheep scattering. "What's chasing them, Joe?"

Joe focused the binoculars on the hill. "There's a dog coming down the road. All ours are tied up, aren't they?"

"Were last night." We were worried it might be a stray.

"Looks mighty like Prince to me."

It seemed Prince was still getting the blame.

Joe went into the office and brought out his .22 rifle. "This'll bring Prince down if it's him. He's gun-shy."

The shot echoed around the hills. The black dog stopped in his tracks and leaped straight off the road, down the ridge, across the lagoon, along the beach in front of the woolshed and up to the dog houses. It scrambled underneath one, and the next thing Prince was standing looking out of his house as if he'd just woken up and was greeting the morning.

"Looks like the old bugger slept in this morning," said Joe.

When we examined his house we found he'd eaten a hole in the back floorboards. The wily dog came and went as he pleased to keep his dates, and I had to ring up and tell the Rowes that there wasn't a stray dog roaming the island after all.

His brains and love of freedom caused his death. All the dog kennels had sliding sash doors, and Prince discovered another way out after we blocked up his back door. He'd put his nose underneath the bottom of the door and push until he could lift up the door with a jerk, then rush out before it slammed down in place. He misjudged, and one morning we found him, half in and half out of his house. The door had crashed down on his back. He was dead.

One of our musters on Wharehunga could easily have ended in tragedy. It was when Joe's parents were overseas and it was an 'all hands and the cook' muster. Another farmer from further down the channel had come to help. During the afternoon it came in southerly with bitterly cold wind and rain. We had the sheep past the point of no return. If we'd given up the muster our efforts would have been wasted. No one wanted to leave the sheep and start from the beginning again when it got fine, so we kept on. Driving the sheep up the hill on the Wharehunga side was miserable but nothing had prepared us for the conditions that greeted us on the ridge when we met the southerly face to face. Six-year-old James appeared to feel the cold the worst. He started crying and I tried to pacify him. "Look, son, you can see our house. We'll soon be home."

"You'd better get cracking with him and Pauline," Joe said. "We'll manage from here. Take Joe and Helen if they want to go."

Joe and Helen were fine. They wanted to help bring the sheep down to the flats and so I began my worst-ever one and a half-mile walk down the farm road to our house. It isn't far as the crow flies but the road twisting in and out of the gullies makes the distance longer. Pauline's solid little legs led the way, and I recalled how she'd been out on the hills with me whenever we were mustering since she could walk. Now and then she'd turn around and tell James and me to hurry. But I couldn't. I now had a son who kept telling me he was tired, and just needed a little sleep. Sheep tracks running off the road into thick gorse took his eye. He kept ducking away and before I could grab him

135

he'd be in a thicket of gorse and I'd be pleading with him to come out and I'd carry him for a little way. I suddenly realised he was suffering from hyperthermia and I had to get him home as quickly as I could.

Uncaring of the prickles I crawled through the gorse and managed to pull him out again. My body was bigger and had a lot more excess fat covering it than his, so I took off my soaking jersey and wrapped it around my son, then picked him up and hugged him close so he'd benefit from my body-heat.

No welcoming smoke greeted us from the coal range or open-fire chimneys, but opening the back door into our house felt like we'd entered heaven. After the cold, the warmth draped around my body like a soft fine woollen blanket and the warmth from the water as I ran a bath soon had my fingers tingling as I sank James into the deep water.

A hot bath and soup supped from a cup while sitting in front of the newly-lit open fire worked wonders and by the time the others arrived home James was his usual self, telling his father that he hadn't wanted to come home with me and his baby sister. We'd made him come.

The experience taught me a lesson about hyperthermia and how quickly it can come on. It is not only the sea that has to be respected. The weather, too, can change so fiercely.

It hasn't always been the weather that has made our musters memorable. Years later, after we had taken over the farm from Ruby and Charlie, Joe and I with much older children were mustering Wharehunga. Joe was doing the bottom beat and the four children and I were spread between him and the skyline. I'd seen him drive his mob of sheep down on to the beach and I yelled out to everyone up the hill to wait until their father came up off the beach. Suddenly he appeared out of the scrub, fingers to his lips and waving with his other hand for us to be quiet. He looked ill, his white face making his freckles stand out.

"What's wrong?" I yelled.

"Quickly! Get to hell out of here!"

Four children, Joe and I scurried around the side of the hill and once out of sight of the bay he told us what had happened.

"When I came down on to the beach this man who rents that bach was waving to me. I thought he was hurt and went to see if I could help him. Closer up I could see he was on the happy baccy. He could barely stand up. His face was red – maybe it was rage – and his eyes were nearly popping out of their sockets. He was waving a knife around and he screamed, 'You know, Heberley, I've a good mind to cut you up into little pieces and feed you to the sharks in the bay!' He was so loaded I could've knocked him over with a feather. I told him if he tries anything five men with me up that hill will be down on him like a shot. I nearly died when I heard you yelling out, asking where I was. Then he raced inside muttering something about a gun. That's when I took off."

136

Any sheep around that bay were left. "Hope they eat his patch," Joe muttered. "Serve him right."

Hidden in the scrub we watched the man stumbling over rocks and finally squat on the point at the entrance of the bay, but it wasn't until we actually saw the sunlight glinting on the barrel of his gun that the Heberleys slipped quietly away, leaving him to his lifestyle and the friends he conjures up in the loneliness of his mind as he smokes his joints.

If life in Auckland is likened to living in the fast lane, mustering in our cattle is like living in the overtaking lane. There have never been many cattle run at Okukari, only those brought in originally to help clear the land of gorse and scrub. It surprised me when I first saw how they'd open up a rough block just by breaking down scrub as they pushed through it in their search for food. Their size and speed, especially when they were covering the distance between them and me, made me very wary of them.

On this occasion Joe and I hadn't been married long. I thought we were still in our newly-married and loving state. The punt was due the following week and Charlie was keen to round up as many cattle as he could to ship out to the Blenheim sale.

"We'll get rid of that old bull if we can get him in to go on the punt. Just keep the younger one." But when Charlie added, "It'll kill somebody one of these days, the bad-tempered old sod," my ears pricked up.

"Well, count me out," I told Joe. "I'm not ready to fill a coffin yet."

But somehow or other I was persuaded to help – chasing cattle is really lots of fun, you'll love it, and anyway I'll look after you – these were the winning words. So I found myself chasing, and trying to keep out of the way of, a mean and enraged bull that made it quite clear he didn't want to leave this place. We'd get him nearly to the yards and he'd wheel around and start pawing the ground while he snorted, then with a disdainful toss of his head he'd take off up the flats, bursting through any gates and fences that were in his way. We gave up for the day when it became dark.

That bull was out for revenge, and just when I was thinking I'd earned my sleep that night, Charlie yelled at the door.

"He's broken the back fence around the houses! We'll have to get him out or he'll destroy your mother's garden."

The thought of the bull trampling over Ruby's beautifully tended flowerbeds and rose garden sent me outside to help. I didn't have a garden then, but four deep holes in the ground with every step the bull took would ruin our lawn.

It was pitch black and I couldn't see a thing. Charlie came out of the generating shed with two burning torches and a bucket of kerosene. I crept behind Joe, trying to melt into his shadow. My imagination was working overtime. There was a hot breath on my neck. I heard a snort. I tugged on Joe's sleeve. "He's right behind me. I can hear him."

I'd be silenced with a curt "Shush!"

We were pushing our way through the long grass that grew between the fruit trees behind the two houses. The rustle of the pine needles jostling each other as the night breeze tangled in the branches of the tall pines around the perimeter of the section became the bull's heavy breaths. The house lights shone invitingly but the bull was all around me and I was too scared to run back to them on my own. The faces of the men were lit up by the light from the flames and I could see they were loving being the mighty hunters. Suddenly thundering crashes sounded in front of us. Down through the trees burst the bull. All I could take in were his glowing eyes, reflecting the light from the flaming torches the two men were holding.

I spun round and took off. Branches slapped my face, but went unnoticed in my fear. I heard Joe and his father trying one last time to get him out of the section and heard their grunts as they threw the torches at him. Charlie took off towards his place and Joe pounded after me with the bull close behind. We burst out into Ruby's vegetable garden and headed for the open window at the back of our house, which adjoined her garden.

We reached it at the same time and both made a dive for the safety of our house. The two of us were jammed in the opening.

"I was here first," I panted, as Joe pushed me. No 'ladies before gentlemen' here, nor a case of a newly-married and loving state. This was a blind fight for survival as we struggled to get inside.

The bull sounded closer. At the same time as the crashing stopped and we imagined him charging over the vegetable garden, Joe and I fell through the window and landed into the concrete wash tub. I slammed the window shut and the noise and the lights from our house stopped the bull in his tracks. He stood his ground for a minute, then took off back into the darkness.

All night I had visions of lawns and gardens completely wrecked but the bull had left the area and by morning my father-in-law had come up with a new idea to get the creature away from Okukari.

"Somehow we'll have to get him into the yards but once he's there we'll be right. I'll duck into Blenheim and see if I can get some tranquilliser. A shot of that and it'll be a damn sight easier to get him over the hill."

We didn't have cattle yards at our wharf but Nan and Gilbert Perano did at Whekenui, and we used to put our cattle on the punt at their place.

"In fact if we give those other bad-tempered sods a shot we'll have more of a chance of getting them over, too."

In the days that followed I found myself laughing more than I had for a long time. Wise now, I sat on the roof of the woolshed and watched, or made sure at least two fences were between me and the wild cattle. A young lad working on the farm looked as if he thought he could walk on water as he ran across the lagoon, trying to get out of one's way, before sinking up to his armpits in the green slimy water.

138

With a "C'mon, Pet," Charlie walked quietly up to one only to find himself running towards the safety of a fence and Pet giving him a hand over with her two curling horns.

The morning the punt was due we had to get the cattle started early to get them over the hill. Gary Kenny had phoned the night before and told us he'd be at Whekenui at 11am, the top of the tide. The bull and some of the more wild stock were standing in the cattle race when my father-in-law arrived down in the yards with his injections.

"I've just got to put it in the rump. They'll be docile in minutes." I stood back as I watched the magic of medicine. The bull swayed on his feet and seemed to have forgotten his ill-humour, and when the gate was opened he joined the other sedated cattle for the walk over the hill.

In every muster there is always one that breaks away and refuses to go in the right direction. We had the usual problems and it took more than an hour to reach Whekenui. The cattle that had been tranquillised behaved themselves, and when we arrived at the beach to drive them along to the yards at the other end I breathed a sigh of relief. This sort of cattle mustering was my sort. But then I noticed the bull and the wild ones we'd sedated were beginning to act strangely. They were tossing their heads around, jumping up and down, and then they'd wipe their faces from side to side on the ground.

"Run!" I heard Joe screaming from behind me. But I didn't have to as the bull wasn't the least bit interested in me. He was after Joe and his father. Joe ran into a shed but the bull kept chasing Charlie up the hill. I watched in horror when my father-in-law turned and faced it. He whacked the stick he was carrying across its nose. The bull stopped in its tracks, stared at its tormentor for a few moments, then turned and ran back down the hill to join up with the others.

We had them all in the yards at the wharf waiting for Gary when he arrived, and were we thankful to see the back of them once they were loaded on the punt. The only mention Charlie ever made of his narrow escape was on the way home.

"You know, son, that bull had bad halitosis."

With motorbikes, mustering has become much easier, even if not quite so safe considering some of the places they are ridden. But at least a bike can outrun a cattle beast.

Wharehunga has been planted in pine trees now and we no longer run sheep on it. It has become the home of wild pigs and the ground beneath the trees, some of which are more than 30 feet high, is ploughed up where the pigs have been rooting in their search for food.

During 1995 Joe spent a lot of time trying to muster off our remaining stock from this block. Only a few cunning sheep and cattle were left. Joe invited me to go over to Wharehunga and see if we could gather up a few more cattle.

We'd had a southerly for three days and I was sick of indoors. As we went up the road on the back of the four-wheeler, memories flooded back. I looked down into the green valley where I'd gazed with such a heavy heart in my first months here, and saw where I'd lambed my first ewe, the place where Lucky, our pet lamb, had become bogged after being worried by pig dogs, and the woolshed, still clothed in multi-coloured sheets of iron.

The creek that runs down the middle of the flats now runs between banks worn steep in many places as huge volumes of water racing down to the sea have eaten deep into the land. It isn't the same creek I used to take four children up, having picnics, building dams and catching the eels that slithered out from under the stones used in their dams.

I thought of the long musters I'd walked before the first bike arrived at the farm. Here is the land I've grown to love. I realised I've got fewer years left to love this place than the years I've already had here, and I had to swallow the lump in my throat.

Through the boundary fence I found myself in another world, sheltered from the southerly. There was only the dark stormy sky above the tops of the trees to tell us of the foul weather on our side of the hill. The noise of the bike seemed rude in the silence as we bumped along one of the firebreaks between the trees. We could see only the track we were on. There were no barking dogs or people yelling at them. Just nothing. The thick scent of pine heightened my senses and turned Wharehunga into a place of long-gone memories.

Joe stopped the bike in a clearing where he'd seen a cow and calf the last time he'd been over. From this clearing I couldn't see any of the beaches on the Queen Charlotte side of the island. While we waited quietly, I thought back to the time, six years earlier, when Joe and Young Joe had sat on a ridge overlooking a bay, and had seen two men shoot one of our cattle beasts before taking it away.

A commercial boat operator had phoned Joe to tell him he'd spotted a beast lying on the beach. Arapawa Island farmers had become sick of high stock losses. I remembered that one farmer had reported the loss of about 200 sheep the previous year. Two or three times a year while mustering we had found offal and other signs of butchering on our property, and although we expected cattle losses through natural causes, our losses were much higher than they should have been.

The local farmers got together and agreed to maintain regular patrols. They also enlisted the help of commercial boat operators to take note of any strange boats in the area.

The first inkling I'd had that anything was wrong that day was when I heard the roar of Young Joe's motorbike as he raced around the farm road, across the flat and up to the house. It was another accident – Joe was hurt and needed help – he was dead. As these thoughts swirled through my mind, Young

Joe burst through the door and yelled for the phone book to phone the police. I let out a sigh of relief – no one was dead.

"What's wrong and where's your father?" I asked a very agitated son.

As Joe looked up the number of Picton police and then waited for the phone to be answered I got a very brief answer. Dad was coming, but it would take him longer on the four-wheeler. They'd watched two men shoot one of our cattle beasts. Then Joe, with James who'd stayed at home, put the speedboat in the water. While they waited for their father, I heard the rest of the story.

Young Joe told me that the cow they'd gone over to check out had fallen over a bank. It was dead on the beach. Climbing back up a ridge to where they'd left their bikes they'd seen a small boat moored on another beach. Through his binoculars Joe watched some men on the beach. Young Joe had crept closer to watch. "I had the breeze up when I heard a shot go off," Young Joe told me. Then they'd watched the two men disappear off the beach and within minutes they'd dragged out a heifer and rolled it into the cockpit of their boat.

"They meant business, Mum. They even put the head in the boat. I'll bet they'll dump that in deep water. Its earmark is the only proof we have that it's our heifer."

After the boat had left they'd gone on to the beach and found the entrails a little way up from the hill and other stock of ours nearby.

"I've left pieces off my bike all the way home. It's never been ridden so fast," Joe said.

When Joe arrived back in the bay the speedboat engine was running and needed no warming up. Three angry Heberley men took off in the speedboat down Tory Channel. The Picton police had a description of the boat from Young Joe and they would intercept it if it passed Dieffenbach, but our men hoped to be at Dieffenbach before the cattle rustlers so they could positively identify their boat for the police. I just hoped for the rustlers' sake that the police got to them before the Heberleys did.

But at Dieffenbach there was no sign of the boat and the police hadn't passed it as they came out of Picton. Everyone felt sick. They'd been so close, and now it seemed the rustlers were going to get away with it.

After a discussion it was decided to check out the deep bays on the Tory Channel side of Dieffenbach. "They may have been a bit faster than we thought and had time to slip in to Hitaua, Maraetai or Onapua," Joe suggested.

The law won. Just on nightfall up in Hitaua Bay Joe saw the boat tied up at a wharf. In a shed on the property was our cattle beast. The head was never found. Luckily for the rustlers, the police accosted them before Joe did.

Salt was rubbed in the wounds when they offered to buy the beast for double its value, in compensation. Our men brought the carcass home but we didn't enjoy it. The rustlers were charged and found guilty. For us there was no true compensation. How do you put value on a heifer that would produce calves in the following years and each of those calves might produce a calf that might produce a calf?

A crashing in the undergrowth alongside us brought me back to the present. It had to be a herd of wild cattle, I thought.

"A grunter," Joe whispered. "Quiet. It might run across the track."

We didn't see any sign of it but down through the trees I could see where pigs had been. It looked as if a giant plough had been over the place.

Out on a knob we saw five cattle beasts. We parked the bike and tried to catch up to them but they heard us and took off.

Pushing our way back through the thick undergrowth, Joe pointed out the places where pigs had been living. In a huge area with a dirt floor and a canopy of bush above, where dead branches and vines hung down, Joe told me that this was where the dogs had got ripped up when James caught a 120-pound boar. I shut my eyes and could picture the frenzy within the thicket as the dogs that had found it barked, and the holders held their prey waiting for the man to stick or shoot the pig. Over all this would be the high-pitched squealing of the pig.

One badly ripped dog had been carried gently to the bike that night and brought home to be stitched, while the gutted pig, now unimportant, was left until the next morning. A few days later the dog was fit again, and in conversation over a cup of tea I had heard another hunt being planned in the cycle of life on the island.

CHAPTER THIRTEEN

Lambing and Tailing

THE GARDEN heralded spring. The haunting perfume of the jonquil-like Earli Cheer mixed with the old-fashioned cream freesias, and bold yellow daffodils waving on their slender stems told us winter was over. The hills were green with spring growth. Hungry lambs bunted at their mums, lifting their back legs off the ground. Impatient mums ate hungrily to keep up the milk for their new offspring. Lambs stretched themselves out, heads laid back, staring at the sun and soaking up the warmth.

Joe noticed one poor old girl up on the face of the hill. "I think she's in trouble. How about whipping up on the bike to check her out?"

"Coming, Judy?" I asked my friend from Nelson.

"Love to."

"Quita, you're staying home. No dogs allowed this time."

The four-wheeler is a godsend. Down from the house, three of the retired farm gentlemen chase us and bark at the bike on the way. At the woolshed they leave us to carry on up the hill. These old-timers know not to come today.

The ewe is in serious trouble. Obviously she has been lambing for some time. A head is presented with two black hooves. The tongue is out, and worst of all it is blue. I have to catch her and do it quickly. This lamb can't last much longer. Judy and I leap off the parked bike. The ewe dives off the side of the clay road. Crazy creature – doesn't want to be helped. They never do. She took off down the hill, bearing down occasionally but to no avail.

"Come on, girl. It's my help or no baby." She doesn't seem to hear. Finally at the bottom of the hill she has nowhere to run. She stands at the gate I've driven through 15 minutes before.

"Stand there, Judy. If she keeps eyeing you I might be able to sneak up on her." The decoy works. She appears to forget about me coming up from behind. I climb up the bank above her, jump on her and both of us fall to the ground. The lamb looks dead. "God, I'm too late." Her pelvis is so narrow. No wonder she is having trouble. I can feel the shoulders catching. The ewe cries out in pain. I hate doing this. I must. I must. I feel the lamb coming. Airways have to be cleaned and the lamp wiped over mum's nostrils and mouth. She won't forget her fine big ram lamb. I feel a quiet sense of achievement.

The first year I was here, lambing was a huge shock. I thought lambing just happened. They just appeared, gambolling about in the spring sunshine, grew up and left the farm. Then I was up the paddock with Joe, collecting pine

143

cones, and he came across a ewe needing assistance. He had to lamb it. The head was tucked back and so Joe had to push the lamb back into the uterus to correct its position before he could deliver it. The ewe maa'd out in agony. Joe's hands are so big. Tears ran down my face. I couldn't stand it and I couldn't do it myself. I ran away from the sound and was violently sick.

"What the hell's wrong with you?" Joe asked when he caught up with me.

"Don't ever expect me to watch that again."

"No? Next time you might be doing it yourself." Over my dead body, I promised myself.

I managed to avoid lambing complications until one day I was home on my own. We had had a lot of rain and the sheep needed to be checked in case any were down and couldn't get up with the weight of their wet wool. Under the pine trees was a ewe, down. I knew she was still alive as I saw her kicking. I ran over to stand her up – and I felt ill. She needed help to have her lamb. No way could I do it. She'll have to die. I could pretend I never saw her. Maybe she'll last until Joe gets home tonight. Turning my back on her I headed down the paddock.

Heather, a voice spoke inside – get back and give it your best shot.

I knelt down beside her. She'll probably die anyway and the lamb's bound to be dead inside. I couldn't tell. One leg and its nose was presented. I watched the nose. Was that a twitch? Perhaps it is alive. The leg got a bit of a tug. Nothing. What else did Joe, do I asked myself? Maybe if I pulled harder – but things still looked the same. Looks like it's just you and me this time, old girl, I thought. I stripped off my jersey and gingerly slipped my hand up into the wet warmth of the ewe and found the problem. The other front leg was bent at the knee and hooked. Once it was freed I knew I could lamb her. I curled my finger around the bent joint and pulled back. The two front legs were free. One pull and the warm slimy body plopped on to the grass, but lay still. Dead. The ewe was trying to sit up and view her baby. "Damn it all, you've got to live!" I cried aloud. I remembered Joe wiping the mucus from the mouth. A few slaps and a shuddering breath shook the wee body. Its mum's tongue soon cleaned the rest of the lamb and before long it stood on wobbly legs to have a drink from the proud mother.

I sang. The Beatles had nothing on me. I leaped over ditches and told the empty paddocks, "I did it! I did it!"

If only spring stayed spring during lambing. Cold wet days come frequently in our lambing period. On the hills there's shelter to be found in the scrub, but lambs on the 100 acres of flat land that run up the valley and foothills have a hard time. Southerly or northerly makes little difference when it is raining and blowing. The wind either whistles up the valley, or down. New lambs dropped in the cold often perish before they can have their first feed. If I can sneak up on a ewe while she is still cleaning her lamb and tip her up, then make sure her lamb has a good drink of colostrum, it improves its survival rate in extreme conditions.

One year we tried plastic lamb coats. If the weather turned nasty new lambs would be warm and dry. In theory it was an excellent idea. We knew farmers in the high country swore by them. Our scatty mothers didn't like their white babies suddenly turning into red plastic ones and they bunted them away. We scrapped that idea. We found out later the coats have to be put on soon after birth, not when the lambs are two or three days old.

After being wet and cold all day, shifting sheep, feeding weak lambs and bringing others into the woolshed, I was always glad when it was time to start preparing the evening meal. One night my forehead pressed against the cold window pane as I watched for Joe. He had been out to the back of the farm checking stock. Through the rain sliding down the glass I saw the bike lights slowly coming down the farm road, made greasy from the constant rain we'd had. Off the hill and through the last gate he picked up speed. The lights flashed two or three times. That's my signal – he has a sick lamb aboard. I fill the tub with warm water and have the lamb reviver ready with warmed colostrum stolen from a ewe earlier in the day. The reviver is the most basic thing but it has saved so many lambs. It is a plastic cylinder which holds three ounces. A rubber stomach tube 16 inches long is joined to the bottom of it. Lambs too weak to drink often died when we attempted to bottle-feed them because the milk ran into their lungs. The tube allows the milk to run directly to the stomach. A "dead" lamb can be up on its feet 20 minutes after we have used the reviver.

Joe sloshed along the back path. He had the lamb tucked inside his coat to keep it warm.

"I had to lamb it. The mother was a stupid two-tooth. She took off. I've raddled her with red so we might find her tomorrow. She's in the hill paddock."

I took the cold, limp lamb from Joe. Its head lolled back but I felt the flutter of a heartbeat under my arm and heard the shallow breaths it dragged in. The mouth was cold when I put my fingers in to see if it would suck. The warm water came up around its entire body as it sank deep in the tub. When the water cooled, I let some out and replaced it with warmer water. I started to feel more life in this water-baby. It doesn't seem to bother a lamb how hard it's rubbed to dry it. The more stimulation it has the better it is. Dipping the end of the tube in milk makes it slide down into the stomach more easily. The warmed colostrum and lambs' replacement milk soon has the stomach bulging.

"Check that the hot water bottle isn't too hot for it," Joe said, "then put it by the fire." Before long the lamb made up its mind whether to live or not. It decided to live. It tried to stand but the front legs were still too weak to hold it up. The bleat sounded disgustingly loud for such a weak lamb. An hour later it was drinking milk from a bottle. We had won that round.

The children soon gave it a name but come morning this was one lamb that never became a pet. In bright sunshine we took it up to where Joe found it. A red raddled ewe was maa-ing frantically. Her udder was bursting with milk and nature was insisting she call for her missing baby. The freed lamb skipped over and with tail happily wagging suckled off its newly-found mother.

A ewe had been brought into the woolshed the day before. The weight of her full fleece from the heavy rain, and the fact she was heavily pregnant, had prevented her from getting up. She had been down for a couple of days and was very weak. To make matters worse, her swollen, reddened bearings protruded from her vulva. Joe had put them back but this morning they were out again and they were huge.

"You'd better inject another tube of penicillin and I'll have another go at putting them back," Joe said. With careful pressure Joe forced the urine from the bladder which is usually within the bearings, and this reduced the size. He cleaned the surface and while I held the ewe's back legs up he gently pushed them back in place.

"She's not far off lambing. She's an old sheep. I might have to kill her and take the lamb. I'll see how she goes this time."

That evening the bearings were out again. The sheep's condition had deteriorated. She lay panting, very sick and in pain. Euthanasia is kind, sometimes.

"Get your box with the hot water bottle and jerseys. I'll have to kill her. We might save the lamb. As soon as I've opened her up grab the lamb. You'll have to be quick or it will drown."

I turned away and attempted to shut down all my senses. I was a long, long way from my old life in Auckland. I heard the blood gurgling through the wooden gratings of the shed.

"Hurry, pull it out." The lamb was monstrous. I held it up by its back legs to let the fluid drain from the airways. It wasn't breathing.

"Slap it. Lie it down and slap it. Hard. Anything to revive it." It still didn't move. I squeezed down its muzzle to clear the mucus away, then it opened its mouth and puffed lightly.

"It's going to live. I can see it breathing." A faint bleat agreed with me. "You are a lucky chap," I told the lamb as I fed it the colostrum we milked from the sheep before Joe killed her. The name Lucky stuck. He became a pet, and, he believed, a member of the Heberley family.

After his shaky start in life Lucky never looked back. He arrived at the house with a belly full of colostrum, and snuggled up in my makeshift incubator that I kept ready for any weak or very sick lambs. In front of the fire, he soon became strong enough to investigate the heat source, and kept trying to jump out. He called out for milk and when he had swallowed that with great gusto he called out louder for company. As long as someone was close by and talked to him, he was content.

146

I was confronted with new house rules. Lucky must sleep in front of the fire tonight. He must be fed every two hours. He must have an extra blanket over him. "Don't forget he's been carved out, Mum, not born out." I could have sworn I saw a smirk on Lucky's face. His needs were met and for his first night he slept in his box, with my clothes basket turned upside down over the top of the box to keep him in. I refused to feed him during the night. I'd served my time feeding my own four babies so Helen and Pauline fed him whenever Lucky thought he needed feeding.

The next day I reminded the girls he was a lamb, and so he moved outside. He stood by the schoolroom window and joined in the lessons with his constant maa-ing.

"Lucky's hungry, Mum. I have to feed him."

"No, he isn't. He's just been fed."

"Well, why is he crying?"

"Just do your maths, Helen. He can be fed at lunch time."

Secretly I hoped we could find a ewe that had lost a lamb and we could mother Lucky on to it. The days slipped by and we never found a ewe desperately needing a lamb, so Lucky stayed. Slowly his metamorphosis took place. He wasn't a farm animal at all. He was human. His name – Lucky Heberley.

We had other pet lambs. They were fed together and lived as lambs should live – in a paddock. Lucky completely ignored them and wouldn't even drink from the feeder bucket with them. He expected his own private bottle. When he started eyeing my garden he was banished from the yard and sent out with the other pet lambs where I hoped he'd start acting like one. But he never joined in the lambs' games or raced around the paddock with them. He'd just sit and wait for Helen and Pauline to come and play. The girls spent hours with him. He grew into the most beautiful big lamb and the following year gave us the best hogget fleece on the farm.

The bigger he grew, the bigger menace he became. He was the boss of all the other pet sheep. If they were in his way he rudely bunted them away. He stood no nonsense.

Our front gate is a pipe gate covered in wire. Lucky still believed he lived in the gold Summerhill Stone house on the hill and whenever he felt like visiting he'd stroll up to the gate, poke his nose through a mesh and pull his head sharply back. The gate would swing open and he'd slip in. If our back door was shut he'd stand outside and maa until it opened. In he'd rush and stand pawing at the door of my store cupboard, waiting for his round wine biscuit. He only ever came in as far as the cupboard but until he was given a biscuit he wouldn't budge. If I didn't want to feed him, the only way to get him out was by force and I'd have to slide him out the doorway. But if he was given a biscuit he'd take himself outside quite happily and plonk himself down on the grass outside.

One day on his way in for his morning tea he was side-tracked and tasted the carnations I'd at last got growing up the front path. He loved them. That did it. Whenever he felt like greens other than lush grass – and it seemed like every few minutes – he'd open the gate and help himself.

"That sheep goes out the back paddock or I'll kill it," I angrily told whoever might be listening. Everyone knew Mum wouldn't kill anything so I doubted if anyone heard. Something must have filtered through sound barriers, however, because the next day a chain was put on the gate. Lucky stood outside, trying to open it as usual, and couldn't understand why it wouldn't spring open. He at last gave up and wandered forlornly up behind the house, lay down on the grass with his head on his front hooves and stared in the window at us, a dejected look on his face. In fact he looked so miserable that I felt like a cruel and rejecting mother, and only the thought of my hard-won garden stopped me from taking off that chain.

Like a dog, he would follow Helen and Pauline whenever he could. The Owen family lived in Fishing Bay where Peranos' whaling station had been. Our girls often visited their four daughters at weekends. It was a good hike over the hill from Okukari. At low tide they were able to walk around the rocks between our place and Whekenui. A good road led from Whekenui to the whaling station. It took them an hour.

On this particular day Lucky decided to go visiting with them. I watched their slow progress up the hill. After the drama on their way home, Mary Had A Little Lamb was rewritten:

> Helen and Pauline had a sheep
> Its fleece was white as snow
> He thought he was a Heberley
> So with the kids he'd go.
> He followed them to Owens' one day
> His steps they didn't falter
> But coming back around the rocks
> He fell into the water.
> He would have drowned if Grandpapa
> Had not seen him and quickly rowed
> To pluck him out of the sea that day
> To him his life he owed.

It was dreadful trying to get Lucky in the yards during sheep work time. He refused to go in with the common mob. We'd finally push him in and he'd stand disdainfully in one corner. At dipping time he'd have to be manhandled the whole distance along the race and into the dip. He'd dig his toes in at the edge and teeter on the brink before giving up the struggle against the enemy.

Then with a huge splash he'd begin his swim along to the other end. He was so fat he floated. His dunk under the water brought forth screams that Lucky was drowning and please save him, Dad. Joe would have to lift up his head with the crook and Lucky would ponderously swim to the end and crawl up the steep race to the draining pen.

But Lucky loved being shorn. As the belly wool was removed, beautiful white teeth grinned up at the astounded shearer. The cream wool peeled effortlessly off rolls of biscuits and carnations but with all his fleece gone he sulked, head hanging down, until he was let out of the shed and on his own again.

The years caught up with Lucky. He came to a sad end. Pig dogs that had wandered on to our property chased him. The girls found him stuck in mud. They dug him out but the cold and his old age, plus the unaccustomed exercise of running around the paddock trying to escape the bounding dogs, were all too much. Lucky died.

My tailing season follows my lambing season. The lambs are getting quite big when Joe announces at breakfast, "We'll start tailing today. We'll just do the mob on the flat and in the hill paddock. Tomorrow we'll muster, and tail the rest the following day."

Mustering ewes with young lambs is the worst muster of the year. Ewes take off, then dart back into the mob, anxiously looking for their youngsters. Lambs break and run off in a totally different direction. There are always six or seven in a group, with a ringleader. They tear all over the place like children in a playground when mothers are trying to get them home. Before tailing, lambs act like youngsters. In the late evening they chase each other up and down the paddocks, bound over the creeks, leap on to logs, then jump up and down on one spot. It's a lambs' world.

Once they are tailed the frolicking loses its enjoyment and overnight they grow into serious adolescents. Driving the mob over the paddock isn't too bad but trying to usher them into the yards creates havoc with the ewes and lambs. Everyone in the bay who can come to help does so, and with sacks, shirts, jerseys or anything we can find to wave around, we finally have them in the yards and can slam the gate shut.

The lambs are drafted off from the ewes and yarded ready for tailing. Mothers are put into the nearby paddock to wait impatiently for their offspring. The constant chorus of maas varying in pitch rolls off long pink-tipped tongues in wide-open mouths. Puzzled lambs don't understand why they can't rush straight to mum and have a drink. Just now they stand to cool down, to prevent bleeding when the tail is cut off with the searing iron. This leaves a clean sealed cut, usually with very little blood loss. Wood gathered off the beach burns well in the fire holding the three alternating irons. The smell of burning driftwood is much nicer in the nostrils than the cooked mutton smell, mixed with the singed wool emanating from the burnt-off tails.

My introduction to tailing was nothing short of barbaric. Picking up my first lamb I heard, "Hold it close in against your body. Sit the lamb up on its tail. Grab the back legs around the thighs and put them between the front legs."

Complicated as it sounded to me I did as I was told and discovered that I had good control of the wriggling body. One jab. I, too, felt that injection for anti-tetanus and pulpy kidney. Next, two square chunks were cut from its ear – the Okukari earmark. The lamb had had enough and leaped from my arms to find comfort from its mother. Joe roared at me, "If you'd held the damn thing properly it wouldn't have got away!"

"Shut up, or do it yourself. I didn't mean to let it go. You'd be off too if you had the same treatment."

The unfinished lamb was pushed back into my arms. "Slide it back so the tail lies across the board." The searing iron, red embers sticking to it and blackening in the colder air, sizzles off the tail. My buttock muscles tighten involuntarily as I feel its pain. This one is lucky. It's female and doesn't have to be castrated.

The day moves into late afternoon. The routine stays the same. Pick up a lamb, slide it along the torture line and drop it into the yard so it can find its mum. The black lamb has the advantage today. His mother finds him immediately and no doubt a drink eases the pain. One old ewe with a huge udder soon has her twins back and quickly takes them out of the noise to lick and soothe them gently. Other lambs try to sneak a comfort drink from any ewe. They are rudely bunted away if they don't belong. Pain causes some of the lambs to pig-jump in reverse in an attempt to get away from the hurt. Others lie still, waiting for their mothers.

Nowadays we castrate the ram lambs using an elastorator and rubber rings, but during the first years I was here a knife was used to cut the tip off the scrotum, and the testicles were pulled out. A farm hand working for my father-in-law was a smart alec and I believe he played on my towniness. I'd look away rather than watch that operation. He delighted in the screwed-up faces I unconsciously pulled. Without warning he bent his head and bit the testicles out with his teeth, then spat them at my feet. Saliva filled my mouth. I felt sick and disgusted. "Lots of old hands do it that way," said Charlie. "The fingers get pretty sore pulling them out by the end of the day."

It certainly didn't appease me. It was the closest thing to cannibalism I had ever encountered. I struggled through my tailing apprenticeship, and, now I've completed my time, I don't hold the lambs very often. I tell my family I'm on the boss's side of the fence now and I enjoy being able to inoculate the lambs.

150

As freak births happen in humans, so they happen in sheep. I was on the lambing beat when I came across a ewe having trouble lambing. Only a head was presented. No feelings of fear now, I knelt next to her to deliver her lamb. I couldn't lamb her. I had the two front legs out but no way was anything else going to appear. Up inside her I felt another lamb. But something was definitely wrong here. I knew Joe was due in from fishing shortly so I left her. When he arrived in I picked him up on the bike and we went back up the hill to see what he could do. The lamb we could see was now obviously dead. "See if the other lamb inside is alive," Joe said. It was. I could feel its heart beat.

"I don't suppose she has Siamese twins inside?"

"Don't be stupid. I've never seen a sheep with them." So Joe killed the ewe. We thought we might have one lamb to rear. When he opened her up I couldn't believe what was in front of my eyes. Lots of arms and legs. One head was already out but there was another lamb with enough arms and legs to make one whole. I tried to remove it from the uterus. I couldn't. It was joined to the other lamb. We had perfect Siamese twins. They were joined from the brisket to the umbilical cord. Of course Joe had never seen this before. A ewe would have died lambing, and he may have found her at some stage and presumed she'd died while having a lamb. Who knows?

These twins, although dead, were exciting. By then Pauline was at Massey University studying veterinary science. "Perhaps Massey might like to have them," I suggested to Joe. A quick phone call affirmed this. We carefully placed them in the bait freezer on the end of the wharf. Pauline had said if we could courier them up to Palmerston North she would pick them up and take them to Massey. I rang a courier. "Can you courier a parcel to Palmerston North, please?"

"No trouble, madam."

"There is a problem. You see it's frozen."

"No problem," the obliging voice at the end of the phone replied. "What is it?"

"A body." Silence. I realised my mistake. "It's actually Siamese twin lambs. We want to send them to Massey University."

"Oh. That's not a problem. Get them up to us and we'll deliver them to Palmerston for you."

They arrived in good shape and it was discovered they each had their own organs. Hence my feeling the heartbeat of the second lamb. They shared the stomach cavity. In humans, we were told, twins joined like this have an excellent survival rate.

We felt our lamb and ewe loss was not in vain if something could be learned from it at Massey.

CHAPTER FOURTEEN

The Power of the Sea

THE SEA. My friend and companion for as long as I can remember. Memories of night sailing in my Auckland girlhood sometimes crowd my mind and I think of the rushing sound the sea made as it swept along the smooth hull, becoming louder as we sailed faster. Now and then a wave would slap against the topsides and land with a plop on the deck, or there'd be the muted crack of a slackened line as it took the strain of a billowing headsail. The night sky draped over the sails and gathered the sea into it until there was no beginning and no end to my sea. I was as one with it.

But in such a short time a bright, smooth, sparkling sea can change to a dark menacing ocean, where giant swells gather force before thundering down into deep troughs, then building up to the next crest.

And it is not only the wind that can generate power to whip the sea into a frenzy. I've sat out on East Head at Tory Channel entrance and watched water seemingly run uphill as strong spring tides have tried to push vast amounts of water through the narrow opening. The seething mass of water is a feeding place for hundreds of sea birds as they scavenge among what is brought to the surface. In the rip formed where the channel waters meet Cook Strait, waves build up out of nowhere even on a calm day, and, when we have a southerly gale, the rip can become a nightmare for the inexperienced boatie.

When I was a little girl I used to lie in the bath and slowly lift my feet until my toes were just popping out of the water. I imagined they were jagged rocks, waiting for a boat to sail over. They'd claw the boat and rip it open. But when the game ended it was only my toes that sank to the bottom of the bath.

When I've been out crayfishing, where they work close to the land and among rocks, I've watched in trepidation as our stern has swept over rocks, so close that I've been able to see the paua, and I've found myself holding my breath until we are clear. The rocks are my long-ago toes in the bath, waiting to tear the bottom out of our boat.

In all this the sea has remained my friend, in spite of its dangers.

With all the call-outs Joe has been involved in, I can always tell what the outcome has been by the way he walks up to the house, or, if it is dark, by the sound of his footsteps. It makes little difference whether or not we know the people. A rescue or a tragedy at sea makes us aware that next time it could be ourselves in trouble.

If the weather is threatening and you see a small boat that looks as if it's heading out into Cook Strait, should you or shouldn't you drop what you're doing and try to get out and intervene? So much, of course, depends on circumstances. Once or twice we've been wretched because – in hindsight – we realised we should have acted, and we hadn't.

One incident involved a small sailing dinghy that had attempted to sail across Cook Strait in the face of a northerly gale. We had noticed it sail past our bay earlier in the day and Joe had remarked how ridiculous it was to be out in a small boat like that in gale conditions.

We were horrified when we had a phone call from the police later that same afternoon, to say the boat was missing. Could Joe go and look for it? The upturned boat was soon spotted but the two occupants were never found.

"Why didn't I go out and try to stop them?" Joe kept asking himself. As I tried to comfort him by saying they probably wouldn't have listened to him anyway, I wondered why I hadn't said he should go out and warn them.

Then again, living at the entrance to Cook Strait and seeing boats passing by has its useful side. When the police have called to tell us a boat is overdue from a trip in the strait, it's wonderful to be able to tell them we have seen it come in the channel.

The years have seen many diving alarms. Most have turned out happily when the missing divers have been found, usually great distances away from where they'd entered the water. The strength of the currents in Cook Strait are often misjudged. Joe's years of fishing in the strait make him useful here. He can read the conditions and calculate the best place to start searching.

A sad search was carried out at the end of 1994. It was a perfect day with ideal diving conditions, but the diver failed to surface where he had been diving at Stella Rock near Koamaru. We knew the diver, and, even though time had gone by and everyone knew there was no hope of finding him alive, Joe stayed and assisted at the scene all day, searching a calm sparkling sea in case the body floated to the surface. The diver was later found on the sea floor.

As I waited at home, the mother in me worried that Young Joe might go diving in the search. I knew he'd want to, but I also knew he hadn't dived for some time and the water around Stella Rock is deep. I breathed a selfish sigh of relief when I heard orders come over the VHF from the police dive squad in Wellington, saying that no more searchers were to enter the water. The missing diver's air supply was exhausted and there was no hope of finding him alive, so no more lives were to be put in jeopardy.

As I felt the sorrow of his wife and family who were aboard the boat from which he'd gone missing, I found myself questioning, yet again, my love of the sea when it can be so cruel.

A large crowd had gathered on the Picton Foreshore and the Waitohi Wharf to watch the cruise ship *Mikhail Lermontov*, with her crew of 330 together with 408 passengers, slowly steam out of Picton Harbour on 16 February 1986. Envy was in many people's eyes as they called farewells to the excited passengers. Joe and I knew people on board and we thought of them as they left their home town behind.

A fresh southerly developed during the afternoon and gradually freshened to 25 knots. In my kitchen the VHF was turned on. Scanning channels 16 and 63, I was so certain that I heard a message saying the *Mikhail Lermontov* had hit rocks off Cape Jackson that I glanced at the clock and noted it was 5.20pm. The disbelief in Joe's voice when I told him nearly made me think I'd imagined it. "No," he said. "It couldn't possibly happen."

But after that he stayed very close to the VHF. A short time later Joe rang the Bakers at Cape Jackson. They had taken over Picton Association Radio from Mrs Kenny in the early 1980s, and ran the base radio from their home. David Baker's words, "If a boat is bow down, stern up, I'd say she was in serious trouble, wouldn't you?" confirmed what I'd heard on the VHF.

David had gone on to tell Joe that he'd been out on the hill and had seen the *Mikhail Lermontov* making her way slowly into Port Gore. "We watched her for a good 20 minutes. I tell you, Joe, it looks bad."

"Is any assistance needed? We can get away now. The wind has freshened in the last hour and it's raining quite heavily."

"No thanks, Joe. A Mayday hasn't been sent out. They've said no help is required so therefore Search and Rescue won't swing into action."

"I'll keep in touch anyway," Joe replied. We hugged the VHF. Other boats were aware of an impending disaster. But still the words, Mayday, Mayday, Mayday were not sent. The Bakers later spoke out about the frustration they'd felt, knowing the situation but not being able to get Search and Rescue to come in because no official Mayday had been given. Betty and Tony Baker decided to alert the local fishermen and they had 23 small boats, private and fishing, standing by.

At last, after being in contact with Wellington Radio, the Bakers themselves declared a Mayday situation.

The senior Bakers, Betty and Tony, controlled the operation. David Baker steamed to Port Gore in the wake of the troubled *Mikhail Lermontov*. Joe, James and Young Joe had left even before the Mayday emergency was declared. "Eric and Phil Wilkes are on that boat. I'm going. Coming?"

"I'd love to, but not this time. If it's a situation where you're ferrying passengers off a sinking ship, if I'm there it'd mean one less you'd be able to carry."

The New Zealand Rail ferry *Arahura*, scheduled to leave Picton at 8pm, was diverted to Port Gore and arrived at 9.30. The LPG vessel *Tarihiko* had been sheltering behind the Rangitotos, 10-12 miles from Port Gore. They heard the VHF conversations and although there wasn't a Search and Rescue situation in place, they came down and stood by the sinking ship. The captain of the *Mikhail Lermontov* had tried to run her aground in the head of Port Gore, but with a gash in her port side 40 feet long and three watertight bulkheads ripped through, seawater flooding in had short-circuited the electrics, the engines had stopped, and the wind had blown her back out into the deeper water of Port Gore.

The night was pitch black, very cold, with a strong southerly and rain blowing straight out of Port Gore. When our boys arrived she was listing heavily and was obviously going to sink. At 8.45pm passengers were ordered to abandon ship. Many elderly people were hurt in their leap from ship to lifeboats. Joe and the boys were asked to locate and take in tow the lifeboats that drifted around the bay. Terrified passengers scrambling on board the *Tarihiko*, and later the *Arahura*, had allowed the lifeboats to drift off so that space was left for the next one to come alongside. Lifeboats and liferafts were all over the bay and the strong wind was taking them out to sea. There was concern that one might be blown out with people still aboard.

The noise was deafening at 10.27pm when the *Mikhail Lermontov* sank to the bottom of Port Gore, 35 miles from Picton. She'd had a list for some time, and as the bow gradually sank down in the sea the stern rose higher. The bow hit the seabed, the stern settled and she rolled on her side beneath the surface. Bubbles more than six feet high belched from the sea, and anything loose on the ship shot to the surface, leaped in the air and then smacked down on the surface of the water. The sounds reverberating from the bowels of the ship were imprinted on my men's minds forever.

Dave Fishburn gave me his impressions of that night. "It was an amazing experience seeing a ship go down. The crashing, banging, hissing, roaring – it was deafening. Then it died. Nothing. Quiet."

At home I'd sat in front of the fire, listening to the VHF. Once close to Port Gore the boats worked a frequency that I couldn't pick up so I had no idea what was happening, and the wind and rain hammering against the windows did nothing to lessen my fears. Joe had called me earlier and told me it was so black they were going up the coast on radar. Now I could only imagine events, and to a wife and a mother they were always the worst. When a news bulletin on the radio told me and the rest of the world of the sinking, I was even more anxious for news of my family.

At last, at 4am, Tony Baker phoned me from Cape Jackson. He'd been speaking to his son, David, and the message from Joe was that everyone was fine and I'd see them later in the day.

All night debris from the ship was picked up, and the next morning nature had dressed Port Gore in a perfect summer's day. Joe said the water above the *Mikhail Lermontov* was a seething mass of little bubbles and looked just like soda water. A scum lay over the surface and hundreds of deck chairs floated around the bay. He said the surface of the water was covered with anything off the ship that could float, and many places in the Sounds had wooden-slatted chairs on sundecks and balconies for the next few years. Joe and the boys were given the task of towing four lifeboats to Picton. The boats were put into the harbour board compound under lock and key until the Marine Department held its inquiry.

There was a lot of criticism of the state of the lifesaving equipment carried on the *Mikhail Lermontov*. Many of the locals towed in lifeboats. They saw for themselves.

Peter McManaway has been running his own boat building business in Picton for many years and he spoke out about it. "In many of the lifeboats bilge pumps were inoperative. They were seized up and had handles missing. There was a radio shack in the bow of one, and it had a hole, one and a half inches by three-eighths of an inch, where battery acid had leaked and eaten through the aluminium. One of the enclosed boats had the exhaust disconnected from the hull and the exhaust discharged into the interior. Many of the lifejackets picked up in Port Gore fell to pieces, the fabric covering them was so rotten. Water containers in the lifeboats had holes in them, and in some of the lifeboats they'd been painted in place. It was hard to find one in good condition."

With all this in front of their eyes, those involved closely in the rescue were stunned when the statement from the Minister of Transport, Richard Prebble, was released. "Allegations made subsequently, concerning deficiencies in the *Lermontov's* lifesaving appliances, have not been borne out by the evidence presented to the inquiry."

Today the 20,000-tonne *Mikhail Lermontov* lies beneath the surface of Port Gore, the grave of one Russian engineer, and the cause of four amateur divers' deaths.

Three months after the sinking of the *Mikhail Lermontov*, my sister Betty was visiting us from Auckland. We were sitting around the kitchen table yarning and enjoying a drink when 19-year-old James stunned us all by saying what was obviously preying on his mind. "Auntie," he suddenly said, "have you ever seen a big ship go down?"

"No, James. I haven't."

I doubt if many people have.

The Baker family became the voices that reassured many boaties and controlled many searches and rescues until they left Cape Jackson on 29 June 1993.

With David their son and his wife Sandra they had kept a listening watch daily. Betty Baker maintained a quiet dignity, and expected and received a high standard of language on the airways. The culmination of this dedication was in 1988 when both Betty and Tony received the Queen's Service Medal.

Betty Baker died on 16 July 1990 after a long battle with cancer. The day of her funeral service in Picton was not unlike the day when the *Mikhail Lermontov* sank, but southerly winds and heavy rain kept very few people from the Sounds away. The church overflowed with mourners and I was privileged to play the organ for this great lady. Many there knew her only through her voice.

"Can't you hear your phone? The *Cook Canyon's* hit the rocks." James's strident voice and the banging against our bedroom window had Joe and me awake immediately. "Your phone's been ringing for ages. Picton Police. She's hit in Wellington Bay."

Joe ran down the hall, pulling his clothes on as he went. This time I wasn't staying home. When I reached the kitchen he'd phoned the police and contacted Ron Smith of Wellington's Cobar Radio on the VHF to let him know we were on our way, and within minutes he was gone, his voice yelling at me to hurry up if I was coming. I glanced at the clock – 12.04am. It was 28 March 1992.

While James had brought the *Fugitive* in from the moorings in our bay, Joe, Young Joe and crew man Darryl Henson had carried the two-inch fire pump along the wharf. As soon as the boat nudged in we all leaped on, lifted the pump on board and steamed out the bay.

On the opposite side of the channel, Scraggy Light flashed its intermittent white light, while the leading lights in Whekenui Bay, Winkie and Blinkie as Charles Godfrey, their first keeper, had affectionately named them, lit up our starboard side. Out in the middle of the channel I felt the push of the tide as it caught under our stern, increasing our speed an extra knot or two. On East Head the red sector light opened to green and we safely headed out into the open sea before turning north.

Joe called Ron Smith on the VHF to let him know we'd be with the *Cook Canyon* in approximately 10-15 minutes. Ron's grim-sounding voice crackled over the airways. "She's making water fast, Joe. I don't like the sound of it – 85 feet of steel slamming into rocks at nine or ten knots. She's got a guts full of hoki and I believe she carries 60-70 tonnes."

In the cabin everyone's face picked up a green hue from the light of the radar as the scanner swept around the screen, searching the darkness for the stricken vessel which would show up on the screen as a blob.

The inhospitable cliffs blocked out the stars as we steamed past. Trees brought to their knees by the prevailing winds grew blackly on the skyline.

It was along this coast that the *City of Newcastle*, a three-masted barque 132 feet long, had foundered in 1872, and looking at the sheer coastline I shuddered as I imagined the fear of those on board. I knew that three children and four women passengers had been lowered into a lifeboat in the darkness with three seamen off the sinking ship. There were no more lifeboats and of the six people who'd remained on the boat, two had drowned while trying to reach the shore.

We were drawing closer to the *Cook Canyon*. It was a fine night. A fresh breeze from the north-west blew out of Wellington Bay and there was only a slight sea running, but all other luck had apparently run out when she had hit land on her way back to her home port of Nelson.

"I've picked her up. Right in the head of the bay. Should see her ourselves soon." James's voice brought me back to the present.

Joe came up to me where I stood in the doorway of the wheelhouse. "When we get alongside of her, Darryl and James and I will go aboard with the pump. You stay and give Young Joe a hand. You'll have to try and tow her out from the rocks a bit, Joe."

As our eyes picked her up, looming out of the darkness, we could see she certainly had a lot of water on board. Her bow was extremely low in the water and her stern was well out.

Four scared faces leaned over the rail as Young Joe steamed the *Fugitive* in close to the *Cook Canyon*. She wallowed in the low southerly swell, the water aboard her obvious by the slow return she made to an upright position as she rolled from side to side.

When the gap between the boats closed the three men clambered aboard the *Cook Canyon* and the fire pump was passed to them. The roar of the *Fugitive's* engine reverberated around Wellington Bay when Young Joe slammed the throttle down to clear the *Cook Canyon* as she rolled in towards us. "Steer her on this course, Mum," I was told, when Joe slowed the engine down. "I'll get the tow-rope ready and take the boat in close, then you take over. I'll throw the rope to whoever's on the bow."

As we came in closer I could see that in the short space of time it had taken Joe to ready the tow-rope, the *Cook Canyon* had settled further down in the sea. I tried not to think what would happen to my husband and James, Darryl and the crew of the boat as I visualised her capsizing with each sluggish roll she made.

Joe stood on the back deck and yelled out directions for me to steer, and with his first throw we were joined to the *Cook Canyon* by a 20-fathom towline. "Head straight out the bay. I'll keep an eye on things out here until we get under way."

Looking over my shoulder I could see her silhouette yawing as she straightened out the line, jerked, then bore down on us from the opposite side until the slack rope tightened once more and the lumbering hull shuddered, before bearing down on us again.

One of the crew called us on the VHF to let us know the fire pump was going but it was barely holding its own. The forward compartment was full of water, and water coming up the stairs had flooded the galley which was situated beneath the bridge. Here there was a foot of water sloshing over the floor – enough to slide the deep freeze from side to side and crash it against the walls.

We were told a bigger vessel, the Physalie, was on her way and would be with us shortly to take over the tow, and also that the police boat from Picton was bringing down a four-inch pump belonging to the Picton Fire Brigade.

The slow tow continued through the darkness and by the time the Physalie arrived we could see the lights at the entrance of Tory Channel. We handed over the towing to the bigger and more powerful boat and before long they were inside the channel where the police boat met them. There they transferred the pump with the fire brigade crew to the *Cook Canyon*.

Darryl Henson is a commercial diver and Young Joe has his diving ticket, and the idea was for the boat to come in to Okukari Bay out of the tide when Joe and Darryl would dive down to find out the extent of the damage to her hull. Joe and I came in on the *Fugitive* to collect his and Darryl's diving gear so they were ready to dive as soon as the boat arrived. I had no ambition to watch for tell-tale bubbles I wouldn't be able to see in the dark – bubbles telling me the two divers were okay – so I jumped ship and went home to sit in the dark, to watch and worry from my lounge window.

Daylight was breaking, pink fingers wiping across the sky and warning us that unsettled weather was coming, by the time the *Cook Canyon* was able to set off down the channel towards Picton. She was towed by the Physalie and escorted by the *Fugitive*.

Later that same afternoon I heard the rest of the story from Young Joe. "It was my first night dive and beyond the glow from the underwater torch I was amazed at so many sea creatures. They were lit up with the phosphorescence in the water as they wriggled and slithered out of our way."

The ship's stem had a split eight feet long, and this split varied in width from one to six inches, he said. They stuffed blankets, towels, sheets – anything they could lay their hands on – into the hole from the outside. Lots of the things they used were sucked straight into the hole, such was the suction with the pumps working from the inside and the water rushing in the gaping hole from the outside. Once they'd stuffed enough in the hole and the pumps started to make headway, they climbed out and the trip to Picton began.

Halfway to Picton they could see that their repair work was failing as the pumps weren't able to keep up with the water again. Darryl and Joe were over the side and the last of their blankets and linen was used as packing. These repairs got the *Cook Canyon* to Picton where more permanent repairs could be carried out. Tired men arrived home just on dark.

But far from being pleased that they'd rescued the boat and there wasn't any loss of life, Joe was livid about our telephone system. "It could have been a tragedy. That boat could have sunk in the time it took to get hold of us," he maintained.

As we were on a party line, sharing it with three others, any extra phones in the house had to have two large batteries to generate the rings. We had an extension phone in our office next to the bedroom so we could hear the phone if it rang during the night on occasions such as the *Cook Canyon* rescue. The phone hadn't been ringing in the office for some time, and after complaining to Telecom we were told the batteries were no longer available. Joe tried to explain the situation and why it was imperative that we heard the phone ringing in the office, but this fell on deaf ears.

"I only hope they don't need help some night and I can't hear the phone ringing," Joe had muttered.

"I might ring the police. If they want me in the Search and Rescue, something's got to be done smartly."

It was. The following week we found ourselves on a private line with not only the phone ringing in the office, but a telephone alongside the bed. We could sleep easier knowing that the police could get hold of us at any time in an emergency. Not that we liked the shrill ring of our newly installed telephone. News in the night isn't often good news.

Labour Weekend 1992 is a weekend the Heberleys will not forget. Years on, and I still get churned up thinking about it. We were woken up with the phone ringing at 1.20am on Labour Day. Auckland Radio passed on a distress call from a Picton fishing boat which had run aground on Dieffenbach Point. Joe and the boys left on the *Fugitive*, gave assistance until the boat floated on the rising tide, and arrived home at 8am. Gale force southerlies were predicted to come in later, and crayfish pots were in close to the shore, so after a quick meal they left to go fishing.

When a southerly is close my painting changes dramatically. Bulging black clouds appear over the hills at the end of Tory Channel opposite Wirikarapa light. They rise higher in the sky and the sea beneath them changes from its usual blue-green to black. Wind that was earlier on the water dies, and a sombre stillness pervades. The southerly hits. Clouds race down the hills and hit the water. Boats fishing in the channel realise there is a wind change and pull the anchor up to run for cover. They hit the wind and are tossed around. Huge sheets of spray are thrown over their bows. Pushing the sea before it, the wind roars into our bay. Waves crash on the beach, and the wind drives clouds of sand up the flats.

That day the southerly hit at 11am. I knew the fishermen would be home soon but I am always anxious until I hear the boat. At 11.30 the *Fugitive* surfed into the bay and I could relax.

"I don't really mind having to come in early. I'm buggered. The early start's caught up with me. Did you see that yacht? It was going out the channel as we came in." Joe stretched out on the window seat as he spoke. I hadn't noticed it, but I don't think he heard my reply. He was asleep.

Wind gusts up to 45 knots lashed against the window panes. Litter off the beach was picked up and bowled along the grass in the wind.

"Mayday! Mayday! Mayday!" echoed around the kitchen. Joe never stirred. This is one time he would have to be woken up.

David Baker from Cape Jackson Radio answered the call, found out the particulars and rang Joe, who was well and truly awake by now. The yacht he had passed going out when they were coming in was in trouble. The fire extinguisher had fallen over and been set off, and its foam had smothered the engine. Then the sails had blown out.

"That's the clown we passed on our way in. It'd got far too tough for us, so why he went out is beyond me, Dave. James isn't home but Young Joe is. We'll go now."

"You can't go out in this. It's crazy."

"We can't sit on our bums while some poor stupid bugger drowns himself, either."

Their engine sound was soon replaced with the savage sound of the wind and sea. I listened to their progress over the VHF. "The ebb tide rip is pretty bad out here. We'll give it a go," Joe reported to the Picton Police.

I hated the people who were putting my husband and a son in danger.

A gale warning had been issued on the marine radio channels at 8am and all morning more warnings had been issued. No one with any sense attempts to cross Cook Strait with the forecast we'd been receiving all day.

The VHF crackled its message from Joe. "We can't reach them. The seas are breaking right over us and pouring off the stern green. God knows what gear we've lost over the side."

I didn't know until Joe told me later that making that decision was hard, but turning the boat around in the heavy seas was harder. The ferry *Arahura* had cleared the channel entrance at 1pm and it stood by the stricken yacht for some time. The yachties refused to abandon the boat and be taken on board the ferry. Joe told the police they would make another attempt to reach the boat when the tide slackened in about an hour.

I didn't want to wait in the kitchen as I knew I'd have to listen to the VHF and so I rang Joy, Young Joe's wife. "I can't bear not knowing what's going on. I'm going out to the heads. Coming?"

From the hill overlooking the entrance Joy and I huddled on the hill, peering through the driving rain. The *Fugitive* sank in troughs so deep she disappeared, and as she climbed back up to the crest of a wave it crashed down on to the boat, to pour over the stern in a torrent of green. As the *Fugitive* leapt out of the water we could hear the roar of the exhaust above the noise of the storm.

There were three aspects of fear on the hill that afternoon. Joy's fear for her husband. My fear for my husband. My fear for my son.

If a boat was suddenly caught in a storm, that I could understand. After all, Cook Strait is notorious for its weather changes. But for people to go out in the face of a storm – this I couldn't and can't understand.

The *Fugitive* reached the yacht and took her in tow. They steamed south of the channel entrance to keep out of the rip and Joy and I watched as they turned and came up the south coast towards the foaming water at the entrance. Seas were breaking over West Head as two small dots tossed in the turbulent seas. Once they were in the calmer waters of Tory Channel, Joy and I headed for our homes.

Inside, on my own again, it suddenly hit me just how serious the rescue that Joy and I had watched had been. Our men's lives could have been lost that day. The more I thought about it the angrier I became. I remembered hearing the idiot telling the Picton Police on the VHF that it was only 20 knots or so out where they were – in the lee of the *Arahura* – when five minutes before Joe had advised the police it was 40-45 knots.

I worked myself up in to such a state that I was shaking when I picked up the phone to call Bill Gibb at the Picton Police. I knew Joe would ring him when he arrived home to give him his report. I also knew from past experience that Joe would downplay the seriousness of it. This time Bill was left in no doubt about my feelings and how atrocious the conditions were. It made me feel much better.

Joe put them on a spare mooring in our bay and invited them up to the house for a shower and a meal. Later two quite unrepentant sailors came to the door. They came inside and sat around our kitchen table, laughing and joking about their rescue. "We'd have been fine. You could have left us. I've done a few trips across."

"What about the other side? You'd have got hell in the rip at Karori Rock." I knew Joe was angry by the tone of his voice and I bit back on asking them why they'd sent out a Mayday if they were fine.

"My boat would've handled Karori rip. No worry."

I was glad when the phone rang. Joe could explode at any minute.

"Bill Gibb here, Heather. Can I speak to one of the sailors? Owner, please."

We knew Bill was furious as we could hear his voice over the phone as he spoke to the owner of the yacht, but after the conversation the man sat down at the table again, shrugged and said he couldn't understand why people were so mad with him.

They both had a shower, then a meal and sat back quite comfortably.

"Use the phone if you want to ring your families," Joe told them. Neither Joe nor I could understand why they didn't do that when they first arrived in the house.

"Yeah. S'pose I should."

That reply was the last straw. We were very pleased to say goodbye to the most uncaring, irresponsible and foolhardy visitors who've ever set foot in our house.

A week later while in town Joe was speaking to Peter McManaway and we heard the rest of the story. They'd got the engine of the yacht going and steamed in to Picton. It had been badly sprung in the seas and was an insurance job. The crew left the boat in Picton and sailed back to Wellington in one of the Cook Strait ferries.

The Tuesday morning after that Labour Weekend *The Picton Paper* phoned me. Wanting to cover the story of the rescue in Cook Strait, the editor had spoken to Bill Gibb. He'd told her to call Heather Heberley. "Get a woman's views on people like that who put her family in danger."

In the next edition of *The Picton Paper* we found Christine Cole Catley had written, under a front page headline of 'Foolhardy' a Gentle Word:

Many people who were involved or who have heard the Labour Day story of the two Wellington yachties who put lives at risk – by trying to get back home in a small yacht in extremely rough conditions – have contacted this paper in incredulity and anger.

Senior Constable Bill Gibb, not a man to mince words, thought he'd better mince them when it came to publication.

Heather Heberley of Okukari Bay, Tory Channel, whose older son and husband Joe risked their lives in the rescue, didn't have quite such inhibitions although she felt that she too should tone down what she really thought.

The eight-metre yacht was probably the only small boat to attempt to make the return Cook Strait crossing. Everyone else had listened to, and acted on, the weather reports.

Tony Baker at Cape Jackson picked up its Mayday at 12.39pm. Southerlies were gusting up to 45 knots and there was a strong tidal rip. The yacht's engine had seized and its two sails had blown out.

Fisherman Joe Heberley and his two sons had already been out once that day, from 1.20am in fact, when Auckland Radio passed on a distress call. A fishing boat had gone aground up the Sound. They did the necessary, and were back home by 8am.

For the second rescue of the day, Joe Heberley and his older son – the younger son was in Picton – went out in their fishing boat, *Fugitive*, to try to tow the stricken yacht back into Tory Channel. "The rip and the weather were simply too bad," Heather Heberley said. "And it takes a lot to make them turn back."

The ferry *Arahura* stood by for some time, and the Heberleys, knowing that the tide would be slackening, made another attempt about an hour after they had abandoned their first efforts.

"I told them I was coming out to watch from the land," Heather Heberley said. "I couldn't stand it, waiting at home." Joe told her later that conditions for the second attempt were calm compared with their first, "but I thought the weather was horrible. The waves were so big the boat would just disappear.

Something like this makes me so churned up."

It would be different, she said, if a yacht were suddenly caught in an unexpected storm. "But for people to go out deliberately, in a growing storm – no."

This time the yacht was able to be towed into Tory Channel. "They put the Heberleys at risk," Bill Gibb told TPP. Choosing his words carefully he added, "It was foolhardy in the extreme."

He paused. "I told them what I thought of them."

Daybreak on 8 June 1993 brought a most unusual request for assistance. *Sea-Tow 22* with barge 17 was on the rocks at East Head. Young Joe aboard the *Fugitive* had left to go fishing earlier than his father on the *Tineke*, and phoned up his father at home. "I think you'd better get out here, Dad. A Sea-Tow barge is in trouble. The tide caught her as the skipper was shortening the tow-line before turning in the channel. She's pushed hard against the rocks."

I left the breakfast dishes. I grabbed my camera and made sure I wasn't left behind. A quick phone call to James in his house, and the three of us were soon punching the strong flood tide, disturbing hundreds of sea birds enjoying their free ride into the Sounds on the fast-flowing tide. They screeched loudly as we passed by when they realised no fish scraps were coming their way.

Only five minutes from home and we were on the scene. A moderate southerly swell lifted the 240-foot-long barge, and then pounded her on to the rocks. We saw her shudder each time she hit. The barge was loaded up with scrap metal bound for the Glenbrook Steel Mill south of Auckland. An unbelievable load of worthless junk it looked, but I was told later it was insured for one million dollars – its value once melted down and made into reinforcing steel.

Our boat certainly could not offer power to tow it. The Sea-Tow tug had plenty of power but Joe and James had the local knowledge of tidal currents and the rocks on which it was hitting. We backed up to the tug and the skipper came aboard our boat so Joe could take him close in to view the damage and see where other submerged rocks lay. Until the tide slackened the barge wasn't going anywhere. After an inspection the skipper knew it was holed and making water. "How many people can you gather up, Joe? Can we start dumping some scrap over the side?

The Heberley men looked horrified. "Is that for real or a sick joke? Imagine that lying on the seabed. Apart from anything else it would ruin our fishing ground." During the crayfish season East Head has a lot of crayfish pots set around the area, and I knew Joe and James were visualising their $400 craypots tangled in among the dumped scrap metal.

We never received a reply. I've often wondered if they were unthinking words, spoken under stress – did the skipper really believe half a dozen men could dump the load over the side of the barge? Or was he cracking a joke to alleviate the situation?

Picton's harbourmaster, John Clark, and two divers were brought up from Picton. The 8am Interislander en route from Wellington to Picton was requested to slow down to prevent her wash causing more damage. On arrival, the divers inspected the damage from the inside of the barge. Their findings confirmed what the skipper thought.

"You'll have to be ready with lines," Joe yelled to the skipper from the barge, "because when the tide changes you'll only have half an hour or so of slack water. It's the only time you'll get to pull her off."

Joe stayed on the barge with some of the crew of the Sea-Tow tug and the harbourmaster. Aboard the *Tineke*, James and I stood off and watched.

The two engines generating 2500 horse power roared ahead and with the slack water she was able to pull the barge slowly off the rocks. As they began to tow into the channel, James and I counted seven steps up the side of the barge. Progress was slow and gradually we could see the steps getting fewer. Water was entering rapidly. Everyone on board was wearing life jackets except Joe. "If she goes down she'll sink low in the water, then roll over," I was told.

God, I thought to myself. Surely I didn't come out to watch my husband drown?

Two more steps disappeared. The barge hardly seemed to be moving now. As our bay came into view it was decided to take her in as far as they could. It was the top of the tide and they hoped a better assessment of the damage could be carried out when it was low tide. *Sea-Tow 22* towed its barge in until it settled on the sandy bottom. I noticed all the steps had gone from view. A tow-rope was pulled ashore and our bulldozer was used as a shore mooring for the barge.

That afternoon Gary Kenny brought his barge out to Okukari with the equipment needed to repair her temporarily. Then once in Picton more permanent repairs could be undertaken.

But Port Marlborough didn't want the barge in Picton in case she sank. Something like this in Picton Harbour would be catastrophic.

We didn't want her to remain in our bay too long. We imagined 3000 tonnes of scrap metal stuck on our beach if a southerly came in. I had a good thought. Maybe I could add to the pile and get rid of some of our junk from the woolshed. Two or three dinghy loads would tidy the shed up nicely. I couldn't believe my ears when I overheard one of the crew asking Joe if he could see anything that he could make use of – some of their junk to add to ours.

"Take anything you want," Joe was told and I watched Joe's eyes as they moved over old bulldozer tracks, train bogies, aluminium steps and broken tools of every description. He decided there wasn't any treasure in that junk. We kept our woolshed treasures, and Sea-Tow kept theirs.

A head man from Sea-Tow Limited flew down and it was decided to pump air inside the barge, thereby forcing the water out, to leave her floating on a bubble of air. This satisfied the Port Authority and the following day she left for Picton, riding high on her bubble of air.

Life at Okukari returned to normal. I no longer had a painting with a mountain of scrap metal stuck in its foreground.

Looking down on the Heberley house sites in Okukari Bay, from the Big Ridge.

My merinos come off the barge from the sale at Blenheim.

Paul Palmer photographer.

Checking off the bales I had classed.

Paul Palmer photographer.

Joe and our dogs.

Paul Palmer photographer.

"Girls can do anything..." Pauline the vet maintains a check on our stock.
Carl and I watch from a distance. And Helen can shear.

Brothers James (left) and Joe prepare the hooks before the line is thrown out in the traditional way.

Young Joe and Joe cut up mackerel for line fishing.

Paul Palmer photographer.

Joe with some of his crays, and Tory Channel in the background.

Paul Palmer photographer.

*The ever-changing picture from my window often features two of the Cook
Strait ferries.*

Paul Palmer photographer.

Playing the organ at Pauline's wedding to Dene Wilson.

Graeme Dingle and Jo-anne Wilkinson, watched by Rachael and Haydn set off from our bay to paddle to Wellington.

My daughters-in-law, Joy and Lisa, repair our burst water line.

*The next generation. Our seven grandchildren, from left, on our farm bike:
Angela, Amanda, Glen, Carl, Haydn, Rachael and Danielle.*

*Family group in 1992. Helen, Pauline, Joe and I, with, in front from left,
James and Joe.*

CHAPTER FIFTEEN

Girls Can Do Anything

I'D HAD more than a taste of exams long before I got my wool handling certificate so I could help at shearing on the farm. That time the exam was to do with the sea.

"If you want to use the boat you're going to have to get your skipper's ticket."

It was a mail day in 1980. Joe was reading a letter from our boat insurance company. "It says a registered commercial fishing boat must have a skipper in charge with a Certificate of Competency."

I thought of the times I used the *Fugitive*. Tailing time, for instance. I always took the boat around to Wharehunga on the other side of Arapawa Island where we tailed our lambs. While I brought the boat down through Tory Channel and up Queen Charlotte Sound, Joe was mustering all the lambs off the block we leased. The boat was used to carry the gates, netting, standards and all the other equipment necessary to build make-shift yards that would hold sheep and everything needed to tail the lambs. There were other times, too, such as when the children came home from boarding school in the weekends I often took them in the boat to Picton on the Sunday night.

The boat was my car. Unless I obtained my ticket I was grounded. The new requirement said if I had an accident and damaged the boat, or if another boat ran into me – no insurance. If we still had our speedboat I could use that, weather permitting, as there were no rules laid down on the use of private pleasure boats. But I knew I couldn't count on the weather. I knew I had to go back to school, nautical school. I took deep breaths and said to myself, "I can do it, and I *will* do it."

The engineer's part of the ticket would be the most difficult so I'd sit that in Picton, then travel to Wellington and study for the nautical side at Pearce House, the headquarters of the Ministry of Transport, and while I was in Wellington I'd sit my first aid exam.

Joe had been required by a new law to sit his Second Class Diesel Engineer's Ticket a few years previously and he still had all the papers at home. "You might as well study for this. The more you know the easier it will be." I didn't need the Second Class Ticket but all the material was there. All I had to do was learn it.

Pauline was then our only child still at home on the Correspondence School roll so my time was not as stretched. I still had to fit this new type of learning around my other activities. Still, after a day spent supervising lessons, I never felt like learning. I discovered that early mornings, after Joe had left to go fishing, were my best times. I'd cook breakfast, see Joe out the door and race back to bed with my book. Quite a change from the historical romances I enjoyed. The generator would be turned off until I got up later and turned it on for electricity to do my housework. I studied by candlelight. I took it section by section and learnt each part of the engine well.

When Joe came in from fishing, conversation around our table suddenly changed. It was no longer about fishing and what sort of day he'd had, but about injectors, oil and fuel filters, or anything else I had studied that particular morning. When the engine room had cooled down after the hours of running it'd had, we'd go on board the boat and crawl around the engine, and Joe would patiently go over what I'd studied that morning. Although it was a totally new kind of learning, I enjoyed it. It took over my life completely. This was the first studying I'd done since I'd left school and I had to teach my mind to learn all over again.

One night I couldn't sleep and in my mind I was going over what I'd learnt. "Joe." I prodded him in the ribs to wake him up. "What pressure is built up in the engine when it's at full revs?" I didn't get a civil answer. He loved telling friends that all the romance had gone from his life since engines had become a large part of mine.

At last I ran out of excuses to make arrangements to sit for my ticket. The day came.

Fear of failure made my heart thump. I found myself tip-toeing along a brown mottled linoleum corridor lit by a single light bulb hanging from the fly-stained ceiling on a black wire. Details burnt into my mind. A brass plaque on one of the closed doors told me I was at the right place. I knocked.

"Come in."

"I'm Heather Heberley. I've come to sit my engineer's ticket."

"I gathered that. This place isn't exactly Paddington Station, you know." I'd heard he was sarcastic and believed women belonged at the kitchen sink, certainly not in charge of a fishing boat.

I took deep breaths to control the thumping in my throat. I knew this work. Joe had spent hours explaining our diesel engine workings to me. I hadn't crawled around a diesel motor changing filters for nothing, or studied by candlelight from 4am just for the fun of it. I will pass. I will. This little man won't get the better of me.

He sat behind a desk, his thinning hair plastered over his bald patch. Black horn-rimmed spectacles accentuated his pale complexion. He swung back on his chair, tapped his ballpoint pen on his bottom teeth and spoke.

"Right, Heather, why do you want your skipper's ticket so badly? Is Joe giving up fishing? Are you taking over?"

168

You sarcastic little shit, I thought. You know damn well why I have to have it. His left eye twitched. Joe had warned me. "Watch his twitch. If he gets annoyed it gets worse." Nervous laughter caught in my throat. I answered sweetly. "Insurance companies have brought in a new regulation. A commercial fishing boat must have a ticketed skipper in charge. If I want to keep using the boat I need my ticket."

His eye twitched. He pulled at his tie and unbuttoned the top button of his pale blue shirt. An open window would have made a difference in the room but the stack of dusty papers sitting on the window sill, with three dead blowflies lying on the top, told me fresh air didn't come from there.

More questions came and I answered. I tried not to count the twitches. Instead I studied the carpet and his black leather shoes. His light grey trousers had a patch of grease on one knee. The air became hotter. Beads of perspiration clung to his top lip and Brylcream oozed from his hair.

At last there was silence. I watched his face for a clue as to whether or not I'd passed. The twitches seemed the same. A half-smile.

"Congratulate Joe. He taught you well." His attitude to women wouldn't let him give me the credit for learning well. I didn't care. Half my ticket was under my belt. Next step was the nautical part, in Wellington. I'd show them.

Twelve days later Pauline and I were on the ferry bound for Wellington. The previous week we'd been mustering for dipping and all the sheep had been drafted ready for the sheep sales in Blenheim. I was on the race gate and a stroppy lamb charged the gate, found it was shut, leaped in the air and hit me on the cheekbone. I had the distinct impression no one believed me when I explained how I got my black eye. Pauline and I were staying with my cousin Jean in Khandallah. She was going to take over from me and teach Pauline her correspondence lessons. Pauline saw more of Wellington in the two weeks we were there than I have ever seen.

First thing on the Monday morning I arrived at the nautical school in Pearce House. I had nine classmates – all male. We had our eyesight test and then it was two days on our first aid, followed by the exam on Wednesday morning. Another part under my belt. Now it was only the nautical.

The afternoon of Wednesday 25 February 1981 is an afternoon I'll never forget. We found the room where we were to spend the next 10 days. Our instructor introduced himself. He was an English retired sea captain. Apparently so were all the others who ran the classes. From the very first words this man spoke it was obvious he did not approve of women doing what I was doing. He must have told us at least six times that afternoon that we could expect a 90 percent pass rate. One of us wouldn't pass – and his eyes always fell on me. He'd quick-fire questions around the room, point to someone, then another, without telling the previous person if he was right or wrong.

I still remember when I was totally confused and he roared at me, "You're

23 1/2 degrees abaft the beam. Are you an overtaking vessel?" I didn't have a clue what he was talking about, and I told him that's what I was there to find out. For the rest of the afternoon he kept on asking me questions. For half of them I had no idea of the answer. At the end of the day as I was going down in the lift I was finding it hard to stop myself from bursting into tears of frustration. "Never mind, Heather," one of the young men said. "If we've learnt nothing else this afternoon we've learnt your name." He understood how I felt. In fact over the next few days I learnt all the class supported me and wanted me to pass as much as I did myself.

Old habits die hard and I was up early studying – only this time I could switch on a light.

This second day I had a wonderful surprise. We had a different teacher. The one we'd had the day before was a stand-in. We still had him occasionally and his behaviour towards me never altered. He was of the old school and believed that women do not run boats. I was always being reminded of the failure rate.

On the day of the exam I was so determined to prove this teacher wrong I wasn't even nervous. I found my way to the Marine Department on The Terrace. Another sea captain was to be my examiner. Things seemed to be going well. I could manage the questions. I relaxed.

Then, "Heather, your boat runs on to rocks. It's dark, she's making water rapidly. You send out a Mayday. All lights have gone as water has covered the batteries. You want to let off a flare. You group around in the dark and find a smoke flare. Explain to me how you'd set it off. Remember, you can't see a thing."

Easy I thought, as I recalled how we'd done it in class. Then I stopped my thoughts. It's dark and it wouldn't be used at night – it's only used in daylight. "I wouldn't use it in the dark," I told him.

I wondered how many more trick questions I was going to be asked. "That's all," I was told. "You have your ticket."

I ran back to Pearce House. "How did you get on?" our usual teacher asked. "I've got it."

"Was he tough?" I told him about the smoke flare question.

"I've heard he sometimes slips in that question but not often."

"Probably saves it for females," I muttered to myself.

Pauline and I flew across Cook Strait to Blenheim. Joe was at Woodbourne to meet us and hear my news. I had my ticket but I felt sorry for the two who'd missed theirs. Our class pass rate had slipped. It was 80 percent.

CHAPTER SIXTEEN

The Biggest Change

ELECTRICITY came to Arapawa Island in 1982. It was costly both in money and lives. Residents in outlying areas of the Sounds already connected to the main grid were in a guarantee system where they paid for a set number of units whether they used them or not, and regular consumers used up their guarantee in a short time. On the other hand, a few bach owners purposely used power unnecessarily. Their excuse was "Why not? We're paying for it," thus making sure they weren't paying for something they didn't receive.

When Arapawa Island was reticulated, the Marlborough Electric Power Board had a new system in place. Guarantees were out and residents wanting power were going to have to pay dearly for it.

The cost of getting power to Arapawa Island hadn't been considered when members of the Tory Channel and Arapawa Island Association met with the Marlborough Electric Power Board for the first time on 17 April 1976, to ascertain what support there was for reticulation of electricity to the area. Our association was told we had to find out how many residents wanted to be reticulated. Then, if there was enough support, they might look into it.

A form was sent out to every landowner whether of a bach, permanent homestead, business or just a piece of land, and 55 people expressed an interest. The power board costed the scheme and the total outlay was estimated at $557,397. This included an undersea cable crossing and a three-phase line around the northern side of the island. It was decided the three-phase line was wasteful and if the site of the undersea cable was altered, the 3.15 km of three-phase line could be deleted. This reduced the estimated cost. We were told in June 1979 that it was $550,730. Half a million dollars. In the late 1970s this was still a huge sum – even for the boon of electricity – when there were so few of us.

Our association formed a committee of local residents and it was their job to work out costs and do the negotiating with the power board. Joe was on this committee and for the following three years the calendar hanging in the kitchen was covered in circled dates reminding Joe of his next meeting with either our committee or the power board. My two or three circles reminding me of school days in town seemed insignificant in comparison with the power circles.

The committee worked out a scale of payment for the capital contribution, and they'd separated baches, permanent houses, forestry operations (small and large), retired, semi-retired, farmers and boat builders. We were told reticulation had been allowed for in the costing.

A big circle was drawn around 1 August 1979. This was to be a meeting in Wellington with the Rural Electrical Reticulation Council and at this meeting our committee was told several times that if our reticulation went ahead it would be a 'guinea pig' scheme. It would need new guidelines, different from the old guarantee system.

All the committee's hard work was worth it when on 10 October a letter came from the power board to confirm that reticulation was to proceed on the basis of promises made by residents in our area.

My electric stove was getting closer. I dreamt of the days when my life wouldn't be ruled by the constant thump of the generator and having to wait for visitors to go to bed so we could run out and stop the power.

One visitor thought he had the answer. Joe and I were both wanting to go to bed after a particularly busy day, and in the end it got too much, especially as the visitor appeared to get more and more engrossed in television. When Joe told him he was going to stop the generator, his reply made our sagging bodies feel much lighter with laughter. "Okay, mate. I'll just sit in the dark and watch the end of the programme before I hit the sack."

Not long after we felt the reticulation of Arapawa was soon to become a reality, I was finishing my ironing before I turned the generator off and began to teach school for the day. I heard the engine surging before I noticed the kitchen lights dimming. It's running out of diesel, I thought as I ran the length of our back path to get to the engine in the shed to try to stop it with the switch before it stopped through lack of diesel. That would mean a laborious job of having to bleed it before it would start running again. I was capable of doing it, but it was a job avoided if I could.

Flames leaping off the top of the engine greeted me. Three feet above the engine there was a shelf, sodden with eight years of spilt diesel, and on this stood a 120-gallon drum holding diesel for the engine. Tongues of flame were hungrily licking the timber of the shelf around the bottom edge of the drum.

I flicked up the switch on the main switchboard for the lighting plant and waited for the engine to stop. It kept on chugging. The flames grew in size and intensity as they found more fuel to consume. I stripped off my baggy sweatshirt and dropped it on to the seat of the fire, hoping it might smother some of the flames. I could see it seemed to be burning from the box on the top of the engine that housed the electrical solenoid that started the motor. Pauline and James were yelling at me to get the hose. "No!" I screamed at them. "It's an electrical fire. We don't want water."

I found a couple of sacks in the shed and these finally smothered the flames but still the engine wouldn't stop. I was on my own and I didn't know what to do.

I raced inside to ring Gilbert Perano and ask him how I could stop the engine. As I reached for the phone it rang. "Gil here, Heather. I can see smoke pouring out your shed. Is everything okay?"

"No. The generator's on fire and I can't stop it."

"Heather," his calm voice came over the phone, "I'll be right over but in the meantime go out to the shed and knock the battery terminals off the batteries. That'll stop it."

I was terrified back out in the shed and my imagination worked overtime as I prised the terminals off the batteries. The smoke caught in my throat and made my eyes water. At last I won and the engine slowly came to a halt. Gil Perano arrived and helped me put out the last of the still smouldering fire, and I whispered quiet thanks under my breath for good neighbours, even if they were in the next bay.

Now we were without any power at all, and I was quickly calculating how long my deep freezer might hold out, and how long the freezer for cray bait would keep the bait frozen, as I didn't expect Joe home until mid-afternoon.

When he arrived in from fishing and had heard the story from James, Pauline and me, he assured us we'd have power by nightfall. "In time for Skippy?" was all Pauline wanted to know.

Since Joe's parents had moved to Nelson earlier in the year their lighting plant had sat in their shed. It needed only to be switched on and it would be away. "I'll run a line from their shed up to ours. When we put on the switch in their power shed the power'll feed back to our shed and we'll have power again." He put his power board hat on and with me pulling and heaving on the wire and passing the tools he needed we soon had a power line running between the two sheds. A power pole was erected temporarily (against the middle of the front fence and spoiling my painting for three years). It wasn't even straight but at least we did get power when Joe started up the generator.

Joe glowed in Pauline's praise as she watched her favourite television programme and we all enjoyed electric lights and hard ice cream.

The next morning Joe was up early and started the power so I could cook breakfast before he left to go fishing. "Don't stop it," I called to him as he walked down the front path on his way to the boat. "I'll stay up and get an early start on school."

The power was fine. Just like it had been when we'd been running our own generator. About 8am we were ready to start school and I set off to run down to my in-laws' shed to stop the generator. I should have slipped into shoes, I told myself when the heavy dew on the grass squeezed up between my bare toes. As I passed the tap on the front of our house I went to turn it on to let the hose run into the Para pool. Our sandy beach with its crystal-clear water looks so inviting but the water is freezing. A cold current of water flows up the eastern coast of the South Island and sweeps around our bay, bringing in the colder water. I couldn't stay in the water long enough to teach our children to swim so we put in the pool. With water all around us I knew I would feel much happier when four children could swim enough to save themselves. Now I reached for the tap.

The tap grabbed me. A huge jolt slammed through my body and I couldn't let go. Pulsating jolts kept me attached to the tap. I was aware of what was happening, and I felt myself becoming quite hysterical when I thought of how our friend Cedric Stewart was always saying how he couldn't believe our power from an engine is the same as town power.

I felt weak and knew I must let go, but I couldn't. Through a black haze I saw that my arm at the tap was rigid, and the tap appeared to be grasping my hand with all its might. I knew things were out of my control and it was up to someone else's intervention, if I was to get away from this.

Then, as suddenly as it grabbed me, it let me go and I fell on the ground.

I had burns on my feet and the fancy design of the tap was branded on the palm of my hand. All day my right side felt weak and I thanked God that one of the children hadn't touched it instead of me. They might not have been so lucky.

Joe was in deep trouble when he came home. My reaction had set in, and he bore the brunt of it. He threw his power board hat away and organised an electrician to come down, who quickly found the problem. The fire had burned the earth wire in the switchboard and we had no earth until I grabbed the tap. It made everyone in the bay very wary of electricity, and taught us all to treat it with respect.

Generator problems didn't seem so bad with the power board dangling its tantalising carrot in our sights. We were sent a circular dated 31 March 1980, which told us that "we are proceeding with the survey of the line routes and the purchasing of the necessary materials for the work. The work should be completed in approximately 18 months." After receiving this news many of the residents in our area had their electrical wiring upgraded in readiness for the power. Some purchased appliances.

But a nasty Christmas present was in store. Ken Forrest, the general manager of the Marlborough Electric Power Board, telephoned our secretary, and told him there were problems with two stages of the line. The Rural Electrical Reticulation Committee, or RERC, wanted to meet those affected. The mainland, on the opposite side of Tory Channel from Arapawa Island, would still be reticulated; but on Arapawa Island the section from Deep Bay to Okukari was the only part of the island which was to receive power.

At the meeting on 15 January 1981 we were told that because of increased costs the board had decided to defer all work on the island apart from the one section. "We feel we have a moral obligation to complete this," they said.

Our committee then met with the affected landowners and it was agreed to write to the board for estimates of the costs of each of the six stages of the line. We were given no figures and in April were told that the RERC couldn't make up its mind if the other stages were viable.

That day, 18 April, should have been ringed in black. At a meeting with representatives of the power board we were told the cost of the reticulation had escalated to $1.215 million. Power was not coming to Arapawa Island.

A ray of light broke through the gloom when the board gave us an alternative. They opted for a single wire, earth return scheme, with an overhead crossing, costed at $908,000 but it would mean the consumers would have to contribute an annual payment of $33,000, or about 200 per cent per customer. Our committee had to contact everyone who had earlier expressed an interest in having the power, and try to get an agreement from them within three weeks, as we were told that the construction had to begin immediately the contractor had completed the first stage on the mainland. With prospective consumers spread over New Zealand it was an impossible task, and all the hard work of our committee seemed to have been in vain. I looked at our calendar and felt like tearing it off the wall when I counted up all the meetings Joe had been to, but I knew it was all part of history.

The only way we were going to get power on to the island was if the RERC could increase its present subsidy of 13 percent. We received a letter from Ken Forrest telling us that the board would make an application for a greater subsidy when they had their next meeting with the RERC at the end of April. A subsidy of 15 per cent on the capital cost of reticulation for a period of 10 years was granted. Joe, with Adrian Perano, spent hours and hours working out a fair scale of payment, and, after many telephone calls and letters, we had a list of consumers with the amount they promised to pay to obtain the power.

An ordinary old mail day towards the end of July 1981 turned into one of celebration with a letter from the Marlborough Electric Power Board. The board had received approval from the RERC for a subsidy on the reticulation of Arapawa Island, and their contractor would be beginning construction there within the next few weeks. Enclosed were legal agreement forms for us to sign and return as soon as possible. Our next mail day couldn't come quickly enough for us to get them back to the power board.

George Lindstrom was the contractor. The reticulation of Arapawa Island was to be the last job George would do for the Marlborough Electric Power Board before his retirement. He was the biggest and one of the strongest men I'd ever met, and his laugh matched his size. With his son Terry and his crew of four or five men he stayed in one of the houses still standing at the whaling station. George bulldozed the roads so his green and white Landrover could reach the site they were working on each day, and every evening it bumped the men back to the whaling station where a flagon of rum was consumed over dinner. They worked hard and played hard.

They dug the holes for the power poles, blasting out many because of the hard terrain, and the poles were placed nearby. A helicopter picked them up and placed them in the holes ready for George and his crew to finish off the work.

One bach owner was always a very tidy Kiwi, and used one of the holes as a rubbish tip at the end of his holiday in his bay. This didn't please the men who had to clean the hole out or else dig another.

All the time our power was creeping closer. One still, fine day the helicopter flew in and lifted the transformers into place on the poles. Then came the time when George was on the ladder at the front of our house, running the wire from the hole to our house. I had just taken a pavlova out of my oven. "Where's mine?" his voice rumbled in the open window.

"When we are on the power I'll be delighted to make you 20," was my happy reply.

His huge hands gave me the thumbs up and his weatherbeaten face broke into a wide grin. "It's a deal."

Electricity had arrived to consumers on the mainland across Tory Channel. A Mr Fisher in Opua Bay was the first customer, then the forestry camp in the same bay, followed by the Agars in Te Weka, then on to Te Weu Weu Bay and Te Pangu Bay. Everyone followed the progress. In May 1982 the line on Arapawa Island was completed. All we needed was the joining of the two by the overhead cable.

The joining had to take place on a day when the tides were neap and there would be little tide movement, and no wind. Weather permitting, 4 April 1982 was to be the day. I circled that in red.

It was a perfect day. Joe and Adrian Perano were going to the site on the island where the lines were to be strung across. On Arapawa the site was above Te Iro, and across the channel it was above Te Weka. This place was selected because here the channel is narrow and the hills above Te Iro and Te Weka are very high.

Excitement was also high. I couldn't see why I couldn't go. "'Fraid not, love. It's a hard hat area, and we haven't enough hats." I was peeved with Joe's reply and he knew it. All the children were at school or away and I was going to be left at home again.

"Take the *Fugitive* up. That's why you got your ticket, isn't it? So use it. Pick up some of the wives on the way and you can watch from the water." I loved Joe's reply. Soon Okukari Bay was deserted and Robyn Perano and Mary Kirk and I were on our way to watch the culmination of all our hard work.

We anchored the boat in a small bay below the crossing, making sure we had the best possible view. This was history in the making, much more exciting than the Americans putting men on the moon. We weren't going to miss any part of it.

From our vantage point we could see the nylon rope snaking through the scrub from the water's edge to the three poles, and braking equipment with the drum of wire on the mainland, and from the water's edge to the three poles and pulling equipment with an empty drum on Arapawa. The rope had been flown in a few days previously by helicopter and placed in position.

With Joe being so involved in the battle to get our power I had learned a lot about our line and where our money was going. I'd read that the wire (conductor) was made up of seven strands so it had to be kept out of the sea or corrosion would set in. The rope was fastened to the pulling and braking equipment and at the beach on each side of the channel two boats took the ends. Then they met in the middle of the channel and shackled them together. The rope was pulled taut by the pulling gear on Arapawa. At the top of the hill on the mainland the wire was fastened to the nylon rope. Tension was on the rope at all times as the braking equipment held it back, while the rope followed by the wire was pulled and slowly wrapped around the drum on the island. Arapawa Island was linked to the mainland by a length of wire that measured one and a quarter miles.

The first wire was hooked to one of the poles, each of which was made up of two 40-foot concrete poles bolted together, and which was seven feet into the ground. The process was repeated three times, and immediately the poles were painted the regulation orange and white stripes required by civil aviation.

The timing for the wires to be lifted had been controlled by the Cook Strait ferry crossings. From the hill on the mainland site the ferries could be seen until they entered Tory Channel. After that the radio telephone kept the men informed of their progress. The channel had to be clear when any ferry was due. If a ferry was coming from Picton, only the radio telephone warned the men when it was due at the crossing.

On the *Fugitive* we ceremonially raised three glasses of champagne as we cruised under the power lines before leaving for home. We felt we were specially celebrating for all the women on the island.

On our way home Mary, Robyn and I decided that the advent of power warranted something more than the 20 pavlovas I'd promised George Lindstrom, and so a power party was born. We'd have it the first Saturday night after we were switched on to the power, so 7 April 1982 became our red letter day.

For the first time in my married life I could switch on a light during the night if I wanted to. My electric stove was nearly a reality. Our fridge and freezer became efficient appliances. The days of engine problems were over. I wondered what we'd talk about instead. Breakdowns and engine antics had always been a main topic.

I remembered the time we'd been to Auckland for two weeks and had come home laden down with stores and frozen foods. Then Joe started the generator.

It tried to run but after a few coughs and splutters it died. Mice had built a nest in the fly-wheel housing, and when the engine turned over the mice became hooked up in the governor around the fly-wheel.

Then there was the time all of us had the flu. It wasn't a 'feeling lousy' strain, but the kind of flu when you want to stay in bed. The engine had to be run for the fridge and freezer so Joe crawled out of bed to start it during the afternoon. When it came time to stop the engine Joe said he'd started it, and besides, he was too sick to go out in the cold night to stop it. I felt lousy – I didn't want to do it. The four children all looked at one another and wondered which one of them would be sent out in the cold. "Well, I've got a brilliant idea," I told them all. "I'll take everyone's temperature. The lowest temperature stops the power." Joe got the job.

And I'll never forget the time Helen and Pauline went to start the generator with the handle as the batteries were getting old and they wouldn't turn it over. I heard the screams above the lighting plant. They'd done the job but had let go of the handle and it was swinging round on the crankshaft with each revolution. I ran to the shed to see them huddling in the corner behind a water tank. As I watched, the handle became airborne and crashed into the tank next to the girls. Nothing like this would ever happen again.

But our lighting plant had one last surprise in store for us. The night before the big day, Joe and I were listening to the beat of the generator, remembering the stories our source of electricity had given us over the years. Suddenly the engine stopped and we found ourselves sitting in the dark. We automatically grabbed a torch and ran down to the power house. It had plenty of diesel. We couldn't see a great deal in the dark but on checking Joe found that the sump had become flooded with diesel. This could be a major. "How much is in the deep freeze?" he asked.

"Heaps. It will hold until we get electricity tomorrow."

For the first time after a breakdown of the generator, we walked away and left the problem behind. It turned out to be not too serious, and as far as I know our generator still runs at Rainbow Skifield near Lake Rotoiti, Nelson.

Everyone who could come to the party came. The simple event that people in town take for granted, just as I did before I was married, came as darkness fell. Lights came on with the flick of a switch. Deep satisfaction and excitement surged through us all. Even the cost was worth it. As well as our initial contribution of $1300, Joe and I were to pay $1930 annually for the next 15 years, plus the units we would use. But there were few thoughts that night of what we would have to pay.

At some stage during the evening Joe sneaked out and turned the main switch off. A cold silence fell on the happy party buzz. "That didn't last long," someone said. Laughter from outside made us realise what Joe had done, and with the lights on again the party continued.

"It was a great job to do. Really exciting, and a great one to finish my working life with," George Lindstrom replied when we formally thanked him and his men. He talked a little about the challenges and satisfactions of the job, but added, "I would have liked to see orange marker balls across that cable, and not just the orange and white tubing marking the wires."

We gave little thought to his words that night, or in the next few years. Then on 4 October 1985 at 12.23pm a Cessna 402B aircraft carrying eight passengers and the pilot from Nelson to Wellington hit those power wires over Tory Channel, and crashed into the sea. Two families were taking children to a gymnastics event. There was only one survivor, 12-year-old Cindy Mosey.

Mavis and Chum Thomas were in the garden of their home on Arapawa Island near the power crossing. There was little wind and the only disturbance on the water was from the bow wave of the ferry, *Aratika*, as she made her way in to Picton. Chum and Mavis said they'd heard the drone of a plane, then two bangs. One was the plane hitting the wire, the second was the smack as it crashed into the sea. "I grabbed some blankets," Chum said, "and pushed my runabout out. Dial 111!" I yelled to Mavis.

Chum's story unfolded. "I saw the *Aratika* was on the scene and thought they'd be handling the rescue so I kept back a bit. But their lifeboat wouldn't go, the engine wouldn't start, so I went over to where I could hear the screams. 'Save me! Save me!' Cindy was in the water and I grasped her arm to find her wrist was broken. I pulled her on board my boat, wrapped her in the blankets and took her back to the *Aratika*."

Mavis had dialled 111 and asked to be put through to the police. The person who had answered the phone called Mavis back, and talked to her through the ordeal, making sure she was all right.

The plane had gone down in more than 160 feet of water. The wreckage had to be located before the plane could be salvaged and the bodies recovered. It took two days before it was located and hauled to the surface. With the modern electronic gear we had on the *Fugitive*, Joe, with our boys Joe and James, had been assisting in locating the wreckage. Divers had managed to fix a line to it and it was towed closer inshore.

For 21-year-old Joe and 18-year-old James this was their first experience of violent death. Before the plane broke the surface of the water the smell made their stomachs churn. When the police asked Joe if he and the boys could help with the bodies, he gave Young Joe and James the option of sitting it out. "You don't have to," Joe said. "It'll be unpleasant. Do what you can."

They helped as best they could. Arriving home all they wanted to do was scrub and scrub their hands. A hot bath made it worse and the evening meal was pushed uneaten around their plates as they valiantly strove to be men.

I sometimes wonder if all the people who read about tragedies, such as this one, can have any idea of the effect of that tragedy on those involved in the rescue.

Power to the island was restored and the wires remain, still marked with only the orange and white tubing. They stand as a memorial to the eight who lost their lives. Their names are still remembered. They were:

Roger Phipps (pilot)
Richard Grayson
Diane Grayson
Kirsty Grayson
Paul Mosey
Julie Mosey
Karla Mosey
Aleisha Mosey.

CHAPTER SEVENTEEN

Sounds People Celebrate

FROM Glee Club parties to a wedding when the bride actually arrived in a stretch limousine – in my 33 years living here I have completed the full circle of parties on Arapawa Island.

My very first party was at my in-laws' house. For the workers at the whaling station it was a night out. For me it was being on show. They'd come to meet the new bride and I was relieved my mother-in-law had suggested they come to their home as we had only four kitchen chairs and the floor to sit on. Once my nervousness had gone I enjoyed the night. The loud and jovial men who'd helped jam my piano in the door were very subdued. I wondered if it was their wives' presence, the unfamiliar clothes they'd put on, or the stranger in their midst. But after a while restraint seemed to vanish, and it turned out to be a wonderfully friendly evening. I felt I now had lots of substitute family, all willing to offer advice when I needed it.

Before long we were invited to a Glee Club party. The workers at the whaling station organised it, and everyone put in towards buying drinks. It was always held in someone's home and was a fun get-together.

The one thing I'll always remember about those whalers' parties were the songs Moira and Trevor Norton sang, with Trevor accompanying them with his guitar. Today when I hear Que Sera Sera – Whatever Will Be Will Be – or the modern version of Maggie, my mind rushes back to the Glee Club evenings when I've sat and listened to one of the Peranos' top gunners harmonising with his wife in a smoke-filled room suddenly gone silent as we listened. Heads would lean against walls, cigarettes held in callused fingers forgotten as they sat with eyes closed or staring at the light, bringing memories perhaps of girl friends or wives left behind while they worked at the whaling station.

Trevor's laughing voice would break the spell. "Another beer, boys. That makes a chap thirsty." A glass of beer would be downed in one go, the guitar picked up again and the tunes would keep pouring out for everyone to join in. Early in the evening we'd be singing Yes Sir! That's My Baby, or Down By The Riverside, and as the night wore on the songs would get more sentimental like When I Grow Too Old To Dream or I Wonder Who's Kissing Her Now. Trevor Norton knew them all. He might have been as one with a harpoon gun by day but by night he was as one with his guitar.

As universities have their famous graduation song, Gaudeamus, the whalers had their special song. Bloody. That's what it was always called. Bloody. It was always sung late in the evening and with great gusto but very little tune – just a few chords strummed on the guitar. Their words were not sung in Latin.

This bloody town's a bloody cuss
No bloody trams, no bloody bus
And no one cares for bloody us
So bloody bloody bloody.

It's bloody awful when it rains
No bloody ditch no bloody drains
The council's got no bloody brains
So bloody bloody bloody.

The bloody dances make me smile
The orchestras are bloody vile
And do they cramp your bloody style
So bloody bloody bloody.

The bloody grog is bloody dear
It's 1/9 a bloody beer
And do they shout? No bloody fear
So bloody bloody bloody.

When whaling finished in 1965 so did these parties. The whaling station became a ghost town and I haven't heard the whalers' Bloody song since. But it wasn't a song you'd ever forget.

Our growing family and fishing took up most of our time. For the next few years our days were swallowed up in work, but birthdays were important and we always made these special days.

As the children grew, so did the population of Tory Channel as new families moved into the area, and birthday parties were a lot of fun with up to 12 or 14 children arriving in boats. Parties were nearly always birthdays and even the adults' parties were family affairs. There were no baby sitters to call on so our children always came with us. They learnt the same songs we'd learnt from our parents – the evergreens they'd learnt from theirs.

A birthday party we'll always remember was at Mike and Pam Davies' place in Onauku at the head of East Bay, named by Captain Cook during his first visit to the area in January 1770. It is at the north-eastern end of Arapawa Island and if we went by boat it took us nearly two hours. It was Mike's birthday and Joe came up with the brilliant suggestion that we'd drive to the top of the hill in the Trekker truck, walk down the hill to the beach in East Bay and hitch a ride with Dave Fishburn in his fishing boat *Nimrod*. "Better than sitting on the boat for two hours," Joe claimed.

Helen and James were home from boarding school for the weekend and Helen had a friend from the Chathams, also from boarding school, with her. The ride to the top of the hill was the easy bit. We reached the boundary gate and everyone found something to carry. There was a crate of beer, wine and a birthday cake I'd made in the shape of Mike's pride and joy – his new boat *Evander*. We had a pavlova, already creamed, our bag with tidy clothes, shoes and make-up, and torches to help us find our way over the hill when it was time to come home.

We scrambled through the scrub down to Puriri Bay to wait for Dave. He came in the bay and put the bow of the *Nimrod* on the beach so we could clamber aboard. The pavlova was covered in bits of scrub bushes collected when its carrier had been down on hands and knees pushing through scrub. These were soon picked off and by the time we arrived in East Bay the pav looked as good as when we'd left home. It had taken us more than two hours to arrive at Pam and Mike's but it certainly hadn't been boring as it might have been sitting on the boat.

The home trip was an experience. Dave nudged the bow of his boat on to the beach and we all dropped over the side into the cold black moonlit water. With our gumboots filled with water we began to squelch our way up the hill to the boundary gate where our truck was waiting. If anyone had been over the limit when we left East Bay this was soon sweated out on the long moonlit trek up the hill. There was no wind but at 2am the beginning of a frost was in the air. Warm air from our heaving chests formed a mist and when we reached the truck we all piled on, deeply grateful for the ride home. Joe turned the key – nothing. "Battery's flat. Everyone push." Except for Joe, we all climbed off the back and pushed while Joe steered the truck along the shadowed road until at last it coughed and started up. Helen's friend, Ngaio, had been to many Chatham Island parties but never, she said, had she ever been to one like the Arapawa Island birthday party.

Church services are always a great get-together. They are interdenominational and people come for all sorts of reasons. But the fact remains they are a social occasion and it's wonderful to get out and meet people. Everyone brings a plate and the afternoon teas are worth making the effort to come, whatever one's strength of faith. Whenever I have to take a plate I make cream puffs. Not a recipe from my *Edmonds Cookbook,* or any other recipe book I have. I use my mother's recipe. It is uncomplicated with fewer ingredients than other recipes I've seen for them, and they never fail.

The Bishop of Nelson has been up Tory Channel on a few occasions but I'll always remember the first time he came. Bishop Peter Sutton is a tall man and through the eyes of three-year-old Pauline he must have seemed to be very imposing indeed as he swept into the room at Te Pangu Lodge, dressed in his regalia and carrying his shepherd's crook. In the hushed room Pauline's whisper was loud. "What's he got a sheep dunker for, Dad?" The bishop quickly answered. "To hook in any lost sheep and bring them home."

Our children loved going to church. Sitting quietly through a service was worth it when the afternoon tea was spread out.

The only wedding in Tory Channel in living memory, at that time, was celebrated at our home on 5 March 1983. Mary Kirk from Deep Bay had lost her husband Ian during 1982. Our community was delighted when we were told she was marrying Frank Williams, a retired lighthouse keeper. It was made even more exciting when they asked if they could hold the wedding at our home.

The wedding breakfast was the gift of their Sounds friends. I became excellent at delegating and found myself with very little food preparation to do apart from icing the wedding cake. I'd borrowed plates and silver cutlery and the tables set for 55 guests looked beautiful with the borrowed silver.

I'd worried myself sick about the weather. "What if it's a southerly? No one'll be able to get ashore. If it's raining we won't fit everyone inside."

"For goodness sake. It's March, not August. It's more likely to be fine than not," was Joe's reply. Nevertheless I found myself whispering little prayers under my breath. "Please God, give us a fine day and no wind."

The morning of the wedding Joe leaped out of bed and pulled the curtains aside. "Your prayers are answered, love, but you forgot about the fog."

We couldn't see a thing. Not even the front fence was visible through the gloom. Young Joe had to go to Picton in his speedboat to pick up the Reverend Fred Greig who was marrying Mary and Frank. The wedding wasn't until 2pm but Fred had asked if he could be picked up early so he could be organised. When Joe left home the fog had started to lift but he had to peer his way through it all the way to Picton. They arrived back in the bay about lunch time to find the fog gone and a flat calm bay.

Our children decorated our truck and painted the words 'Getting Married' on it. When Mary arrived at the wharf it was down there to meet her and bring her up to the house. Frank, the bridegroom, had to walk.

The celebrating went on well into the evening and the bride and groom were waved to as they left the wharf to go to Deep Bay where they were to stay for a couple of days before leaving for a holiday in Australia.

Wedding or no wedding, Sounds life goes on as Frank was to find out the next day. Mid-morning the phone rang. "Joe, there's a fire on the other side of Arapawa. It's pretty bad. Can you get a crew up to it as soon as possible?"

As Joe is the fire officer for our area he has a crew he can call on. Frank had offered his services, and honeymoon or not he was called up. We didn't see any of our men until the following day. Frank arrived home just in time to pack his bags for his holiday in Australia.

184

In 1988 Joe and I had been married for 25 years. Early in the year I'd lost a very special aunt and uncle (husband and wife). At their funeral services it was decided it was time a happy event took place. "Let's get together and celebrate Heather and Joe's wedding anniversary," someone suggested. The May school holidays would be a good time, so a reunion was planned.

Invitations were sent out:

Greetings.
On 14 May at Okukari Marae there is to be a hui to discuss the legality of the relationship after 25 years of Heather Tupawere Macauley and Joseph Wailer Heberley and their joint claim to that area of land situated adjacent to the traditional fishing ground of the Fletcher Consortium tribe.

Elders will be given beds. Otherwise sleeping will be marae-style and guests are asked to bring sleeping bags. As we have to arrange the trips to Picton in the Te Arapawa sub-tribe fishing canoe, your plans would be much appreciated. Hope to see you.

Joe and Heather
Ngati Heberley tribe.

We had a lot of laughs with some of the replies we received. Dave and Kath Fishburn would not require beds. They were bringing their own 'water' bed.

Mike and Pam Davies from Onauku regarded it as their solemn duty to attend the important hui at Okukaro. Chief and Wahine Davies would sleep on *Te Evander Onauku* as was respectful to their tribe.

Heather and Peter McManaway would be honoured to be present to discuss the Wailing Tupaweres and their claim to their fishing ground.

Diana and William of the Willis-Birdsall tribe of Auckland were arriving in Blenheim via 'the great white bird' and were happy to sleep marae-style. They hoped to catch the Te Arapawa sub-tribe fishing canoe from Picton.

A special aunt in Hamilton wrote: "I don't know what I'll wear to the 'do'. I had planned to wear my feather cloak but so far I've only got two sparrow feathers I've collected on my tribal lawn." She'd signed it Aunt Tupawere Willa Shaw.

We didn't have a hui and it was not held on a marae, but all who came were of the opinion that Joe and I were truly married. About 40 people from three months to 70 years came. My wedding dress was brought out and I squeezed into it. I think the 25 years may have shrunk it slightly. Joe couldn't have fitted into his suit so I didn't feel too bad. From our wedding party of seven, four had made it to Okukari for our 25th anniversary. It was a great weekend.

"You know, Mum, we should have a barn dance. The woolshed would be ideal." Pauline was always coming up with these bright ideas. It sounded fun, and under the banner of our local Tory Channel and Arapawa Island Settlers' Association she organised the dance. We bought decorations and our woolshed got a new lease of life dressed in bright crepe paper streamers and coloured lights. Pauline had phoned people in our vicinity and asked them to tell others about the dance. Shane Murray from Te Pangu in Tory Channel was a willing disk jockey, and well over 100 enthusiastic dancers boogied on down in our shed that night.

Fear of fire was paramount in our minds so we'd asked people not to smoke in the shed, but the ban didn't seem to bother anyone. They were too busy dancing, anyway. It may have gone on all night if a southerly buster hadn't come in around midnight.

Cinderella had nothing on the barn dancers when the southerly came in. Boats tied at the wharf strained at their mooring ropes, trying to break free in the seas that soon built up. Everyone was scurrying to their boats and backing out from the wharf into the already breaking seas. Within half an hour the shed was once more just the old woolshed squatting in the middle of the bay, the streamers blown down when the wind came in the door, and the music silent.

Most of the memorable parties we've had at home have had a name attached to them. One such was Joe's Fish Hanging Party. Joe and I had flown to Hawaii in July 1986 with Kath and Dave Fishburn. While there we had gone out on a charter boat and Joe had caught a Pacific blue marlin. It was quite a small one, but all the same the excitement was great when it was landed in the cockpit of the boat, and as we headed for port the flag went up to tell the world we had a blue marlin on board. It was Joe's trophy and he was having it mounted and shipped back to New Zealand. The finished product looked great (if you liked that sort of thing) and I was relieved it was only 91 inches long and weighed 113 1/2 pounds when I saw it on my wall.

We had it shipped to McManaway Marine, and the plan was for Heather and Peter McManaway to bring it down on their boat the night of the fish hanging. It had arrived from the States in a large box, but to carry it up to the house everyone had met them on our wharf, and, with arms wrapped around the prize, they'd walked it up to the house. It was here the arguments started. I didn't want a fish hanging in my lounge. I didn't care what it had cost to get it to New Zealand – I didn't want it in the lounge.

It had to be seen, I was told, so for the moment I lost that battle and it was triumphantly hung on the lounge wall. Many glasses were raised to the poor fish which was no longer enjoying the tropical waters of Hawaii. Actually, if it had had any feelings it would have felt very welcome that night.

Two weeks later Joe was in Picton, painting the *Fugitive* on McManaways' slip. "I'll shift the fish while you're away," I'd threatened before he left. The following day he rang me up from Picton. "How's things?"

"Good. I've moved the fish."

"I told you to leave it where it was."

"I have. I've shifted the wall." Silence.

Until Joe got home he never knew where his Pacific blue marlin was. I did shift it from the lounge into another room, but I'd left the wall standing. I heard later he'd told the men in the smoko room he wouldn't have been surprised if I'd sawn the wall down because I was so fed up with having it hanging in the lounge.

A party with a difference was a hangi we had for a 21st birthday. The fact that Joe has some Maori blood doesn't make him a hangi cook. So he phoned Bluey Hebberd, better known for his shearing abilities. "Pauline wants a hangi for her birthday. I'd hate to try and put one down. You couldn't come down, could you?"

"Haven't done one in years, mate. I'll talk to a cobber. We'll both come down."

The day was perfect. Bluey and his friend arrived. They dug out a hole with the bulldozer. Old chains and iron were wired together and placed in the hole, and a massive fire was lit over it all. When the fire died down they brought in the tractor and lifted the hot iron out with the tractor bucket. The hot ashes were shovelled out, the iron lowered back into the hole and the prepared food was arranged over wet sacks and lots of watercress. The men carefully covered it with more wet sacks, then dirt, and we waited for the end result.

Chooks, mutton, wild pork and vegetables. The food was cooked to perfection. I found the taste bland, but there were no preparation dishes and I most certainly had no complaints. And it was all prepared with so little work, at least from me. But as they dug the hole with the bulldozer I imagined the Maori digging their oven pits with their tools. I thought of some of the artifacts we've found on our property and I was glad I wasn't a Maori living in pre-European times and digging out my oven to cook my evening meal. It could be a week late.

A wedding is always exciting, but none more so than your own children's. Helen and Pauline had both thought it would be nice to be married at Okukari. If a fine day could be guaranteed it would have been wonderful, but that was impossible so all our children's weddings have been in Picton. We have enjoyed them all, even the mammoth task of getting everything to Picton. And there is a bonus with our wedding celebrations lasting over a weekend. The thought of that early morning start to arrive in Picton early enough to iron all the dresses, assemble the cake, run through the music I'd be playing as well as having time to treat myself at the hairdressers, besides catching up with friends and family, sent us to Picton on the Friday before each Saturday wedding.

The year Helen was married, James with Greg Stewart were given the job of going home on the Saturday morning to milk Trudi, our house cow. As they sped up the Sounds I enjoyed a rare lie-in and breakfast in bed. I never eat a cooked breakfast at home but when it's brought to me, piping hot and the crisp bacon with eggs and tomatoes arranged on a plate, I love it. The best part is when I've finished and I can wriggle down into the warm bed, shut my eyes and not have to get up immediately.

After my breakfast on the morning of Pauline's wedding I lay in bed in my Picton hotel while behind my closed eyes a camera shutter clicked its way through the photographs in my mind as I relived our previous family weddings and saw once again Helen, and my daughters-in-law Joy and Lisa, walking up the aisle. I'd made all the girls' dresses for their weddings and each girl had chosen a completely different style.

Joy, Young Joe's wife, I saw in her deep cream heavy satin and perfectly plain dress. The features of her dress were the full sleeves that cascaded from her arms and fell into deep folds over the skirt. These were edged with guipure lace, and a lace insert with its scalloped edge was sewn over the bodice.

Helen had tried on my wedding dress and thought she'd like to wear it, but the years had yellowed the Chantilly lace even though the white satin still gleamed beneath. The yellowed lace was very fragile and tore with the slightest pressure. I copied my dress, and Joe walked his oldest daughter up the aisle in a dress identical to the one he'd seen me wearing when my father walked me up the aisle, in Northcote's St Aidan's Presbyterian Church.

Lisa, James's wife, chose cream satin and lace. The lace bodice overlay with its long lace sleeves fitted to just above Lisa's knees and it drew up to a V at the back and formed a bustle finished off with a cream satin bow.

The shutter on my mind's camera worked faster as pictures flashed through my mind of the night of Marlborough's Bride of the Year contest. Lisa had seen it advertised and jokingly said, "Perhaps I'll enter. I'd love the sewing machine." The joke became a reality when Lisa was placed third out of 45 contestants, and claimed her prize – a Bernina sewing machine.

My private film ended and I thought about Pauline's wedding to take place later that day. Pauline's traditional dress with its long train had been made during the year in between her trips home from Massey University. Her dress was white satin, with different lace motifs on which I'd sewn more than 8,000 beads before cutting them up to create our own designs.

I'd loved sewing those four wedding dresses. Working with the beautiful fabrics gave me such pleasure. It seemed such a long time ago that I'd been sewing the children's clothes, using the many cast-offs I was given. What new materials I bought usually became their one set of town clothes.

For every wedding I'd treated myself and bought something to wear, and my latest outfit was now hanging in the wardrobe waiting for me to put on and become the mother of the bride.

188

I never got used to the idea of cramming all the dresses into suitcases, loading them on to the tractor and passing them on to the boat. My heart was always in my mouth, imagining a case falling in the sea.

Before I was married I went to night school at my old school, Northcote College, and learnt cake decorating. I've been able to ice fun birthday cakes and, more recently, the wedding cakes. Pauline, too, has had lessons in cake decorating and she iced Lisa's and James's wedding cake, and I helped her ice hers and Dene's.

Getting the wedding cakes to Picton in one piece has been a nightmare. The two- and three-tiered cakes had to be carried down to the wharf and put on the boat with a few spare pieces of lace and flowers in case of breakages. One cake had to be taken down in pouring rain. It went from the house to the truck under an umbrella, and from the truck to the boat under the same umbrella until it blew inside out. Another cake was carried along the wharf in a southerly gale but all of them have reached the reception in one piece.

The farm dogs and cats are easily taken care of for the time we are out of the bay, with extra water and food, but young pets are not as easy to leave overnight. The Heberleys going to Picton for a family wedding travel like a circus. Pauline's was the last wedding and, as well as the dresses, three-tiered cake and buckets of flowers for the church, there was my little dog, and an angora goat that still needed a bottle.

A wedding when one lives in the Sounds is certainly different. Paula and Peter Jamieson who lived at Te Pangu and ran a guesthouse and a charter boat – the *Tory Trader* – were married in their garden on 9 May 1993. Paula and Peter had each lost their previous husband and wife. Now locals celebrated with them. I found myself sitting at a very special instrument that had been Paula's first husband's love. It was an old harmonium and as her father walked her down the front steps and out on to the lawn to Peter, I played Here Comes The Bride.

On 11 February 1995 our family was invited to another wedding, only the third wedding in Tory Channel in living memory.

The new owners of Whekenui, Mike and Antonia Radon, had bought the property from the Perano family in 1993. New Zealand-born Antonia had met Mike in the States six years earlier, and although they were married in the States at Lake Tahoe in 1994 they'd decided to be re-married in New Zealand so their New Zealand family and friends could celebrate with them. Where else could they find a more picturesque setting than their new home in Tory Channel?

Antonia was to get dressed in the 'bottom house', the house that had been Gilbert and Nan Perano's family home. The ceremony was to be held outside at the 'top house'. Joe and Pattie Perano, the founders of Perano Whaling and parents of sons Joe and Gilbert, had built the house in 1945 and named it Gunyah.

As they waited for the bride to arrive, wedding guests were already feasting and drinking – not with food and drink but with the panoramic views overlooking Tory Channel and the entrance. Shrill screeches of seabirds, as they hovered overhead before diving into the disturbed water around Wheke Rock straight below in their continuing search for food, replaced the organ music. The *Lynx*, the controversial fast ferry of the Interisland Line, came in the channel entrance. Viewed from the bow on, she looked like a ship one would expect to find in a science fiction story. Below us we could hear only the crashing of the wash she created as she sped past on her way to Picton.

"The bride's on her way. She's coming!" Everyone waited.

"I heard she was coming by tractor."

"It'd hardly be by motor bike."

"She'll be hot and dusty if she walks."

Around the last bend in the road, past the concrete gun pit that had been built during World War Two to house a 1500 mm P3 naval gun to guard the entrance of Tory Channel, under the leaning branches of old macrocarpa trees, swept – of all things – a black stretch limousine. It pulled up on the lawn alongside the concrete path that led up the side of the house and across the front to where Mike and Antonia were to re-affirm their wedding vows.

The bride's father had arrived at Whekenui only three hours earlier and he'd found himself in a stretch limousine curling its way round a dusty farm road, hills rising up on one side and the edge of the road dropping steeply to the sea on the other. Peter McPherson, Whekenui's farm manager and better known to all of us as Dingle, rode next to Keith Offord, the owner of the car and chauffeur for the day. Without his working clothes it was hard to recognise Dingle in this spruced-up man in high-waisted black dinner trousers, braces and white shirt as he opened the car door and the bride and her father stepped out.

Stunned silence greeted the bride. Her old-fashioned cream lace and tulle wedding gown made me feel Pattie Perano would have felt in perfect harmony with Antonia as she walked to meet Mike. But the amazement was not for the bride. It was for the black stretch limousine, dressed in white ribbons with two white toy bears clasping each other tightly and sitting on the bonnet of the car that had glided up the dirt road. Whatever was this? It couldn't drive to the island. No one had seen it. How had it arrived at Whekenui? People's minds worked overtime. After the ceremony the plan was revealed.

Antonia, although she didn't know it at the time, would get dressed at the bottom house. Keith Offord would bring his stretch limousine to Whekenui. Peter McManaway who owns and operates a barge would provide transport. This was all to be top secret.

The road from the bottom house where the bride was going to be dressed, to the top house, Gunyah, was checked and quite a few places had to be smoothed off before the car could drive on it. "Not a problem," Dingle assured Keith. "I'll whip the bulldozer over it during the week."

Mike had other ideas. He didn't think the road needed smoothing so close to the wedding. He had other things for Dingle to do. To keep his job, Dingle had to let Mike in on the secret. And so the road was made ready for the bridal car.

Antonia and Mike were in town the day before the wedding, ready to help load the barge with the equipment they'd hired for the wedding. "I'll help you guys load. I'll give you a ring to find out what time."

Keith never turns his cell phone off but that day Antonia couldn't get hold of him. It was off, so she couldn't find out what time she should help the men load up in Picton. She didn't realise all this had been carefully planned. No way did they want her to see the car already sitting on the barge, waiting for its midnight ride up Tory Channel.

Antonia stayed in Picton because she was picking up her father the next morning. Mike had come back to the farm that evening. As he hadn't let on that he knew about the car, Keith and Peter waited until after midnight when they stealthily steamed the barge in to Whekenui, and drove the car off at the breastworks where the cattle yards used to stand. It drove quietly along Dingle's newly bulldozed road, parked in the woolshed and was covered with a tarpaulin. They moored the barge on one of our moorings before going across the channel to Keith's Tory Channel holiday home.

Antonia's story unfolded. "I couldn't understand why I had to stay in one room. Why couldn't I have got dressed at Gunyah? I'd get so dusty going up the hill. I knew the guests were on their way to Gunyah and I was still a prisoner in the bedroom in the bottom house."

Antonia wanted to peer out the window but 10-year-old Hinewai, Dingle and Katherine's daughter and who was to be the ring bearer, wouldn't let her. Were they dressing the tractor for her?

As she told it, "At last it was time for me to leave the room. Driving over the bridge and up to the front steps was this limo. I couldn't believe my eyes! I was flabbergasted, speechless and so emotional. I knew the effort involved in getting anything to the island – anything at all – and here was a limousine brought in just for our wedding! And we'd only just met some of the people who'd gone to so much trouble for us.

"The only words I could say were, 'Oh my God, oh my God.' I felt I was the luckiest girl on earth. Before we arrived at Gunyah, Keith stopped the car and he and Dingle dusted it so I'd arrive in true style. It is a day I'll remember for ever."

For the guests, the bride's arrival made it a day they'd also always remember. For me, another surprise was still to happen.

Walking back to the bottom house, everyone was still talking about the way in which Antonia had arrived. The limousine had stolen the show. We passed the schoolhouse which had been built for the whalers' children. Nostalgia drew me in. Joe had spent his primary school years here, and at the height of the whaling season the roll swelled to 32.

Silent since December 1964, the school looked very spruce with its newly painted pale blue walls and dark blue trim. No children's windbreakers or oilskin coats hung on the coathooks, and the classroom reminded me of ones I'd been taught in. The walls were lined with bookshelves built so young children could easily reach the book of their choice. Above these, three walls were lined with blackboards while the fourth wall let in the light through small, square, wooden-framed windows. A pot-bellied stove stood in a corner, its life nearly eaten away by the salt air. On its top was a pile of blackboard slates, some still with names on the top. There had been a Toni and an Alec in the class at some time.

On a shelf under a thick coating of dust I saw a stack of *Sea Spray* magazines. Some dated back to 1963 – the year I was married. I excitedly flipped over yellowed pages, hoping to read of a boat or person I'd remember from my yachting days in Auckland. In the July 1963 *Sea Spray* a heading caught my eye. The names *Mangawai* and Tom Macauley, my father, jumped out of the page at me. I read the article for the first time, 32 years after it was written. For the second time that day I was stunned. Whales and Sheep for Auckland Girl, said the headline. It read:

> Auckland yachtsmen who know the yacht *Mangawai* will miss seeing Tom Macauley's daughter at the helm next season. Heather is now married to Joe Heberley and living on a farm just inside the entrance to Tory Channel, surrounded by sheep and whales. Although a busy girl, she always found time to help her father with the boat. In the dark hours of the morning when most young girls would be getting their beauty sleep, Heather would be helping her dad to grid the boat, then over the side in the chill water to scrub off. She would even be seen scraping the top of the mast or painting the topsides. Heather loved her yachting and the *Mangawai*.
>
> Joe Heberley was working at the Whaling Station, Great Barrier, as a gunner when they first met. Although a seafaring man then in fast chasers, he took to sailing on the *Tango* and later *Mangawai*. Joe is again whaling, this time for Peranos in the Tory Channel.
>
> We wish them both fair weather and good sailing.

I stood in the silence of the schoolroom, reading and re-reading the article, and feeling the wash of happy memories as they surged over me in waves. I had truly travelled 32 years this afternoon.

CHAPTER EIGHTEEN

When Fishing People Meet

WHEN I walked into the foyer of Auckland's Centra Hotel and saw the words, 'New Zealand Federation of Commercial Fishermen's Conference' listed on the function board, my mind flew back to the earlier conferences I'd been to with Joe. Each has grown bigger and better over the years as the fishing industry has grown to the stage it is now, a tough business to be in, not the enjoyable way of earning a living that it used to be.

With the introduction of quotas in 1986, fishermen suddenly found themselves worth money as they were given a catch history, worked out on the quantity of fish they'd caught over the previous years. Fish quota could be bought and sold throughout New Zealand, and many big companies began buying up quota as they became available from people wanting to get out of fishing. Other fishermen opted to sell their quota, but still stay in the industry. They'd lease quota from owners who didn't want to fish, but wanted money from the quota they held.

Fishing became big business. Many wives found themselves, as I did, struggling to manage the monthly Quota Management Reports and hoping they would balance with the Licensed Fish Receiver Reports and their own quota balances. If a mistake was made and quota overfished, fishermen could expect a Deemed Value Invoice from MAF, the Ministry of Agriculture and Fisheries, and the amount payable would be more than the value of the caught fish. Responsible fishermen – and there are now a few women fishing skippers and crew, too – knew there was a need to conserve fish stocks. But this business of quota with the mountainous paper work involved has completely upset the age-old business of fishing. What's more, mostly the paper work ends up as the responsibility of the wives.

Familiar faces were getting fewer and fewer at each conference we went to and I knew as we registered for this one, the 37th national conference, that if it weren't for our two sons being involved in the industry and working as a partnership with Joe and me, we too might have bowed out and left it up to the younger generation to catch fish using all the latest electronic equipment on the boat. With echo sounder, radar and GPS, the fish in the sea haven't much chance to get away.

The conference is a very intense three days of sitting in on seminars followed by the annual general meeting on the last afternoon, and Joe claims it's more exhausting than three days' fishing. But at the end of each day the evenings are relaxed and happy times to catch up with old friends, and there is always a time of remembering those fishermen lost at sea since the last conference.

The women have one day out, and mixed with the hilarity after a few glasses of wine is the talk about their share of the work – how we all feel about the work most wives or partners have to do just to keep MAF's papers up to date, and so make a fishing business possible. I've never heard talk of the apprehension or fear most of these women must have felt at some time, when loved ones have been caught out at sea in stormy weather. I've watched happy faces and thought that we've all got to have a horror story about fishing in our minds, but that belongs in the past. If we were to dwell on the near disasters our men have experienced we couldn't enjoy what we have in the present.

During the conference two sessions are set aside. One is for a fundraising to pay for the running of the conference, and the second, a wind-up function on the last evening, is when all the money raised goes to the New Zealand Shipwreck Relief Society. This is a body in its own right, formed in the late 1880s with its office in Dunedin. Its aim is to provide immediate short-term financial aid to wives, children or dependants of seamen lost at sea.

The main fundraising for the conference is usually an auction. Sponsors are generous with donations of fishing gear and boat equipment, and as the auction progresses the odd tie or shirt is likely to go on offer to the highest bidder. Raffles are run occasionally and any excess money is put towards the final cheque for the Shipwreck Society.

In 1995 we enjoyed our auction above the Maritime Museum on Auckland's Hobson's Wharf. A walk up Albert Street to our hotel would have been enjoyable if Joe hadn't had a large roll of monofiliment fishing line that weighed 30 pounds – his spoils from the auction. We met up with Jan and Graham Webb, also from Picton, just as we were leaving and we decided a taxi among us all would be a great idea. Seeing a taxi phone in the entrance Jan picked up the handpiece. "We'd like a car, please. Four, to go to the Centra."

"Certainly madam. Where are you?"

"Where are we, Heather? What do I say?"

When Jan told them at the Maritime Museum on Hobson's Wharf she said they sounded rather vague, but she told them it was for Webb and hung up.

"I'll try again and say it's by the yacht that was in the America's Cup. They must know where I mean."

This time a different voice answered the phone and soon we had two taxis ordered. We waited outside and a taxi came along and we heaved a sigh of relief. It was getting cold and we were all thinking a meal would be good.

"Sorry, folks. This car isn't for Webb," we were told. "I'll call base and get them to send one for you. It'll only be a couple of minutes." Now we had three taxis ordered for Webb. By the time our first taxi arrived there was quite a crowd waiting. We suggested to those nearest that they take the next couple of cars that should soon arrive to pick us up. "They'll all be under the name of Webb," we called out. The crowd looked at us as if we were from the country.

The last conference night is always the best. Fishermen are pleased the business side of the conference is over. They are looking forward to getting back home and to work, and an evening of fun and relaxation is in front of them. It's usually a dinner followed by dancing and the fundraising, which is always a time that you have to be prepared to laugh at yourself in the same way you've laughed at others.

It's hard to recognise many of the fishermen we've met on their boats when in port. Dressed in tidy clothes with shiny, new-looking shoes, clean-shaven with their hair combed, they look totally alien and uncomfortable out of their woollen bush shirts, yellow smockies and gumboots. They dance with exuberance, their weatherbeaten faces showing their enjoyment as they stamp and sing along with the band.

I sat apart during a bracket of dances and as I watched I couldn't help feeling sorrow when I thought how possible it was that some of that happy group mightn't be here next year, and it might be their wives and families who would be benefiting from their generosity tonight. That night a galvanised bucket had been passed around the tables and we were asked to put our change into it. Approximately 160 people gave nearly $4000.

One of the most memorable fundraisers was a Karaoke night. It was worked like quota. If you were called up to sing on the Karaoke you had the option to FARQ it (authority to fish against another's quota) and pay into the fund for the Shipwreck Society if you could get someone else to sing in your place. Or you could sub-lease the right to sing and the person taking your place had to pay to sing.

Neither Joe nor I had ever seen a Karaoke machine before. We'd heard of them and what a lot of fun people had singing on them in the pubs, but we couldn't believe how professional it made ordinary singing sound. The better performers weren't nearly as much fun to watch as those who just paid up and sang, no matter how they sounded. "Let's hope I don't have to do it," laughed Joe as we clapped and cheered the latest fisherman and hoped he wasn't dreaming of giving up fishing for a singing career.

I'd looked through the books with the hundreds of song titles that the machine could play and found there were country and western, rock, all the evergreens and even nursery rhymes. When Joe was out of the room I caught up with Dick Hall, one of our Picton members and the president of the federation. "I'll give $50 if you can get Joe up to sing. No trade-offs or FARQs. He has to do it himself. He knows Twinkle Twinkle Little Star."

When Joe was called up his hand shot immediately into his pocket. "I'll pay. I'll pay."

"Bad luck, Joe. There's conditions to this one. C'mon."

Still protesting, Joe was led to the stage. "But I don't know any of them."

Next thing the words of Twinkle Twinkle flashed up on the screen and the red ball bounced over each word Joe had to sing. He really got into the swing of it, tapped his foot, held the microphone like a professional and sang with great gusto as he swayed back and forth in time to the bouncing ball. For a time he had the nickname of Twinkle.

A common ice shovel became one of the biggest fundraisers for the Shipwreck Society for many years. It started at an auction when three ice shovels had been donated at a time when one MAF person was causing a lot of hassles in conference. Two shovels were auctioned earlier, but the third was kept for the final night and offered during the evening as the shovel that shovelled the MAF person off the conference floor to stop him taking up valuable time. Everyone wanted it but a Te Anau fisherman, Peter Squires, better known as Swack, was the proud owner. He maintained it was a bargain at $150.

Next year the shovel was brought back to the conference and put up for auction once again. The second buyer paid $2500 for the privilege of owning the shovel that had swept MAF away.

Peter Stevens, the secretary of the Federation of Commercial Fishermen, got it chromed and every year the bidding got higher for the right to hold the trophy for a year. Fishing companies and groups bid for it. The huge amounts were invested for a year at the end of which the Shipwreck Society received the interest and the donors received their money back without the interest.

In 1992 a plaque was put on the ice shovel and it was given in memory of John Lowe, who had died during the year, for the work he'd done in forming the Leigh Fishermen's Association, and which then had one of the highest memberships in New Zealand. It hangs on the wall in a display cabinet in the foyer of the Leigh Hotel. The Fiordland Association holds a golf and shooting tournament every year, and a cheque from the tournament proceeds is added to the Shipwreck Society's fund.

The generosity of those at the conference always makes me think of a line in the prayer of St Francis:

'For it is in giving that we receive.'

Perhaps when they get home the elusive crayfish will be fighting to crawl into the crayfish pots. Shark, groper and other line fish will be queuing up to take the baited hooks, and schools of fish will be waiting to swim into nets. Whatever these men of the sea are thinking now as they relax, they know that in a few days their lives will once more be ruled by the weather and the sea. Verses 23 and 24 from Psalm 107 say it for them:

'They that go down to the sea in ships, that do business in great waters;
These see the works of the Lord, and his wonders in the deep.'

CHAPTER NINETEEN

Visitors to the Bay

ANTICIPATION is what sends fishermen to sea in all weathers. The anticipation of a good catch closes their minds to the wet and cold conditions they often have to put up with.

Mornings in Okukari always have an edge of anticipation. Mondays and Thursdays, before my parents died, meant mail day and letters from home. Today the mail bag and the daily papers still generate excitement. Papers are soon spread all over the kitchen table or lounge floor, along with letters on good days, and bills on bad. Always there's the huge pile of junk mail. Town visitors are always amazed at the quantity that finds its way to our place.

I've always woken up wondering what the day will bring. For many different reasons people have arrived in our bay, and as well as those we've met after rescues – some of whom I've written about – there have been enough other callers to Okukari to make up a book of their own. One reason is that our bay is a natural jumping-off place for many events.

In May 1995 Joe and I were watching the New Zealander of the Year Awards on television. We were delighted that Graeme Dingle of Auckland, founder and director of the Sir Edmund Hillary Outdoor Pursuits Centre, won the category of Recreation and Sport. Dressed in a dinner suit, he was a very different-looking Graeme from the man we had come to know during his stay with us a few months earlier.

On 16 January Joe and the boys had been putting the last of the gear on board *Te Wai* and *Fugitive* before setting off to chase the tuna up the west coast of the North Island as far as Manukau Harbour, which was to be the port they'd be unloading into. From the wharf we watched a white kayak turn into the bay and skim smoothly over the water before coming to a halt on the beach.

A man with a bearded and weatherbeaten face framed with a bush of greying hair, and a lively dark-haired woman, climbed out of the beached canoe. The man's eyes gleamed through crevices etched deeply into his skin, obviously from years of being out in the sun, as he introduced himself and his companion. "Graeme Dingle and Jo-anne Wilkinson."

We soon heard about the latest journey Graeme was undertaking, with Jo-anne. They had left from Nelson, and during the next two months they intended to paddle across Cook Strait, traverse the central North Island ranges to the Waikato and then journey on to Auckland which they hoped to reach in early

March. The pair were hoping to raise awareness, and money, for Project K, something which they'd devised to help 'directionless' young people.

Cook Strait was to be the next hurdle but for the rest of the day and that night they had time to catch their breath. It took very little persuasion for them to leave their tent packed and to stay in the house with me, so my day, which had started out with an empty feeling as I knew I wouldn't be seeing Joe for six weeks, ended with a master of adventure bringing his world into my lounge.

The weather in Cook Strait was too rough for Graeme and Jo-anne for the next two days. In those two days, from my armchair, I travelled 28,000 km around the Arctic Circle, and through Europe. I climbed the Andes, the Himalayas and the Southern Alps. Graeme made the world so small as he re-lived some of his incredible journeys for us, journeys where I guessed he'd pushed himself not just to the edge of human endurance but far beyond.

When I waved goodbye to Graeme and Jo-anne, something he'd said in reply to a question kept running through my mind. He'd been asked, "How important was the journey itself to you?" His answer was, "What's more important to me is that I do things that are worthwhile to me and other people. It's called filling the cup rather than draining it."

As the kayak went out of sight I wished a silent godspeed to them both and their Project K. If only all our visitors could be as nice. Sometimes we get people who fit Graeme's definition of 'directionless' – or rather they are heading in the wrong direction.

On this occasion Joe was in Picton for the day and I knew he wasn't going to be home that night. As the four children and I sat at the kitchen table we watched a scruffy boat steam into the bay. Another one waiting for the right conditions before venturing out in Cook Strait, we all decided. But when I took a closer look at the boat I was sure they must be up this way fishing. It certainly didn't look seaworthy enough to take on Cook Strait.

The boat was about 36 feet, and looked as if it hadn't seen a paint brush since the day it was built. The wheelhouse looked as if it was built from plywood, some of which was layering, and there was a hole where glass should have been. Altogether it was one of the most battered and unloved boats I have ever seen. The steering, we found out later, was tied up with thin rope, and they had neither navigational aids nor a radio of any sort.

Later that same afternoon I was working in the garden, a million miles away as I do a lot of thinking and sorting out of problems among the plants and weeds, when two black gumboots appeared next to my bucket. No greeting, no cough or excuse me. I lifted my eyes and took in the man who stood there – this intruder on my thoughts. I saw filthy blue jeans, a baggy jersey covered in grease and full of holes, and shirt sleeves hanging loosely below cut-off jersey sleeves. His thin, sharp-featured face needed a shave, and his lank brown hair hanging to his shoulders was hooked around his ears in an effort to keep it off his face.

I asked if I could help and the only answer I received was, "Is your husband around?"

Once again my fertile imagination was working overtime. Where were my children? "No," I replied. I found myself being as abrupt as he was. "But my father-in-law is. Why?"

"Just wondering what the weather is going to do. We want to get to Wellington. Will he be home tonight?"

I was feeling very uneasy in this person's presence so I lied and told him my husband would be home later and I had no idea what the weather was doing until I saw the TV map later that night.

He left as silently as he'd come but called out from the front gate that he'd be ashore that night. "I'll come and watch the TV weather map myself. That'll give me an idea."

At times like this I feel very vulnerable. Only my in-laws to hear screams for help, and they quite likely wouldn't hear. And this man gave me the creeps.

"You'd better come down and spend the night with us. You shouldn't be alone with the children," Charlie said after I'd told him about my visitor. "If he'd really wanted to know about the weather surely he'd have come and asked me. Perhaps he's checking the place out for easy takings."

Now I was terrified, but, as I told my father-in-law, I wasn't leaving my house for the likes of him to walk in and help himself. He'd have to get past me first.

As the time rolled on towards the television weather report I'd schooled my children. "Don't speak unless spoken to, and if you do, tell them Dad's in bed, exhausted, after mustering over the back all day and our TV isn't going tonight." The TV lie could easily have been true because when it's been windy the aerial often flies to pieces, or the wires from the aerial to the top of the ridge to our house plait together in the wind.

This time a woman as unkempt as the man arrived with him. They knocked and let themselves in. Four children threatened with dishes for a week if they said the wrong thing soon filled them in: TV wasn't going and poor old Dad was in bed fast asleep. But somehow between all this I got them out the door and smartly locked it.

At bedtime I had to go outside to stop the generator. I sauntered out to the shed. I wasn't scared. The axe I used for cutting kindling lay by the shed door and I picked it up – just in case. Then I stopped the generator. In the sudden silence and blackness I tore along the back path, reached the safety of my house and slammed the door shut behind me.

I lay in bed, sleepless. I'd bravely made the statement earlier in the day about protecting my home, and now I was too scared to close my eyes. The axe inside the back door and Joe's .22 alongside me in bed gave little comfort as I lay in the darkness, not knowing what I was waiting for.

At 2am I heard an engine start up. Thank God, I thought, they're off. But the sound went on and on. They were running the motor without going anywhere. About half an hour later, in the stillness of the night, I heard the motor clunk into gear and I leaped out of bed. Through the bedroom window I watched the lights on the boat come into view as the boat came alongside the wharf.

I rang my in-laws. "They're at the wharf."

"I'll go down and see what the hell they're up to," Charlie said. "Don't worry."

I sat at the kitchen table, straining to see through thick blackness and wondering what was going on down at the wharf, when the sound of the front gate opening had me around the table and pushing the window open to see who it was. I could see it was the woman close to the house. "What the hell do you want?" I yelled. I might be a fisherman's wife but it flashed through my mind that I must be sounding like a fish-wife.

"We wanted to let you know we're off to Wellington."

This left me speechless and she turned around and all I heard were her running footsteps fading in the dark.

Meanwhile, at the wharf, Charlie with the light of his torch found the man snooping around in the boatshed. Mac, one of his sheepdogs, had followed Charlie, no doubt wondering what the nocturnal jaunt was all about.

"I could have booted the dog in the behind," he told me after they'd gone. "When I yelled at him to get himself and friend back on to the boat and out of my sight or I'd put my dog on them, old Mac padded up to him, put his paws on his shoulders and began to lick his face. The man didn't say boo. Just walked along the wharf and when she arrived they took off. Let's hope it's the last we'll see of them."

Did we judge strangers too harshly? But the story didn't end with their departure.

Next morning Charlie rowed out to his boat to go fishing. Habit had him dipping the fuel tank although he knew he had plenty. That morning he found it empty. It seemed our visitors had been busy in the time I'd heard their engine running. Their fuel tank was full, at Charlie's expense.

Marjorie Stanley, owner of the guest house Te Pangu down the channel from us, had also had visitors that morning. Roger, her husband, was in Wellington and she'd been alarmed to find the pair on her doorstep before 8am. Once again they'd wanted to know what the forecast was, as they were hoping to get across the strait.

They either got their bearings wrong or changed their minds because in our newspapers the following week we read of the same people, found living aboard a valuable launch in the Picton Marina. They'd tied their own boat up, broken into the launch and were living very cheaply as the owner's uninvited guests.

But then the Peter Buttons of this world who keep dropping in to Okukari quickly make us forget people like that.

Peter Button OBE, often called The Magic Button, was a frequent caller to Okukari in his helicopter. Many of the rescues he was involved with were in Cook Strait, and weather conditions, usually fog or darkness, meant he'd put down on our flat and wait for an improvement, sometimes staying overnight. Peter and Joe too, were often involved in the same searches and rescues and I often heard Joe say that if he was ever in need of a rescue he hoped Peter was there plus his helicopter.

One search Joe was involved in was when a police diver went missing while diving on Wash Rock, in central Cook Strait. Joe was told to search north of Wash Rock but he told the police that would be a waste of time. His local knowledge of tides and winds gave him an idea where to start the search, and it wasn't north of the rock when it had been ebb tide for the last hour.

A grid search began and although it wasn't as far south as Joe would have liked, it wasn't as far north as he was told to go. Late in the afternoon and with no sightings, Peter Button was called in.

He started well south of Joe, where Joe had wanted to go in the first place, and just on nightfall, three and a half miles east of the channel entrance, one extremely lucky diver owed his life to Peter Button. Peter spotted him in his diving gear, bobbing up and down in the open sea.

In the late 1970s a plane went missing. It was a small, single-engined plane which had left Nelson for Wellington. Thick fog filled the strait, and Wellington Airport was closed so they had to turn back. The plane slammed into the cliffs on the edge of the bushline in Wellington Bay on the Cook Strait side of Arapawa, and their locator beacon had alerted Civil Aviation to the fact that a plane had gone down.

Joe and his father had been sent out to search for it, but they had been told by someone, who made a geographical error, to search in Puriri Bay on the Queen Charlotte side of Arapawa. From above Puriri Bay Joe and Charlie saw Peter Button circling in Wellington Bay and they realised they'd been sent to the wrong place.

They arrived back down to the flat at the same time as Peter in his helicopter.

"We've found it. There's three in it. All dead. I had to drop the police away from the crash site. Too steep to touch down where it hit. I'm wondering if you have some spare woolpacks I can use to bring the bodies in? I'll have to bring them in below the chopper."

I'd gone down to see Peter but talk of bodies being pushed into woolpacks and then dangling them below the helicopter was more than I could bear. It wasn't long since my parents' deaths and my grief was still too raw.

In the house I heard the helicopter take off, and later land again. Peter made one more trip out to bring back the two police.

The police had to stay with us that night as Peter had a full load in his helicopter. I felt much better when I was told the bodies had their dignity returned and that they'd been flown back to Wellington inside the helicopter, on stretchers. "There was no other way I could fly them out from the crash site," Peter had told me when he saw how upset I was.

Peter Button was a man who always replied to thanks with the words, "I'm only doing what I hope someone would do for me." So it was with disbelief and deep shock that we heard on the news that he was dead, dead after his helicopter had hit power lines and crashed while he was following an escaped prisoner in April 1987.

Only three days before his death, Peter and his son Clive had been awarded the Queen's Gallantry Medal in recognition of their courage when the police boat *Lady Elizabeth* had capsized in Wellington Harbour. In winds of more than 60 knots they'd plucked two police from the upturned hull as they hovered three metres above the six-metre waves. Two lost their lives, but if it hadn't been for the chopper all four would have drowned.

Peter Button had a dream which he made a reality. It is still with us – the Life Flight Trust and the Westpac Rescue Helicopter. It continues to fly seriously injured or sick people to hospitals.

In October 1995 Peter's dream landed on our beach. Another day in the woolshed was about to begin, and as I ran from the house about 7.30am our phone rang. A local fisherman was bringing his crewman into our bay. The youth had breathing difficulties and his feet and arms were tingling. Ron Smith of Cobar Radio, Wellington, had arranged for the Westpac Rescue Helicopter to fly from Wellington to our beach.

In less than 15 minutes the helicopter had landed and a doctor was checking out the young man. He was able to walk to the helicopter. As it lifted off the beach and flew out of the bay and on to Wairau Hospital, I thought with warmth of the man whose vision had made it possible. The man who loved to do good for other people lives on in the Life Flight Trust.

Over the years we've met hundreds of strangers who have become friends after their visit to Okukari, and we have also become fond of many who were previously casual acquaintances before visiting. But a few people – a minority – have invited themselves on some pretext or another, and I've felt they've abused our hospitality. They've expected to be waited on and never lifted a finger to help, giving me the impression we should be grateful to have them stay with us. When visitors like this leave, I wave goodbye to them vigorously.

A more typical example of the kind of person we got to know and like very well was a pilot who brought his helicopter down for a number of years, spraying the gorse on the farm. One year we had a lot of spraying to be done, but windy weather was holding it up. With a dying southerly and fine weather predicted for the next few days, it seemed the right time to have the helicopter down. It would fly from Nelson but Joe had to steam in to Picton and bring home the jet fuel and drums of spray. I was on my own.

I was organising dinner. As the wind died away and the sun streamed in the kitchen it became stifling. My clothes stuck to me, and something the children had said when we'd first put in our Para pool kept swirling through my head. "Gee, Mum. You've got to try skinny-dipping. Your body slips through the water. It's neat."

I'd decided long ago that I wasn't going to become a skinny-dipper. My body couldn't slip through water. It had too many bumps. But as the afternoon wore on the idea began to appeal. Just once, I thought, when nobody was at home to catch me out. I imagined my naked body stepping down the rungs of the ladder into the coolness. At last I gave in and, without more thought, I left my clothes in the bathroom and sank into the pool.

It was as wonderful as I'd been told. I lay on my back, floating and staring up at the blue silence, watching dandelion seeds as they floated past. I closed my eyes. The water caressing my body made me forget my misgivings about skinny-dipping. I felt I was floating in space. Time was forgotten.

Dully at first, I heard a persistent thump thump thump. It seemed to be getting closer and I opened my eyes. I saw a helicopter coming in the bay, obviously to land. He's not supposed to be here yet, I thought as I came back to reality and went to leap out of the pool.

My heart sank. My clothes were inside and I hadn't brought a towel outside with me. Now I could see he was going to pass right over the pool so I slid in behind the ladder hugging the side. This must be how a paua feels when it senses someone coming to prise it off the rocks, I giggled to myself as I tried to become part of the side of the pool. At last the helicopter was out of sight, landing in the paddock, and I rushed inside to get dressed before anyone arrived up at the house.

Nothing was mentioned about a naked swimmer being seen in the pool. The gorse was sprayed and the day they finished the job the pilot invited me for a flight over the farm as a thank you for the meals.

This was my first helicopter flight and the take-off as we flew forward and I saw the ground rushing past before we lifted high over the farm was breathtaking. This was a bird's-eye view, land and sea, so unbelievably beautiful, and everything so clear. As we swooped over the house on the way in to land, the clarity of the water in our pool took my breath away. But it wasn't until the pilot said, "Don't you get a great view?" that I knew.

In the 1960s the P & O Shipping Line sponsored the Cook Strait surf lifeboat races from Wellington Head to Island Bay, Wellington. Joe skippered the *Heather*, one of the escort boats, and the day before there would be 10-15 lifeboats on our beach, with crews camping overnight in the woolshed. Early morning would see the boats being towed out by their escort boats to begin their race across the strait.

Robin Judkins, of the Coast to Coast race fame, brought his competitors to Okukari for part of the Xerox North Cape to Bluff Challenge. They were meant to paddle across Cook Strait, but bad weather and time running out caused them to catch the ferry across the strait and come up to Okukari on board Bill Hicks's *Beachcomber*. Southerly winds were too strong for the kayaks to be off-loaded so they were taken back to a bay the Picton side of Dieffenbach Point. Joe was to escort them into Picton, and at the last minute I jumped aboard.

The further down the channel we got the calmer it became, and in the bay where they were to leave from it was deceptively calm. Now and again little ruffles of water circled the bay, and Joe warned the competitors. "Be prepared for strong gusts once you're around the point. The wind will sweep out of the next three or four bays."

I really don't think anyone believed him. I imagined them thinking here was a silly old man being over-cautious. But by the time Picton Point was reached, past those three or four deep bays, and three miles out from Picton township, every kayak and person had been taken aboard the escort boats. That day, the sea was the winner.

Since November 1962, when Barrie Devenport became the first European to swim Cook Strait, the strait has been conquered more than 100 times. We went out in the boat to cheer many of the swimmers on over the last couple of miles, and shared their excitement or heartache – Keith Hancox, John Coutts, Perry Cameron. But the biggest satisfaction was when I watched an American marathon swimmer, Lynne Cox, become the first European woman to beat Cook Strait. She landed on the rocks of the South Island, and if she later raised her glass to the American flag I raised mine to women everywhere.

Then 16-year-old Karen Bisley broke the women's record in 1982. Late in 1984 Karen approached Joe, asking if he'd be willing to pilot her in an attempt to swim from Cook Strait to Picton, through Tory Channel.

Karen entered the water off West Head just before 7am on 12 January 1985. The flood tide had started and this was going to push her to Dieffenbach. Here the wind had got up and it was very rough for the swimmer. Karen became seasick and above the noise of the boat engine I heard her gurgling heaves as her stomach emptied. She was exhausted, hungry and – I couldn't believe – thirsty.

Although the sea conditions were tough for the swimmer, on board the *Fugitive* there was little movement and from the shelter of the wheelhouse I watched a body being pushed to the limit, then further, as she was tossed around by the waves. Someone threw a plastic bottle to Karen and she rolled on her back and gulped down the mixture of flattened lemonade mixed with high energy food.

Stroke after stroke. I watched Karen moving through the water with very little propulsion from her legs. All her energy came from the upper part of her body with only an occasional flick of her legs.

Close on 5pm Karen crawled ashore on the Picton Foreshore to be met by the Mayor of Picton. Another stretch of sea had been conquered – and it had been done by a woman.

Then there was the Arapawa Island goat issue. This was between Betty Rowe, who lived on the other side of the island, and the Lands and Survey Department. It had been simmering for a couple of years.

Betty maintained that the goats were purebred Old English milk goats, now extinct in Britain, while local farmers (Joe included) believed they couldn't be purebred because many farmers had introduced other breeds to the island when the land was first being broken in.

The Marlborough Sounds Maritime Parks Board, funded by the Department of Lands and Survey, was concerned when they inspected the native bush on the coastal areas of Arapawa. Goats were destroying one of the few remaining examples of Cook Strait vegetation, and now native trees such as the taupata, ake-ake, ngaio and manuka were battling for survival against more than the prevailing westerly wind.

Since the bounty had been removed from goats their numbers had increased. Whenever we mustered we'd find ourselves with mobs of goats among the sheep, and, as Joe said, for every goat we could run one more sheep. And sheep don't destroy native bush.

The New Zealand Forest Service was to do the culling and a date was set. Betty Rowe said "No" to this, and she set up a campaign to stop the culling going ahead. During this time the farmers got on with farming and all the while Betty Rowe was working on the goats' behalf.

The issue boiled up in the mid-1970s. The voice for the goats was heard on the radio, in the paper, on television. Suddenly it became our issue as well, and we realised that unless we started to stir this pot, too, we'd be finding ourselves over-run with goats.

It all got too much for Joe one day. He'd been at home mending fishing nets in the woolshed when, for about the fourth time that morning, he'd heard the news about how we must save these goats and how they must not be killed. By the time he reached the house he had a full head of steam, and he tore inside and rang Television New Zealand. After introducing himself he said to the voice at the other end, "I'm sick and tired of hearing one woman's side of the story. It's time you came and got the farmers' side." Two hours later a helicopter landed in the paddock next to the house. Television visited our bay and Joe was given his chance to put his views, as a farmer, to the people of New Zealand.

Joe was fuming and he was angry to think that, because he'd kept out of the issue, it was now quite likely every goat would be protected, and our farm would be over-run with goats. At the end of the interview Joe stated, "As far as I'm concerned the only good goat is a dead goat."

Four bright and shiny scrubbed faces watched their father become a television star that night. His punchline made our mail days even more exciting as all his fan mail poured in. One letter he kept. It was addressed to:

Mr Farmer Heberley
Killer of Goats
Arapawa Island.

Much of his mail came on postcards and we could imagine the mail room in Picton laughing over some of the crude comments.

The goats were culled amid bitter confrontation between Betty Rowe's supporters and the cullers. There is now an uneasy peace. Betty protects the goats on her own land, which is fine by us. Cullers keep the numbers down in an area of reserve that has been fenced off, and we can graze sheep without the numerous goats coming in from the bush on to our farm land.

People who want to fish are, perhaps, our most frequent visitors.

Captain Laurie Collins, one of the Cook Strait ferry skippers, needed a break. He'd spoken to Joe and asked if he could camp in our woolshed. He wanted to bring his young son down with him and take him out in the dinghy fishing. We had plenty of spare room so persuaded Laurie to stay in the house with us.

The weather was perfect and father and son spent many hours fishing in the channel. I watched them as they drifted in with the tide. They'd still be out there when the tide changed, and they'd drift out.

A visitor in another bay gave Laurie Collins his party piece for the next few years. They were drifting past Te Awaiti, enjoying the sunshine and catching the odd blue cod, when a small boat came alongside Laurie and his son.

"I wouldn't fish there if I were you, old chap. Those mad buggers on the ferries'll run you down."

Laurie was still grinning when he came back to our place and told the story.

One of our most enchanting visitors was Japanese. A friend had brought him to our place as all he wanted to do while in New Zealand was to fish and eat fish. We took him fishing and his enthusiasm over whatever he caught was infectious. He didn't moan if it was fish generally used for bait. It was quickly filleted into thin slivers and eaten, I'll swear, while it was still quivering.

One English word he seemed to know well accompanied his feast. "Beautiful. Beautiful." Everything was beautiful. He spoke very little English but we all made ourselves understand one another, and an interpreter with him bridged the gap.

On his last day he cooked a Japanese meal for us with ingredients he'd brought with him. Rice, which he washed and washed. The most important part, the washing, the interpreter told us. A roast of beef, which had had my taste buds watering every time I'd opened the fridge, was rinsed in salted water and then put in a pot and boiled. Boiled, not roasted. His sauces were added to the water and, when the meat was cooked, eggs were cracked into the simmering water and lifted straight out again. I felt myself developing an allergy to eggs, an allergy which quickly grew serious when I was told our friend would be offended if I didn't eat his meal, and I was excused the raw egg.

I felt laughter stick in my throat as I watched Joe's raw egg stick in his. Slimy egg dribbled down his chin as he nodded his head and assured the cook it was "Beautiful. Beautiful."

My favourite meals are when I'm able to cook with ingredients fresh from the sea, our sea.

CHAPTER TWENTY

The Island Changes

MY 33 YEARS on Arapawa Island have seen many changes. Perhaps the most important is being in touch with the world. Telephone lines have been replaced and we no longer have to wind a handle to generate the rings. We just dial our numbers. There are still party lines but these have fewer subscribers on them. Because Joe is in the Search and Rescue organisation we are lucky to be on a private line, and our phone is as good as those in towns. The wind sometimes plays havoc and brings the lines down but we remind ourselves that other places in New Zealand also lose their phones in extreme weather conditions.

Not long after we'd been switched over to the new telephone system, with new numbers to dial to reach our usual people, Joe was trying to ring James's house to wake him up to go fishing. Twice he dialed and slammed the phone down without speaking.

"What's wrong?"

"Must be crossed wires or something. A bloody woman on the other end keeps telling me, 'You have dialed the wrong number. Please try again.'" Through laughter I explained to Joe who the strange voice belonged to, but I expect he can be forgiven as it was 3.30am.

The world has come to Okukari in more ways than one. Even the beach has changed. Glass floats and bottles no longer seem to wash up on the beach. Instead plastic in many shapes and forms is washed ashore after three or four days of gale-force southerlies. When it is piled into one heap and burnt I sometimes wonder which is the worst pollution – the thick black smoke, or the plastic littering the beach.

But plastic does have its good points, specially at lambing. Two plastic fish tubs, with one inverted over the other, make wonderful lambs' beds. With an old woollen jersey and a hot water bottle in the bottom, a weak lamb is kept warm as well as having plenty of room. When I look at the fish tubs lined up against the laundry wall they remind me of the bad old days when newborn babies used to be taken away from their mothers and lined up in their cots behind a window in the hospital nursery, and parents lined up to point out their offspring to admiring friends and relatives.

Our farm motorbike, too, has brought changes during lambing. If a ewe is having problems lambing she can easily be brought down to the woolshed, and after a storm weak cold lambs can quickly be brought into the warmth. The bike itself undergoes transformations during the season, becoming Grandma's lambulance.

Tory Channel traffic has increased over the last five or six years as more and more fishermen target hoki, a deep water fish caught mainly by trawling. Its soft, moist flesh flakes easily, and its delicate flavour makes it an excellent fish to use in reprocessing for such things as crabsticks. Hoki is a major winter fishery in the waters of Cook Strait, and the trawlers pass our bay constantly during the season.

Hoki is a huge resource and there have been both near-losses and actual losses of some of the fishing boats involved in this fishery. The 1995 season saw the loss of the *Caskade*. She had filled up and was on her way into port when she listed and sank. Her crew was rescued by Wellington Rescue Helicopter. I listened to the search and rescue run by Ron Smith of Cobar Radio in Wellington. At least it was a fine morning, but it was freezing cold and there was a big swell in the strait that day. The Interisland ferry on its way from Wellington to Picton was diverted, and when at last I heard that the fishermen had been spotted by the helicopter, among floating debris from the boat, I felt the relief that every other fishing family must have felt. How easily it could have been them.

Thirty-three years ago, when I first stood inside the woolshed watching dust particles dance in the shafts of light that filtered through the skylights, I never imagined that 31 years later I'd be standing in the same woolshed watching a fish scientist set up a mini-laboratory on our wool table.

This scientist had phoned Joe to explain what he wanted to do, and why, and to ask for our help. Hoki is a very important commercial fishery in New Zealand but the catch was arriving for processing in poor condition, with bruised and mushy flesh. His main objective was to find a 'benchmark'. Once he had this, guidelines could be set for improving hoki fishing and handling practices.

Joe and the boys were long-lining out in Cook Strait, catching groper, and they also caught a few hoki. The scientist hoped to be able to get these fish for research. After careful handling and being placed in cases and iced, the fish would be transferred to a speedboat and brought into the 'laboratory' in our woolshed as soon as possible.

Murray, a commercial launch operator from Motueka, brought the man down to us and used his boat to transport the hoki. I watched, fascinated, as each fish was examined. Its sex and length were recorded before it was skinned and filleted. Discolouration and the number of bruises or bloodspots were also recorded.

A thin slice of flesh was removed from each fillet and placed on two very small freezing plates to hold it. One of these plates moved along teflon runners and, as it did, the sample of fish was pulled part and broken. The strength taken to break each sample was recorded. The scientist told me, "The fresher the fish, the more strength in the fillet."

I had bags of very fresh hoki fillets in my freezer. We tried it in many ways but its comparative lack of flavour, when we had plenty of groper cheeks on offer, made it a poor second choice. It did make nice fish cakes and fish pie, and the cats in Okukari Bay enjoyed fish for months.

I no longer have to take my life in my hands and go out to meet the mail boat in a dinghy. I'd often sat cringing in the dinghy as Bill Kenny charged into the bay in the *Reo Moana*, and prayed that it would stop when he pushed the gear lever into reverse. Having our own wharf put a stop to that.

Our speedboat of the last 12 years has become my mini-car. Weather permitting I can shoot into Picton whenever I feel like it.

Motorbikes instead of our feet have saved hours and hours out mustering. The sight of the bike sitting on the road, waiting for me to ease my tired body on to it after mustering and bring me home, makes me thankful for changing times.

The advent of electricity has made the biggest difference of all to our lives. It has given me the time to write this book. I had my story to tell, but so did my mother-in-law's generation, and their mothers and grandmothers. If these women had been able to find the time to write, what inspiring stories theirs would have been.

When I first decided to write this book and told Joe, he said, "What are you going to fill a book up with? You go to bed, get up, cook my breakfast, do the housework, cook, garden. I hear you playing your piano. I can't see how that can make a book."

"You've forgotten to mention sex," I shot back at him.

I've re-lived my life as the chapters have taken shape and between laughter and tears I've enjoyed every minute. In my mind I've travelled millions of miles, without going far from Okukari.

Recently when Joe was away chasing tuna I found myself in the Blenheim saleyards bidding on 120 merino wethers Joe wanted. He couldn't be there but he trusted me to be in his place. After the sale I could have sung and danced all the way to our car, as happy as on the day I'd lambed my first ewe.

I've learnt to understand diabetes, even to help. Our daughter-in-law Joy was 17 years old and a mother of only three months when, after a stay in hospital with appendicitis, she was found to have high levels of sugar in her urine. Initially she was treated through diet. Back at Okukari Joy tested her blood sugar regularly and kept in touch with the diabetic nurse at Blenheim's Wairau Hospital. With rising sugar levels it was obvious diet alone wasn't enough and she was told she needed two injections of insulin each day. I had no idea how to give comfort to a 17-year-old girl who could only feel scared of what her future held. "It's horrible," Joy cried, as I tried to understand while at the same time thinking back to myself at her age. I'd been working for a year in the Auckland office of Berlei Ltd, enjoying dances at the Khyber Pass hall of the Church of the Holy Sepulchure – always known as St Sep's – and yachting in the *Mangawai*.

Joy stayed on two doses of insulin daily until 1984 when she was told that if she wanted another baby she must go on to three doses daily. This would control her blood sugar levels better. They had to be as normal as possible at conception and while she was carrying a baby.

Angela was born in 1985. She weighed in at 10 lbs 9 oz, her heavy weight not uncommon for babies with a diabetic mother – our second grandchild after Rachael.

All this time I wished that I understood diabetes better. Joy was here in the bay, with family all around, but not one of us understood this 'thing'. I didn't even know how to describe it. Is it an illness, a disease or perhaps a type of virus?

Then my niece, studying medicine in Auckland, arranged for Joy and me to spend a week in Auckland at Diabetic House. Joy was able to spend time talking with other diabetics and learning more about coping with diabetes. I, too, learnt about it and the staff took me aside and explained what to expect if ever I found Joy in a coma. I was taught how to recognise and treat it, and how to give Joy a glucose injection. For the first time in four years Joy had someone in the bay to talk to about her condition. And, best of all – I understood.

We discovered it wasn't only Mayday calls that had one of our sons pounding on our bedroom window in the middle of the night because we couldn't hear our phone ringing in the office.

"Mum! Mum!" I heard through sleep. "Joy's unconscious."

I pulled my dressing gown over my shoulders as I tore down the passage, not even stopping to put on sandals. My mind flew as I remembered all I'd learnt while at Diabetic House.

"I think she missed her supper," Young Joe panted as we ran down to his house.

She'll probably need the glucose injection, I told myself as I went over in my mind how I'd prepare it. I was terrified. In Auckland I'd injected an orange for practice, but this was my daughter-in-law who needed it now – not an orange.

Joy didn't need the injection. She was in the state my family told me I was in after getting hit in the woolshed – "at home with the lights out". I was able to feed Joy a thick glucose drink to raise her sugar level while trusting it would rouse her enough so I could follow it up with a sandwich. Then, pricking the tip of Joy's finger I took a blood sample. Her blood glucose testing machine enabled me to find the level of her blood sugar. It was zero.

The glucose I'd given Joy brought her around enough so I could make her eat the sandwich. The glucose would give only short-term relief – she had to follow it up with carbohydrates.

It was a great relief when Joy became lucid and we were able to sit and enjoy a cup of tea together before going back to our beds.

Accidents and sickness aside, the greatest of my anxieties in this place I've made my home has been how well I could guide four children through their Correspondence School years. The most important part of their education has been in my hands. I always worried over whether I'd given them enough time. On 'bad' school days I worried over the fact that by bedtime I wanted my children out of my sight as I'd had enough of the constant bickering and fighting over lessons that, I felt, weren't up to standard. And, I'd ask myself, what is this standard I set? I wasn't a teacher. Maybe it was too high. Or it could be too low.

The respect and caring my parents taught me have bonded our family into a close unit. As I have watched our four children grow up, get married and have children of their own, I have been given answers to the questions I'd so often asked myself over the years.

Pauline as our youngest always seemed to be last on my time-sheet and by the time I'd got the other three children started on their lessons and got back to her she'd have finished the work she'd started and be waiting for me to spend time with her. How can I divide one body into four equal parts, I'd ask of Joe? His answer was always the same. "They'll be fine, love."

As a child Pauline was never going to get married. She was going to be a zookeeper. Dene Wilson, Marlborough's professional tennis coach, changed her mind. They were married, and instead of a zookeeper she has become a vet.

Not long after Pauline had completed her veterinarian science degree I had the chance to watch her perform a caesarian on Kelly, an 80 lb bull mastiff cross.

I watched her X-ray and prepare the dog for surgery. Stretched out on the table, the bitch looked nothing like the big creature which had come bounding in.

I watched Pauline's hands make the first incision while Kerry, the nurse, cauterised bleeders. Before long the first puppy was handed to the owner's wife. Very quickly came six more puppies with their squashed-up and frowning faces and tightly closed eyes, oblivious to the bright lights. Amidst snuffles and squeaks they were rubbed dry and swaddled in a blanket to keep warm until they could be with their mother.

As Pauline stitched up Kelly my mind went back 15 years. A grubby child wearing odd socks, jersey on back to front and her hair needing a good brush ran in late for lunch. As she reached across the table for a piece of bread Joe noticed the tops of her hands and wrists.

"You're filthy. Go and wash."

"I did wash my hands. How can they be all clean when I've just put a uterus back in a sheep?"

"Where's this sheep?" Joe said into the silence.

"In the woolshed. Strung up by her back legs. I'll check her after lunch. I washed the uterus with Savlon, squeezed the fluid out and put it back in the sheep."

"Who told you how to do that?"

"I read it in your book on lambing problems in your office."

The vet within the 11-year-old child had stirred although we weren't aware of it at the time. Joe was still amazed a few days later when Pauline proudly let the ewe back out with the main mob.

Years later I thought of this episode again when Pauline was operating on our farm, not in a surgery in sterile conditions but in the sheep yards at Okukari.

"I never thought I'd see the day when Dad would let us operate on one of his cows while he lay in the yards," Helen laughed. She was washing her hands after helping Pauline cut a cancerous growth from a cow's eye.

Two weeks earlier when we'd mustered in the cattle Joe had noticed a black, cauliflower-like growth over the eyelid of a pale red and white cow. When he'd spoken to Pauline about it she'd told him it would probably be a cancerous growth, especially with the cow's colouring. "I'll be down next weekend. I'll bring what I need with me to operate."

When we mustered the cow in for Pauline to have a look at her we were horrified. The growth had grown rapidly and was now like a fist covering her eye completely, and it had been bleeding. "I've no doubt it's cancer, Dad."

"Well, let's get on with it and cut it off," was Joe's answer.

I had to be in the thick of it, even if I was only the fetcher and carrier. This was Joe's beast. He'd supervise, and Helen, who was staying with us, was Pauline's assistant.

First attempts to sedate the cow enough to be able to operate on her in the race failed, so a lightly sedated cow was led out into a bigger yard where she was roped and pulled to the ground. Pauline told her father she wanted to keep the cow sedated only enough to be able to operate as she was heavy in calf.

I still had memories of sedated cattle chasing everyone in their sights so I kept my distance until she was obviously not going to leap up. As Pauline cut further in to the growth she had to sedate the cow more. Part of the eyelid was cut away and she found it was worse that she'd thought. She had to scrape the bone around the eye.

"Look at this, Dad." I looked with my eyes shut, but I quickly opened them when I heard Joe muttering he had to go and get something from the woolshed. He was green, and as he staggered into the shed I asked him if he was okay. All we heard was, "Go and get Joe to help hold the cow's head."

An SOS was sent out to Young Joe who came and finished off his father's job. We all pretended not to notice Joe when he quietly came outside and stretched out on the tractor tray, staring at the sky.

The cow recovered and the next time she was in the yards she had a healthy calf at foot.

Our other children also had their ambitions. James, our third, once told me that the only reason he was doing school lessons was so he'd learn how to sign his name and then he'd be able to write out cheques. All he wanted to be when he grew up was a fisherman. When school was out for the day he'd be out in the dinghy netting, catching mostly butterfish – or greenbone as it is called in some places – and before he left home to go to college he'd saved his earnings from his catch and bought himself his first farm bike.

He was the quiet one in our family. If he could use one word instead of two or three he would. As a little boy he loved to go hunting with the men, and today he spends a lot of his spare time hunting the wild pig on Arapawa. He says he loves going on his own and sits in his special places, waiting patiently for the big one.

He must have learnt more than signing his name on cheques. He certainly signed a lot of deposit slips because by the age of 23 James owned his own home which he'd had built in the bay and where he brought his bride, Lisa Wilson, Dene's cousin, from Marlborough's Rai Valley. Their two children, Haydn four and Danielle two, are seventh-generation Heberleys.

Helen, our second child, is very much a Heberley. She picked up my mother-in-law's housekeeping skills, certainly none of mine, and her house is always neat and tidy. Her first marriage broke up and she was left with three young children; Amanda now nine, Carl seven and Glen four. She was strong enough to weather the turbulent times she faced and now laughs again, with Peter, her new partner.

When Helen left school all she wanted to do was work on a farm. We had the farm, Helen came on to the payroll and on the farm she stayed until she left home to be married.

Helen ran the farm as well as any man could have done, and worked alongside men shearing, fencing, mustering and doing all the other jobs of a farm. I had my own personal butcher and whenever I needed meat she'd have it in my freezer the next day.

And Joe – my firstborn when I was 21. I wasn't much more than a child myself and so I feel I can excuse myself if I say, as I'm sure other mothers all over the world feel of their firstborn, that he was my special child. Time has moulded them all into one golden block, warmed from holding it in my hands, and I love all four, and their partners, the same.

Young Joe didn't go far to pick his wife when he married Joy, Dave and Kath Fishburn's daughter. Living in Dryden Bay, Joy had also learnt by correspondence lessons, so she knew all about them when she came to teach their two girls, Rachael now 12 and Angela 10.

Like James, Young Joe also lives to fish. Fishing has moved into the age of electronics and the boys understand this much better than their father. But although Joe is of the old school when it comes to the modern equipment, he still has knowledge to pass to his sons – knowledge which has come from more than 30 years of fishing in Cook Strait. With the two boats, fishing has become our main income while the farm is a way of life for three Heberley families.

As Rachael and Angela are older than the other grandchildren, and living on the farm, they are learning to love the way of life many Heberleys have chosen to live. This past year Rachael has taken over a lot of the work involved in lambing. It has given me more time to write. We have extra helpers in the yards as all our grandchildren like to help out.

Each January we drive all the sheep through the race and keep a tally.

"Angela!" Joe shouted. "Can you count?"

"Course I can, Grumps." Angela was then nine.

"Well, sit by the gate and count the sheep as they go past."

An important Angela counted. Her eyes in her dusty face watching each sheep never blinked. Her only movement was an imperceptible nod of her head as they ran through the gate.

"When the yard was empty Joe turned to Angela and asked how many.

"Five thousand and two."

"How many?" asked a surprised Joe.

An eyelid never blinked. "Five thousand and two."

Our usual 400-500 tally seemed very small.

During the summer of 1994-1995 some of the greatest changes took place in Tory Channel with the introduction of two fast ferries, the *Lynx* and the *Sea Shuttle*. When all the regular ferries were also running there were 25 ferries passing through the channel daily, each creating its own wash.

Situated just inside Tory Channel, Okukari is exposed to the south, and the seas that crash on the beach whenever there is a southerly storm have weathered the beach to the point that the wash created by the fast ferries has little effect. But further down the channel, where the waters remain calm in a storm in comparison with our bay, the ferries' special wash has left a path of destruction. Bays where the biggest waves had only ever broken gently on the shore were suddenly having great walls of water smashing over them, lifting rocks and dumping them up high on the beaches.

At Chum and Mavis Thomas's home near the power line crossing, the narrowest part of Tory Channel, the wash was extreme. The first time they saw the wash they were terrified. A wall of water crashed over their jetty, up their path and through the front gate. Whenever a ferry passed at high tide they'd be left with rocks covering their path and front garden. Over the summer the quantity of rocks spewed from the seabed beat the elderly couple. No sooner had they shifted one lot than another ferry passed, leaving another heap of rocks. To reach their wharf they had to clamber over a path which was buried beneath three feet of gravel, stones and clay.

Chum had been a pilot in the RAF who had flown Kitty bombers in the Western Desert with the Shark Squadron until he was shot down and became a German prisoner of war. He and Mavis were going away to a special Anzac service so Peter and Paula Jamieson came up with the idea that some of the channel residents might like to help clear the mess from their place now that the ferries weren't operating over the winter months.

Our men were out fishing and Joy was away, but Lisa and I were joined by Marcia Rowe, daughter-in-law of Betty and Walter Rowe. She had walked over the hill from Aotea. Paula and Peter picked up Judy Brain from Deep Bay so there were six of us, armed with wheelbarrows and shovels. As there are no creches down our way, Lisa had brought Haydn and Danielle with her.

I knew it was bad at the Thomas's place but I wasn't prepared for the huge pile of rocks I saw when we pulled up at the jetty. The beach had disappeared beneath the rocks and boulders and as my eyes swept over the rubble I wasn't surprised that it had beaten Mavis and Chum. It looked daunting for five women, and Peter.

It took all morning. Amid rain, thunder and lightning crackling round the bay, and our laughter when we looked at one another, soaking wet, hair plastered to our heads and splattered in yellow mud, we cleared the path that led from the wharf to the front door steps. We shifted more than 50 barrow loads and built a wall twelve feet long and two feet high from the bigger rocks, along the outside of the front fence.

Peter brought Mavis and Chum back to their bay. He told us the look of sheer delight on their faces when they saw what had been done in their absence was worth all our efforts. But we wondered when neighbours would have to come to their aid again.

In writing this book I have lived again through each of the years since Joe and I married. If I had known what was ahead of me, would I have married Joe Heberley and gone to live in Okukari Bay, in the Marlborough Sounds? Could I have come to our relationship as a different type of person, and survived?

I was young, very naive, and knew nothing about farming. I remember making a bold statement before our wedding. "I don't care where I live as long as it is with Joe and I can see the sea."

Joe had been brought up in the old tradition where the male was the head of the family who earned the money while the wife stayed at home and cooked, cleaned and brought up the family.

I believe our marriage worked because I was young when I married. I didn't realise it at the time but I was moulded into the type of wife Joe wanted. And all through the ups and downs our love grew. Not into a heart-stopping, cymbals-clanging relationship, but into a deep, strong feeling for each other, built on respect.

In striving to become myself over the years I have gone out and done things I would never have done if I'd lived in a different environment, and all these things have helped build up increasing confidence in myself. I have grown to be equal to Joe, not just his wife.

But it is Joe I have to thank for making me want to do these things, and my parents, Tom and Rene Macauley, who brought me up to believe I could learn to do them. I think, though, that if I had been the person I am today, our marriage would not have survived in Okukari. As it was, I learned on the job, as it were, and I like to think that Joe has too.

While looking through old photo albums and books I found my autograph book from schooldays. My sister Betty had written for me, in 1953, that old verse about life bringing thorns with all its roses, "but aren't the roses sweet". I thought about this in terms of my own life. The responsibility of teaching our four children, the work involved in getting electricity to the island, the fear when Joe has gone to sea in extreme conditions, the hours I put in when I was studying and bringing up four children so often on my own... The list could go on and on, but at the end of every single trial or hurdle, or time of apprehension or dread, there has been a reward like that sweet rose.

No. If I had the chance to live my life again I would live it in exactly the same way.

As I've got closer to the end of this book my normally placid Joe has made a few sharp comments about how the garden looks overgrown, the cupboards are untidy, the windows need cleaning and – saddest of all – the cake tins aren't full any more. When I did get around to some baking I got quite a shock. I had to clean out my sponge-roll tin as it had gone rusty.

I've been told I've changed since I began my book. I know I have become much more assertive and my time hasn't been as freely available as it used to be. I have learned to say no. For this I don't feel the slightest guilt. In the years I brought up my family my time was all theirs, and now I am revelling in finding a new me. And I'm understanding more about who we are and where we've come from.

A link in my children's and grandchildren's past was broken on 20 August 1995 when Albert Guard of Kakapo Bay in Port Underwood died in Blenheim in his 93rd year. He was Captain Jacky Guard's grandson, nephew of John Guard (the first white child born in the South Island) and uncle of my mother-in-law, Ruby Heberley.

At the time of Albert's death, Helen's three children, Amanda, Carl and Glen, were staying with Joe and me.

The morning of the funeral Okukari turned on one of its fierce northerly gales with driving rain. As Joe rowed out to the *Te Wai* and brought her alongside the wharf I took the three children down to the boatshed on the motorbike. I struggled along the wharf with our bag of 'good' clothes to change into, the children's bags, and three children, at the same time making sure they were all hanging on to one another in the wind, and suddenly I felt my life had completed one cycle and I was now beginning the second.

And my thoughts raced back to that terrible day, not long after I began writing this book, when we had a dreadful northerly gale. We'd watched the violence from the window. A sheet of iron peeled off the woolshed and sliced across a power line, causing it to arc. Showers of sparks and melting plastic fell to the ground. Two of my favourite proteas gave in to the wind and broke off at the roots. Tree limbs lay broken.

Joe was nailing the side of the shed which was threatening to blow away when the end blew right out of it.

Then the hatch blew off the *Fugitive*, moored in the bay. Rain would be driving in on the electronic equipment.

Young Joe volunteered to row out. The dinghy was at the end of the beach, straight in from the *Fugitive*. With the wind behind him, catching the boat as he whistled past was the hardest part. His voice crackled over the VHF in the kitchen. "If I don't appear in 10 minutes, come looking. I broke an oar in half on the way out. It'll be grim rowing in."

I tore out to the bank above the beach. The wind had strengthened. Through the spray I saw my son clinging to the side of the boat, feet in the dinghy, waiting for a lull so he could make a start. Rain poured down and willy-waws raced over the water and whipped up huge seas. I couldn't see him at times. I was scared to watch, and scared not to. If I didn't watch I'd miss him if he was blown out of the bay. No one could help if anything happened. *Te Wai* was straining her lines tied off the end of the wharf. She definitely couldn't be pulled in to rescue Joe. For a second, the wind died down. I saw him digging in the oars hard. He was using the short oar on the lee side. A sheet of water hit Joe side on. The dinghy was on its ear. I screamed. Tears ran down my face. He's gone. No, he's still rowing. Hurry Joe, hurry. Please God take care of him. Gusts pounded the dinghy, slowing his progress in the frenzied sea.

At last he reached the shore. I watched him climb out and slowly pull the dinghy up.

That day over the years I heard and felt my mother's cries of terror from my own childhood at sea. This day, as Joe and I and three of our grandchildren set off through the storm to celebrate the long life and work of their pioneer forbear, Albert Guard, I knew that at last I truly understood.

218

RECIPES

OUR VISITORS so often ask me for recipes that I thought I should include all those I happen to mention in the course of this book.

They are old, tried and true recipes. Where there are weights, I use the old, pre-metric measurements.

HEATHER'S FISH PIE

I use any fish for this but if I have groper cheeks and throats, especially if they've been in the freezer, I use these as there are no bones. I have also used hoki fillets.

Simmer the fish, removing bones if necessary.

Make a thick white sauce using some of the fish stock. With bland hoki, I grate a small onion into the sauce.

Season, including a pinch of curry powder, particularly if the fish is hoki.

Mix the flaked cooked fish into the white sauce. Add freshly ground black pepper and grated cheese (optional). Cover with fresh breadcrumbs and dobs of butter.

Heat through. Turn on the grill to brown breadcrumbs before serving.

Sometimes I leave off the breadcrumbs and pile mashed potatoes over the fish and white sauce. Cook in the same way.

MY LAZY FISHCAKES

Any fish can be used but I prefer groper cheeks and throats as they have no bones. I prepare the cakes using only one saucepan which means no fuss.

Peel and cut up potatoes and one onion. Place in pot and just cover with salted water. I put the fish I'm using over the top of the potatoes to steam.

When the potatoes are cooked, lift out the fish if it has to be boned, and drain the potatoes. Mash all ingredients in the pot together, with one or two eggs to bind.

Add seasonings. I add my little pinch of curry powder and lots of chopped parsley.

Spoon on to floured paper. Coat with the flour and form into fish cakes.

Fry in oil.

HEATHER'S FISH CHOWDER

I use groper cheeks and throats, or blue cod, but any fish can be used to make stock. I simmer it, then remove the cooked fish, and in the stock I put celery, diced raw potatoes, onions, carrots, leeks. When these are just cooked I add the flaked fish, a medium can of whole kernel corn, one cooked and diced crayfish tail and a tin of salmon.

Then I add milk, salt and pepper to taste and simmer about 20 minutes. Thicken a little. A pinch of curry powder lifts the flavour without people being aware this soup has curry in it.

Before serving add parsley. Depending on seasons I have left out the crayfish and added, instead, oysters, mussels or scallops.

OVEN-FRIED FISH

Fish – own choice	3 level tbsp flour
1 egg	½ tsp cooking oil
pinch salt	shake pepper
½ cup breadcrumbs	

DRESSING
¼ cup salad oil	2 tbsp white vinegar
pinch salt	shake pepper and marjoram

Cut fish in portions. Toss in flour. Combine all dressing ingredients in bottle or blender. Add marjoram if desired.

Mix egg, oil, salt and pepper. Dip fish in this egg wash, then crumb.

Pour a thin film of dressing over base of baking dish. Place fish in a single layer. Sprinkle the remainder of dressing over this.

Bake until golden brown, 200°C (400°F) 20 minutes. Serve with lemon or tartare sauce.

PAUA PATTIES

I bring the paua to the boil first as this makes it easier to remove them from their shells and mince. I remove the green stomach and the black frill from the edge of the shellfish, and cut the paua into pieces.

Then I use my food processor and mince the paua, two or three rashers of bacon and an onion. Add this to a batter and cook in the usual way.

Paua is tasty and also very high in iodine.

CRAYFISH CASSEROLE

After drowning the crays in fresh water, simmer for about 15 minutes. Remove the flesh and place it in an oven-proof dish. Make a white sauce, add salt and freshly ground black pepper to taste. Sprinkle with toasted breadcrumbs. Heat through.

When I make this, Joe insists we have it with mashed potatoes into which I've stirred raw diced onion.

MUM'S CREAM PUFFS

2 oz butter	1 breakfast cup water

Bring to boil. Add 2 heaped tbsp flour. Stir till the mixture leaves the side of the pot. Cool. Add 2 eggs. Beat together until shiny. Place in spoonfuls on tray.

Cook at 450°F 30-40 minutes. Prick with a knitting needle as soon as they are removed from oven. Leave on oven tray to dry out.

To serve, cut the top almost off and fill with whipped cream.

MUM'S SULTANA CAKE

8 oz butter	8 oz sugar
3 eggs	12 oz flour
1 lb sultanas	1 tsp baking powder
lemon and vanilla essence.	

Cream butter and sugar. Add eggs and beat. Add flour, baking powder, sultanas and essences.

Then add 1 dsp cornflour mixed in cold water. Fill cup up with boiling water. Add last.

Cook 1½ hours at 375°F.

My failure at making a sponge cake like my mother-in-law's daunted me. I just couldn't make a sponge cake like Ruby's. I followed her recipe exactly but still the only guarantee I had was that it would make a trifle. Then I found a recipe for a sponge which I tried and have used ever since.

GOLDEN SPONGE

3 eggs	½ cup sugar
5 tbsp custard powder	2 dsp flour
2 tsp baking powder	

Beat eggs till fluffy. Gradually add sugar and beat till very thick. Fold in sifted dry ingredients. Place in two eight-inch greased and floured tins. Bake at 190°C for 15-20 minutes.

MAUREEN'S PAVLOVA

3 egg whites   1 cup sugar
Beat until stiff.
Add 1 tbsp water, 1 tsp vinegar, 3 heaped tsp cornflour.
Bake at 125°C for 1 hour.

STEAMED PUDDING

4 oz butter   6 oz flour
4 oz sugar   1½ tsp baking powder
2 eggs

Cream the butter and sugar. Add the eggs and fold in the sieved flour. Mix to a soft dropping consistency with a little milk or water. Put in greased bowl with golden syrup, jam or condensed milk in the bottom of the bowl.

Cover and steam for 1½ - 2 hours.

On no account let the water in the saucepan or steamer go off the boil. If more water is needed, ensure it is boiling. (Remember Isabelle the pig and her ball.)